ROCKY MOUNTAIN FLORA

James Ells

The Colorado Mountain Club Press
Golden, Colorado

D1040475

Rocky Mountain Flora
Copyright © 2006 James Ells

All rights reserved.

This book may not be duplicated, copied, transmitted, or reproduced in any
manner or by any means, including electronic, mechanical, photographic,
or optical, including methods not invented or in common use at the time
of this publication, without the express written consent of the publisher.

PUBLISHED BY

The Colorado Mountain Club Press.

Founded in 1912, The Colorado Mountain Club is the largest outdoor recreation,
education and, conservation organization in the Rocky Mountains. Look for our
books at your local bookstore or outdoor retailer or contact us at:

710 Tenth Street, #200, Golden, Colorado 80401

303-279-3080, ext. 2

Email: cmcpress@cmc.org

DISTRIBUTED TO THE BOOK TRADE BY

Mountaineers Books

1001 SW Klickitat Way, Suite 201, Seattle, WA 98134, 800-553-4453

COVER IMAGE

by Aaron Locander
Indian Paintbrush in the La Plata Mountains, southwestern Colorado

We gratefully acknowledge the financial support of the people of
Colorado through the Scientific and Cultural Facilities District
of greater metropolitan Denver for our publishing activities.

First Edition

ISBN 0-9760525-4-7

Printed in China

Contents

❦ *About this Book* ❦

BACKGROUND

This book is as much a surprise to me as to those who know me because none of us had ever thought of me as an author. So now I'm trying to recall the events that lead up to this book.

I've had an interest in plants since childhood and thought, as I grew up, that I would become a farmer since that seemed a viable option back in the late '30s and '40s when a large percent of the population was still living on farms. However, the postwar era brought an unprecedented upheaval to American agriculture. Farmers that had survived the war found they could not survive the postwar agricultural revolution that dictated that they had to get big or get out. As farm prices fell, the farmers had to produce more, and to do this they needed more land. More land required larger and more efficient equipment. The new economics of large-scale farming dictated fewer crops, greater debt and more efficient production and marketing.

I was in the educational system while this revolution and exodus from the land was taking place and it became apparent that I needed to review my plans. With a few stops to explore different avenues, I returned to the educational elevator and rode it to the top, getting off with a Ph.D. in horticulture. This provided me with the credentials needed for an academic career that involved teaching, extension and research in horticulture at Colorado State University for 35 years.

After the children had grown, I found myself with a little time and money that I had not known earlier, and I used some of it to venture afield on day trips. On these trips I carried a camera to document what I had seen and to help recall the occasion. Among the pictures I acquired were pictures of wild flowers that

I identified with date and location and a name if I could find one. Flowers became my main interest and I found myself hiking trails for the express purpose of collecting pictures of flowers. It was not until I realized I had a collection of several hundred pictures that the idea of a book entered my head. Recalling the difficulty I had in establishing the identity of the plants in the pictures I had acquired, I decided that if I was going to write a book, it would need to be written so that one could use it to establish the identity of any common plant in the field or from any good photograph of the plant away from the field. This meant including close-ups of leaves, or flowers and fruit in such a way that they would provide positive plant identification.

ESTABLISHING PLANT IDENTITY

When Dr. Asa Gray wrote the first edition of *Gray's Manual of Botany* in 1848, there was no electricity or photography. The only way to include a picture was to make a hand-carved wood cut from a line drawing. Since this was prohibitively expensive, there were very few if any pictures, leaving only verbal descriptions as a means of identifying plants. I have a treasured copy of the 8th ed. of *Gray's Manual of Botany*, all 1,632 pages of it and I am in awe of this man who acquired the knowledge of the thousands of plants included in this manual and developed keys for identifying them.

The identity of a plant may be established by keying it out. To key out a plant, one needs the proper key, a glossary of botanical terms and either the whole fresh or dried plant. It also helps to have knowledge of botanical terms and experience at keying out plants. If only a picture is available and the key asks for the number of stamens or the length of the awns, the question cannot be answered, and perhaps the plant identity will go unconfirmed.

Bringing a manual having the necessary keys is a good way of identifying plants, if one is proficient at using the manual and hiking alone. However, one should not expect others, who may not share an avid interest in plants, to patiently wait while the plant's identity is being established. And digging up the plant and taking it home is now a no-no.

Another way of establishing identity is to consult a book that has colored pictures of plants. I have quite a few of these and in some cases they have been helpful; however, they usually emphasize the showy plants and picture the whole plant instead of showing enough detail to firmly establish its identity.

Hiking with someone who knows the plants is an enjoyable way to learn plants. Guided tours of this type are conducted in some parks. However, the availability, scheduling and cost of these tours could limit their usefulness.

PURPOSE AND SCOPE

This book is supposed to identify the common plants that are encountered in any of the parks, forests or trails in the Rocky Mountains, although the examples are from the mountains, foothills and plains of Colorado and Wyoming. It is intended for field use and it should reside in a daypack or vehicle and not permanently on a library shelf. No discrimination has been used in selecting the plants included in these pages. If the plant was encountered on any of these trails, it has been included without regard to its flowers type or if it was a weed, a non-native, or an escapee from cultivation. As a result, better than 90% of the plants one finds on these trails are to be found in these pages. This is a conservative claim because I have hiked for miles without finding any plant not already included.

CATEGORIES

The most obvious character of a flowering plant is the color of its flowers. This being the case, there are sections on White

Flowers, Yellow Flowers, Red Flowers, Blue Flowers, and Purple Flowers. There are a number of flowering plants with flowers that do not fall into these categories and they are included in the section of Flowers of Other Colors. In this section will be found most of the wind-pollinated plants including many of the trees. The remaining sections are specific to certain plant types and they are: Grasses, Sedges and Rushes, Mushrooms, Ferns and Fern-Like Plants, Lichens, and Mosses. Within each of these 12 sections, the plants are grouped, alphabetically, by family, then by genus, and then by specie.

USER GUIDE — TIPS AND TOOLS

The flowers in this book are first classified by color. Within the color section they are arranged alphabetically first by family, then by genus and finally by species. For example, Colorado's state flower, the blue columbine, would be found in the Blue Flowers section under the family of *Ranunculaceae*, the genus *Aquilegia*, and the species *coerulea*.

Any plant encountered while hiking in the Rocky Mountains is probably in this book, and all you need to do is find it. If it has a white flower, it will be in the White Flower section. If it has 4 petals, it is likely to be found in the *Brassicaceae* family, if 5 petals in the *Rosaceae* family, if many petals, in the *Asteraceae* family, and if bi-symmetrical, in the *Fabaceae* family. These are the major families, but there are many others all of which should be checked if not found among the 4 families cited.

In regard to color, there is no agreed upon point where off-white becomes pale yellow, or where purple becomes blue or red becomes purple. So if the "red" flower is not found in the Red section, try the Purple section. Flower color is affected by sunlight, age, genetics and elevation, and allowances must be made for these factors.

The description that accompanies each plant provides:

1 – the common name;
2 – the Latin name;
3 – the family name;
4 – a statement that characterizes the plant (e.g., Perennial), then brief comments on the STEM, LEAVES, FLOWERS, FRUIT, and SEED or other features;
5 – ECOLOGY cites the conditions under which it is found;
6 – LOCATION gives the date and place where the picture was taken;
7 – LOOK FOR suggests the characteristics you should observe to identify the plant; and
8 – LIFE LIST for noting which plants you have encountered, where the flower was observed, and a number key to your own Life List (see page 299).

This description is not intended to detail all that is known about the plant. For this information, one should consult other books, some of which are cited in the Reference section.

After identification, it would be well to note the date and place where the plant was found; an expanded Life List can be found toward the back of the book. In this way, the book becomes a checklist or Life List of the plants encountered, and can be used as a measure of one's progress in plant identification.

Although it is not as sure a way to identify plants, a camera can be used to photograph the plant for later identification. If this method is used, take several close-up pictures including the flowers, leaves, and fruit, and, of course, one of the whole plant. This will give a pictorial documentation of the plant and serve as the basis for producing your own keepsake book or collection.

✎ Acknowledgments ✎

It strikes me as ironic to see a wheelbarrow and an automobile sharing the same garage, separated by only a few feet in distance, but by over 5,000 years in development. While I have no idea why the automobile is there, I can guess that the wheelbarrow is there because it is the most maneuverable, practical and economical vehicle ever invented for a man to carry a load. This comparison and others that could be made serve to remind me that we, as individuals, do not do very much. Sir Isaac Newton was aware of this when he was lauded for his contributions to the sciences of mathematics and physics, and he gave credit to his predecessors by insisting that he "stood on the shoulders of giants." I don't intend to dwell on the things that I haven't done, even though they are more impressive than what I have done, but we all need to be reminded that I (we) didn't invent the language, the book, photography, the automobile, or the computer, nor did I establish the parks and forests and recreation areas, all of which were used in putting this book together. All I did was make use of what was available, and that includes people.

First of all there is my family, wife Marleigh and daughters Marcia and Mary. Had they voiced strenuous objections to my spending the time and money involved in photographing and writing this book, it, quite simply, wouldn't have been done.

Then there were my two hiking and biking buddies John Waddell and Joe Manalo who logged many miles of trails with me over the years. John is a botanist with the National Seed Storage Laboratory and Joe was in charge of their greenhouses until he retired. Both had an interest in plants that reinforced the interest I already had. John being the botanist already knew a lot of the native plants, and those he didn't know he could quickly key out in his well worn copy of Ruth Ashton Nelson's book on

Plants of the Rocky Mountain National Park. Joe didn't have the formal training, but was good on the common names and together we learned a lot.

Another botanist with the National Seed Lab was Leigh Towill. Leigh didn't have his Saturdays free like John and Joe, but he was very good at looking at my pictures and naming the plant. Over coffee, he would go through the pictures and I would write down the names, after which I would verify the identity and spelling.

As luck would have it, I acquired a son-in-law, Bryan Leary, who was both knowledgeable and proficient at computers. In the early stages of this project, I was planning to arrange the photographs on poster board along with the descriptions and photograph them as pages. I had a word processor but no computer or scanner. Bryan saw the problem and he and Mary set me up to scan and burn the scans onto compact discs. As it turned out this would have had to be done anyway because no publisher would have used photographs of pasteboard pages, but then, I didn't know that.

Having worked in the same building that housed the herbarium at C.S.U., I was familiar with its function and knew the various curators over the years. I sought and received permission to verify all the entries in this book with herbarium specimens. Jennifer Akerfield, a former student of mine, has been the assistant curator of the herbarium for the past five years and was very helpful in identifying some of the more difficult plants. She also provided me with web sites to verify Latin and common names.

Finally, I would like to thank Alan Bernhard of Boulder Bookworks who designed and composed the book and Steve Garvan of Garvan Marketing who found a home for the book at the Colorado Mountain Club Press. This book would not have been possible without their superb work and advice.

JAMES ELLS
Fort Collins, Colorado

ROCKY MOUNTAIN FLORA

White Flowers

SPANISH BAYONET
Yucca glauca
Agave family *Agavaceae*

SHRUB to 5´; flower STOCK erect and leafless; LEAVES linear to 28″x½″, pale green, and thread bearing; FLOWERS greenish-cream to 2½″ long; buds pink; racemes to 2´ long.

ECOLOGY: Plains and foothills in dry areas.

LOCATION: Bitterbrush Trail, Hall Ranch, Lyons, CO 6/00 6000´

LOOK FOR sharp pointed, bayonet-like leaves.

■ LIFE LIST Where _____ NUMBER _____

ARROWHEAD
Sagittaria latifolia
Water Plantain family *Alismataceae*

PERENNIAL vine to 3´ long; STEMS submerged; LEAVES to 2½´ tall with winged blades to 10″x4″ at petiole junction; wings to 5″ long; FLOWERS white to 1″ wide with 3 petals, in racemes to 10″ long.

ECOLOGY: Plains, in moving water.

LOCATION: Spring Creek, Ft. Collins, CO 8/02 5000´

LOOK FOR large arrowhead leaves.

■ LIFE LIST Where _____ NUMBER _____

GIANT ANGELICA
Angelica ampla
Celery (Parsley) family *Apiaceae*

PERENNIAL to 7´ tall; STEMS stout and purplish; LEAVES divided into twice-toothed leaflets; FLOWERS white, tiny and many, borne on large, flat umbels to 8″ across.

ECOLOGY: Foothills to subalpine in wet places.

LOCATION: Boy Scout Rd. (68C), at Elkhorn Ck., Larimer County, CO 7/04 8000´

LOOK FOR a large flat umbel, a purpling stalk, and celery-type leaves.

■ LIFE LIST Where _____ NUMBER _____

POISON HEMLOCK

Conium maculatum
Celery (Parsley) family
Apiaceae (Umbellifera)

BIENNIAL to 6′ tall; STEMS gray-green in clumps of 5–8 forming a vase-like shrub; LEAVES twice pinnate with lobed leaflets; FLOWERS white in umbels to 2″ wide; BERRIES to ⅛″.
ECOLOGY: Plains to montane on moist sites – poisonous.
LOCATION: Dowdy Lake Rec. Area, Red Feathers, CO 7/01 8000′
LOOK FOR a shrub-like plant with gray-green stems.

■ **LIFE LIST** Where _____ NUMBER _____

COW PARSNIP

Heracleum sphondylium
Celery (Parsley) family
Apiaceae (Umbelliferae)

PERENNIAL to 8′ high; LEAVES large, with coarse, toothed leaflets; FLOWERS white, tiny and grouped into many umbels to form a head to 8″ wide.
ECOLOGY: Foothills to subalpine in wet places.
LOCATION: Isabelle Glacier Trail, Brainard Lake Rec. Area, Ward, CO 7/00 11,000′
LOOK FOR a large, succulent plant on wet ground.

■ **LIFE LIST** Where _____ NUMBER _____

LOVAGE

Ligusticum porteri
Celery (Parsley) family
Apiaceae (Umbelliferae)

PERENNIAL to 3½′ tall; STEMS hollow, reddish, stout, curved, with few leaves; LEAVES to 10″ long, divided into toothed segments; FLOWERS small, white and grouped into flat-topped umbels to 3″ wide.
ECOLOGY: Montane and subalpine in forest clearings.
LOCATION: Sheep Lake Trail, Medicine Bow N.F., WY 7/00 11,000′
LOOK FOR a white-flowered umbel and carrot-like foliage.

■ **LIFE LIST** Where _____ NUMBER _____

FERNLEAF LOVAGE
Ligusticum tenuifolium
Celery (Parsley) family
Apiaceae (Umbelliferae)

PERENNIAL to 2′ tall; STEMS slender and erect, bearing 1 or 2 small, fern-like leaves; LEAVES mostly basal and fern-like to 6″ long; FLOWERS white, tiny, in clusters of umbels forming a dome head to 3″ across.

ECOLOGY: Subalpine on grassy slopes.

LOCATION: Pawnee Pass Trail, Brainard Lake Rec. Area, Ward, CO 7/00 10,500′

LOOK FOR an erect stem bearing a white terminal umbel and fern-like leaves.

■ **LIFE LIST** Where ＿＿＿＿＿＿ NUMBER ＿＿

SALT AND PEPPER
Lomatium concinnum
Celery (Parsley) family
Apiaceae (Umbelliferae)

PERENNIAL to 10″ high; STEMS usually leafless; LEAVES to 6″ long with deeply incised leaflets; FLOWERS white or pink to ⅛″ across in terminal umbels.

ECOLOGY: Foothills in early spring.

LOCATION: Lory S.P., Ft. Collins, CO 5/01 5500′

LOOK FOR gray-green, carrot-like foliage and reclining stems.

■ **LIFE LIST** Where ＿＿＿＿＿＿ NUMBER ＿＿

COWBANE
Oxypolis fendleri
Celery (Parsley) family
Apiaceae (Umbelliferae)

PERENNIAL to 2′; STEMS hollow and weak; LEAVES to 8″ long, bearing 7–9 ovate, soft, blunt-toothed leaflets; FLOWERS white to 1/16″ wide in domed umbels to 2 ½″ across.

ECOLOGY: Montane to subalpine in wet areas.

LOCATION: 4th of July Trail, Eldora, CO 8/99 11,500′

LOOK FOR a white umble and pinnate leaves with well-spaced leaflets.

■ **LIFE LIST** Where ＿＿＿＿＿＿ NUMBER ＿＿

INDIAN HEMP
Apocynum cannabinum
Dogbane family   *Apocynaceae*

PERENNIAL to 4´ tall; STEMS reddish with forked branching; LEAVES opposite, ovate, to 6˝ long, ascending and short-petioled; FLOWERS white to greenish, urn-shaped, to ⅛˝ long, with 5 tiny lobes.
ECOLOGY: Plains, in moist areas.
LOCATION: S. Platte River, Denver, CO 5/92 5000´
LOOK FOR clusters of white cylindrical flowers and opposite, leathery leaves.

■ **LIFE LIST** Where _____ NUMBER _____

SIBERIAN DOGWEED
Apocynum x floribundum (medium)
Dogbane family   *Apocynaceae*

PERENNIAL to 4´ tall in thickets; STEMS leafy, milky and upright; LEAVES elliptic, appressed, pale beneath, milky and sessile to 4˝; FLOWERS white, erect, berry-like, in umbels; PODS slender to 4˝ long and often paired.
ECOLOGY: Plains, near water.
LOCATION: Prospect Ponds, Ft. Collins, CO 8/02 5000´
LOOK FOR a thicket of red stemmed plants with upright, milky leaves.

■ **LIFE LIST** Where _____ NUMBER _____

WILD SARSAPARILLA
Aralia nudicaulis
Ginseng family   *Araliaceae*

PERENNIAL to 3´ tall; STEMS slender and leafless up to the crown; LEAVES pinnate with 3–5 ovate and serrated leaflets; FLOWERS greenish-white in ball-like umbels.
ECOLOGY: Foothills to montane in wet, shady places
LOCATION: Lion Gulch, Roosevelt N.F., Rt. 36, CO 7/00 7500´
LOOK FOR ball-like flower heads.

■ **LIFE LIST** Where _____ NUMBER _____

TANSY YARROW
Achillea millefolium (lanulosa)
Aster family   *Asteraceae (Compositae)*

PERENNIAL to 3´ high; STEMS erect, reddish, with alternate leaves and nodes 1–2″ apart; LEAVES twice pinnatifid, stem leaves sessile, basal leaves petioled to 8″ long; FLOWERS tiny, pinkish to white, in flat-topped clusters.

ECOLOGY: Foothills to alpine in dry areas.
LOCATION: Bike trail, Copper Mt., CO 8/91 10,000´
LOOK FOR feathery-soft foliage.

■ **LIFE LIST** Where _____ NUMBER _____

PEARLY EVERLASTING
Anaphalis margaritacea
Aster family   *Asteraceae (Compositae)*

PERENNIAL to 3´ tall; STEMS erect, leafy and woolly; LEAVES alternate, sessile, narrow, to 4″ long and greener above than below; FLOWERS white, berry-like to ¼″ across, forming heads.

ECOLOGY: Foothills to subalpine in dry, exposed areas.
LOCATION: Arthur's Rock Trail, Lory S.P., Ft. Collins, CO 8/05 5500´
LOOK FOR clusters of white pearls atop erect stems 1´ or more tall.

■ **LIFE LIST** Where _____ NUMBER _____

TALL PUSSYTOES
Antennaria anaphaloides
Aster family   *Asteraceae (Compositae)*

PERENNIAL to 16″ high; STEMS hairy and silvery; LEAVES narrow-lanceolate to 6″ long and fuzzy on both sides; FLOWERS white, round, to ¼″, in small clusters.

ECOLOGY: Foothills to subalpine in open, dry areas.
LOCATION: Young Gulch, Poudre Canyon, CO 5/02 7000´
LOOK FOR 4–7 fluffy, ball-like, white flowers clustered atop stems 1´ tall.

■ **LIFE LIST** Where _____ NUMBER _____

SMALL LEAVED PUSSYTOES
Antennaria neglecta
Aster family   *Asteraceae (Compositae)*

PERENNIAL to 14″ tall, in patches; STEMS erect
with small linear leaves; basal LEAVES bright green,
spatulate, to 1″ long, stem leaves linear, to 1″ long;
FLOWERS white, cylindrical, to ¼″ wide, forming
loose clusters with up to 10 upright heads.
ECOLOGY: Foothills and montane in association
with pines.
LOCATION: Arthur's Rock Trail, Lory S.P., Ft. Collins,
CO 6/99 5500′
LOOK FOR white pussytoes.

■ **LIFE LIST** Where _____ NUMBER _____

SUNLOVING CATSPAW
Antennaria parvifolia
Aster family   *Asteraceae (Compositae)*

PERENNIAL to 6″ tall, woolly and mat-forming;
STEMS woolly with tiny, alternate leaves; basal
LEAVES to 1″ long, spatulate and woolly; FLOWER
clusters to ½″ across with pinkish-white bracts.
ECOLOGY: Foothills to subalpine on dry, sunny
slopes.
LOCATION: Cow Creek Trail, McGraw Ranch, RMNP,
CO 6/10 8000′
LOOK FOR patches of gray-green foliage with
cotton-like balls on stems less than 6″ high.

■ **LIFE LIST** Where _____ NUMBER _____

ALPINE PUSSYTOES
Antennaria umbrinella (alpina)
Aster family   *Asteraceae (Compositae)*

PERENNIAL to 4″ high, forming mats; STEMS
woolly and leafy; stem leaves to ½″ long, sessile and
linear; basal LEAVES to 1″, spatulate and pointed;
FLOWER heads in clusters on stalks with brown
bracts.
ECOLOGY: Montane to alpine on slopes and in
meadows.
LOCATION: Mueller S.P., Divide, CO 6/04 9000′
LOOK FOR in-folded leaves to distinguish it from
A. parvifolia.

■ **LIFE LIST** Where _____ NUMBER _____

NORTHERN BOG ASTER

Aster borealis
Aster family   *Asteraceae (Compositae)*

PERENNIAL to 20″ tall; STEMS slender, leafy and branching at the top; LEAVES narrow-lanceolate to spatulate to 3″ and reduced upward; FLOWERS purple going to white, to ¾″ wide.
ECOLOGY: Foothills to montane.
LOCATION: Parvin Lake Rec. Area, Red Feathers, CO 8/01 8000′
LOOK FOR purple buds opening into white flowers.

■ **LIFE LIST** Where _____ NUMBER _____

CAMPESTRIS ASTER

Aster campestris
Aster family   *Asteraceae (Compositae)*

PERENNIAL to 18″ tall; STEMS erect, leafy and branched at the top; LEAVES spatulate, to 2″ long at the base, becoming lanceolate, sessile and wavy upward; FLOWER heads few, white, to 1″ wide.
ECOLOGY: Foothills to subalpine.
LOCATION: Lower Poudre Canyon, CO 7/02 6500′
LOOK FOR a daisy-like flower with many rays and a long stalk.

■ **LIFE LIST** Where _____ NUMBER _____

MANY FLOWERED ASTER

Aster (Virgulus) ericoides
Aster family   *Asteraceae (Compositae)*

PERENNIAL to 3′ high; STEMS curved, leafy and hairy; basal LEAVES spatulate to 3″ long, stem leaves linear to 1″ long; FLOWER heads white to ½″ wide, in clusters.
ECOLOGY: Plains and foothills on dry, sandy soils.
LOCATION: Avery Park, Ft. Collins, CO 8/01 5000′
LOOK FOR a clump of bottlebrush stems with cylinders of tiny white daisies.

■ **LIFE LIST** Where _____ NUMBER _____

ROUGH WHITE ASTER

Aster (Virgulus) falcatus
Aster family   *Asteraceae (Compositae)*

PERENNIAL to 4´ tall, in patches; STEMS woody,
wiry, leafy and hairy; LEAVES narrow, twisted and
bristly on the underside, to 3″ long; FLOWER heads
to ½″ across, numerous and white.

ECOLOGY: Plains and foothills on open slopes.

LOCATION: Well Gulch, Lory S.P., Ft. Collins, CO
8/01 5500´

LOOK FOR a plant covered with tiny white daisies.

■ **LIFE LIST** Where _____ NUMBER _____

WILLOW ASTER

Aster lanceolatus (hesperius)
Aster family   *Asteraceae (Compositae)*

PERENNIAL to 18″ tall; STEMS yellowish, leafy and
branched; LEAVES alternate, narrow-elliptical to 2½″
long; FLOWERS white or purple to 1¼″ wide with
25–40 petals.

ECOLOGY: Plains in wet places.

LOCATION: Avery Park, Ft. Collins, CO 8/01 5000´

LOOK FOR daisy-type flowers with narrow petals.

■ **LIFE LIST** Where _____ NUMBER _____

PORTER ASTER

Aster porteri
Aster family   *Asteraceae (Compositae)*

PERENNIAL to 18″ high, the most common white
aster of the mountains; STEMS slender, crooked,
branched and leafy; LEAVES narrow and pointed to
4″ long; FLOWER heads white, ¾″ wide with 3 tiers
of reflexed bracts.

ECOLOGY: Foothills to subalpine.

LOCATION: Well Gulch, Lory S.P., Ft. Collins, CO
8/01 5500´

LOOK FOR an abundance of daisy-like flowers and
grass-like leaves.

■ **LIFE LIST** Where _____ NUMBER _____

KNAPWEED

Centaurea (Acosta) diffusa
Aster family   *Asteraceae (Compositae)*

ANNUAL or perennial to 2´ tall; STEMS rough and
   much branched; LEAVES to 1˝ long, rough, hairy
   with lower leaves lobed; FLOWERS numerous, white
   or purplish, to ¾˝ wide, with narrow, unruly rays.
ECOLOGY: Plains and foothills on disturbed ground
   – a European weed.
LOCATION: Boulder Creek Trail, Boulder, CO 8/05
   5500´
LOOK FOR cocoon-like buds and disarrayed petals
   of uneven length.

   ■ **LIFE LIST** Where _____ NUMBER _____

FROST BALL

Cirsium scopulorum
Aster family   *Asteraceae (Compositae)*

BIENNIAL to 2´ high; STEMS erect and leafy;
   LEAVES are narrow, to 6˝ long, deeply incised into
   spine-tipped teeth to ⅛˝ long; FLOWERS white and
   hidden by cob-webby hairs and spiny bracts.
ECOLOGY: Subalpine and alpine on rocky or gravely
   slopes.
LOCATION: 4th of July Trail, Eldora, CO 7/01
   11,500´
LOOK FOR comb-like leaves and a white fluffy
   flower head.

   ■ **LIFE LIST** Where _____ NUMBER _____

AMERICAN THISTLE

Cirsium tioganum (coloradense)
Aster family   *Asteraceae (Compositae)*

BIENNIAL or perennial to 3´ high; STEMS erect,
   reddish and unbranched; LEAVES deeply incised and
   spiny; 3 or 4 FLOWER heads form a terminal cluster,
   with white hairs and spine tipped, purple bracts.
ECOLOGY: Montane and subalpine.
LOCATION: Herman Gulch Trail, Bakerville, CO 8/99
   11,000´
LOOK FOR smooth, purplish stem, well-spaced
   alternate leaves and several terminal flower heads.

   ■ **LIFE LIST** Where _____ NUMBER _____

HORSEWEED

Conyza canadensis
Aster family   *Asteraceae (Compositae)*

ANNUAL or biennial to 4´ tall; STEMS erect, leafy and unbranched; LEAVES alternate, crowded and linear, to 3˝ long; FLOWERS white, tiny and numerous.

ECOLOGY: Plains in pastures, cultivated fields and disturbed places.

LOCATION: Dixon Reservoir, Ft. Collins, CO 9/01 5000´

LOOK FOR a plant that resembles a bottlebrush.

■ LIFE LIST   Where _____ NUMBER _____

CUTLEAF DAISY

Erigeron compositus
Aster family   *Asteraceae (Compositae)*

PERENNIAL to 10˝ tall; STEMS ascending or erect and nearly leafless; basal LEAVES clumped, consisting of string-like lobes, stem leaves linear, few, and tiny; FLOWER heads to ¾˝ across, white or sometimes pink or blue.

ECOLOGY: Foothills to subalpine in dry areas.

LOCATION: Top of Rist Canyon Rd., Larimer Cty., CO 5/04 8000´

LOOK FOR spaghetti-like foliage.

■ LIFE LIST   Where _____ NUMBER _____

COULTER DAISY

Erigeron coulteri
Aster family   *Asteraceae (Compositae)*

PERENNIAL to 1´ tall; STEMS erect and leafy; lower LEAVES elliptic to 3½˝, and petioled, upper leaves sessile and clasping; FLOWER heads single to 1½˝ across with up to 100 white or pale lavender rays.

ECOLOGY: Montane to alpine.

LOCATION: Herman Lake Trail, Bakerville, CO 8/00 11,000´

LOOK FOR tulip-like leaves and single, terminal flower heads.

■ LIFE LIST   Where _____ NUMBER _____

SPRAWLING DAISY

Erigeron divergens (colo-mexicanus)
Aster family *Asteraceae (Compositae)*

BIENNIAL to 10″ high; STEMS ascending, with a few tiny leaves; basal LEAVES linear to 1″ long, in many, little tufts; stem leaves linear and sessile to 1″ long; FLOWER heads are 1″ across, singular, with white rays showing pink beneath.

ECOLOGY: Plains and foothills in dry areas and gravely slopes.

LOCATION: Rabbit Mt., Lyons, CO 5/01 6000′

LOOK FOR a single, terminal daisy flower with more than 50 rays.

■ **LIFE LIST** Where _____ NUMBER _____

TRAILING DAISY

Erigeron flagellaris
Aster family *Asteraceae (Compositae)*

BIENNIAL to 16″ tall; STEMS smooth, slender, erect, and yellowish; basal LEAVES linear to 2″ long with winged petioles; stem leaves sessile and reduced upward; FLOWER heads white, terminal, solitary, to ¾″ across, with over 50 rays.

ECOLOGY: Plains to subalpine.

LOCATION: Bear Creek Nature Ctr., Colorado Springs, CO 6/04 7500′

LOOK FOR an upright stem with regularly spaced leaves and a single terminal flower head.

■ **LIFE LIST** Where _____ NUMBER _____

BLACK-HEADED DAISY

Erigeron melanocephalus
Aster family *Asteraceae (Compositae)*

PERENNIAL to 5″ tall one of the most common dwarf daisies on subalpine slopes; stem LEAVES linear to ½″ and basal leaves spoon-shaped and petioled, to 1½″; FLOWER heads are single to 1″ wide with blackish bracts.

ECOLOGY: Subalpine and alpine in moist, open areas.

LOCATION: Sheep Lake Trail, Medicine Bow N.F., WY 8/99 10,500′

LOOK FOR blackish bracts.

■ **LIFE LIST** Where _____ NUMBER _____

LOW DAISY

Erigeron pumilus
Aster family   *Asteraceae (Compositae)*

PERENNIAL to 8″ high, in clumps; STEMS reddish
and leafy; LEAVES linear, rolling inward, to 2″ long,
sessile and reduced upward; FLOWER heads solitary,
to 1¼″ wide with purple rays bleaching to white.
ECOLOGY: Plains and foothills.
LOCATION: Arthur's Rock Trail, Lory S.P., Ft. Collins,
CO 5/01 5500′
LOOK FOR purple rays on new flowers and white
rays on older flowers.

■ **LIFE LIST** Where _____ NUMBER _____

HAWKWEED

Hieracium albiflorum
Aster family   *Asteraceae (Compositae)*

PERENNIAL to 2′ high; the only species with white
flowers; STEMS slender, mostly leafless, branching at
the top; LEAVES mostly basal, spatulate, with or
without serration, to 5″; FLOWERS white to ¼″
wide.
ECOLOGY: Montane.
LOCATION: Mill Creek Trail, RMNP, CO 8/99 9,000
LOOK FOR a cluster of small, white, rayless flowers
atop a slender stalk.

■ **LIFE LIST** Where _____ NUMBER _____

OXEYE DAISY

Leucanthemum vulgare
(Chrysanthemum leucanthemum)
Aster family   *Asteraceae (Compositae)*

PERENNIAL to 2′ tall; STEMS erect and
unbranched; LEAVES alternate, narrow, toothed and
reduced upward; FLOWER heads to 2″ across with
30–40 white rays.
ECOLOGY: Plains to montane.
LOCATION: Young Gulch, Poudre Canyon, CO 7/02
7000′
LOOK FOR daisy flower heads with diameter of the
disc equal to the length of the rays.

■ **LIFE LIST** Where _____ NUMBER _____

WILD CHAMOMILE
Matricaria perforata
Aster family *Asteraceae (Compositae)*

ANNUAL to 2½´ tall; STEMS smooth and branched; LEAVES string-like to 2½˝ long; FLOWER heads terminal, solitary, to 1˝ across with 20–30 white rays.
ECOLOGY: Montane and subalpine in diturbed areas.
LOCATION: Berthoud Falls, CO 7/02 10,000´
LOOK FOR a daisy with string-like leaves.

■ **LIFE LIST** Where _____ NUMBER ____

TALL TOWNSEND DAISY
Townsendia eximia
Aster family *Asteraceae (Compositae)*

PERENNIAL to 8˝ tall; STEMS reddish with leafy whorls under the heads; LEAVES linear to 3˝ long; FLOWER heads single, bowl-shaped, to 1½˝ across with white rays and sharp, tiered bracts.
ECOLOGY: Plains and foothills.
LOCATION: Arthur's Rock Trail, Lory S.P., Ft. Collins, CO 7/05 5500´
LOOK FOR leaf whorls under the flower heads.

■ **LIFE LIST** Where _____ NUMBER ____

SHOWY TOWNSENDIA
Townsendia grandiflora
Aster family *Asteraceae (Compositae)*

PERENNIAL to 6˝ high; STEMS LEafy and reddish; LEAVES linear, pointed, in-folded, and wavy to 1½˝; FLOWER heads in bowl form, to 1½˝ wide with white rays.
ECOLOGY: Foothills to subalpine on gravely slopes.
LOCATION: Timber Trail, Lory S.P., Ft. Collins, CO 7/93 5500´
LOOK FOR a group of bowl-shaped daisy heads with greenish centers.

■ **LIFE LIST** Where _____ NUMBER ____

EASTER DAISY
Townsendia hookeri
Aster family *Asteraceae (Compositae)*

PERENNIAL to 2″ high, prostrate and mat-forming;
STEMS short and woody; LEAVES linear, alternate,
to ½″ long; FLOWER heads sessile to 1″ wide; rays
unruly, white above and pinkish beneath.
ECOLOGY: Plains and foothills.
LOCATION: Pawnee National Grasslands, Keota, CO
4/00 5000′
LOOK FOR small patches of green with several little
daisy heads.

■ LIFE LIST Where _____ NUMBER ____

MOUNTAIN CRYPTANTHA
Cryptantha cana
Borage family *Boraginaceae*

PERENNIAL to 2″ high; STEMS short, upright, and
leafy with terminal flower clusters; LEAVES linear to
½″ long; FLOWERS to ¼″ wide with 5 overlapping,
white petals, yellow centers and long bracts.
ECOLOGY: Plains on open, dry ground.
LOCATION: Pawnee National Grasslands, Keota, CO
4/00 5000′
LOOK FOR a tiny patch of gray-green leaves with
dried remnants from previous years.

■ LIFE LIST Where _____ NUMBER ____

BRACTLESS CRYPTANTHA
Cryptantha crassisepala
Borage family *Boraginaceae*

ANNUAL to 10″ tall; STEMS hairy, leafy and purplish;
LEAVES linear, upright and in-folded to 1″ long;
FLOWERS ⅛″ wide with 5 white petals and yellow
centers.
ECOLOGY: Foothills and montane.
LOCATION: Hall Ranch, Lyons, CO 5/02 6000′
LOOK FOR a slender plant that branches in the form
of a "Y".

■ LIFE LIST Where _____ NUMBER ____

SMALL CRYPTANTHA
Cryptantha minima
Borage family   *Boraginaceae*

PERENNIAL to 16″ high; STEMS multiple, leafy and ascending; LEAVES alternate, hairy and in-folded; FLOWERS white, 5-petaled, to ⅛″ wide.

ECOLOGY: Foothills and montane in dry disturbed areas.

LOCATION: West Lake Rec. Area, Red Feathers, CO 6/02 8000′

LOOK FOR a clump of ascending stems with alternating, upright leaves.

■ **LIFE LIST** Where _____ NUMBER ____

MINER'S CANDLE
Cryptantha (Oreocarya) virgata
Borage family   *Boraginaceae*

PERENNIAL or biennial to 2′ tall; STEMS erect, stout and leafy; LEAVES linear and hairy to 3″ long; FLOWERS white, ¾″ across and bowl-shaped.

ECOLOGY: Plains to montane on dry slopes.

LOCATION: Fish Creek, Estes Park, CO 6/92 8000′

LOOK FOR a plant that suggests a white candle.

■ **LIFE LIST** Where _____ NUMBER ____

CURVED BORAGE
Heliotropium curassavicum
Borage family   *Boraginaceae*

ANNUAL or perennial to 5″ high; STEMS succulent, prostrate, leafy to 10″ long; LEAVES fleshy, wavy, sessile to 1½″x ½″; FLOWERS white, 5-lobed to ⅜″ wide with yellow or purple centers.

ECOLOGY: Plains in drying mud.

LOCATION: Boyd Lake S.P., Loveland, CO 7/02 5000′

LOOK FOR gray-green, leathery leaves and clusters of white flowers with colorful centers.

■ **LIFE LIST** Where _____ NUMBER ____

FALSE GROMWELL
Onosmodium molle
Borage family   *Boraginaceae*

PERENNIAL shrub-like plant to 2′ tall and 5′ wide;
STEMS hairy, ascending, branching and leafy;
LEAVES hairy, lanceolate to 3″ long with prominent
dark green parallel veins; FLOWERS white.
ECOLOGY: Plains and foothills on dry, open sites.
LOCATION: Coyote Ridge Rec. Area, Ft. Collins, CO
7/01 5500′
LOOK FOR a clump of reclining stems that branch at
the top into multiple flower spikes.

■ LIFE LIST Where _____ NUMBER _____

HAIRY ROCKCRESS
Arabis hirsuta
Mustard family   *Brassicaceae (Cruciferae)*

ANNUAL, perennial, or biennial to 30″ tall; STEMS
erect, slender, branched and leafy, LEAVES mostly on
stem, lanceolate, clasping, to 1½″ and reduced
upward; FLOWERS white, 4-petaled, to ½″ across,
clustered in a terminal head; pods wire-like to 2½″
long.
ECOLOGY: Foothills to subalpine.
LOCATION: Lost Lake Trail, Eldora, CO 6/02 9000′
LOOK FOR an upright stem with a terminal cluster
of 4-petaled flowers.

■ LIFE LIST Where _____ NUMBER _____

HOLBOELL FALSE ARABIS
Arabis holboellii (Boechera refracta)
Mustard family   *Brassicaceae (Cruciferae)*

BIENNIAL or perennial, to 20″ tall; STEMS erect,
slender, and leafy; LEAVES linear, upright to 1″ long;
FLOWERS white, ⅜″ long and ¼″ across with 4
petals; PODS drooping, slender, to 3″x ⅛″.
ECOLOGY: Foothills and montane.
LOCATION: Well Gulch, Lory S.P., Ft. Collins, CO
5/02 5500′
LOOK FOR a spindly stem, pinkish-white flowers
and drooping wire-like pods.

■ LIFE LIST Where _____ NUMBER _____

HOARY ALYSSUM
Berteroa incana
Mustard family   *Brassicaceae (Cruciferae)*

ANNUAL, biennial, or perennial to 3´ tall; STEMS erect and branching; LEAVES lanceolate to ½″ long; FLOWERS white with 4 cleft, petals, borne terminally on racemes.

ECOLOGY: Plains to montane.

LOCATION: Alderfen Park, Evergreen, CO 9/99 7000´

LOOK FOR a slender plant with several ascending racemes bearing terminal flowers clusters.

■ LIFE LIST Where _____ NUMBER _____

SHEPHERD'S PURSE
Capsella bursa-pastoris
Mustard family   *Brassicaceae (Cruciferae)*

ANNUAL to 2´ tall; STEMS leafy and branching; basal LEAVES deeply lobed to 3″ long, stem leaves sessile and linear to 1½″ long; FLOWERS white, 4-petaled, to ¼″ wide; PODS triangular with a notched base.

ECOLOGY: Plains, on disturbed ground.

LOCATION: Avery Park, Ft. Collins, CO 5/02 5000´

LOOK FOR the triangular purse.

■ LIFE LIST Where _____ NUMBER _____

BITTER CRESS
Cardamine cordifolia
Mustard family   *Brassicaceae (Cruciferae)*

PERENNIAL to 30″ tall in patches; STEMS erect and leafy, LEAVES petioled, heart-shaped, to 2″ long; FLOWERS to ½″ wide with 4 white, indented petals; borne in clusters to 2″ wide.

ECOLOGY: Montane and subalpine.

LOCATION: Mitchell Lake Trail, Brainard Lake Rec. Area, Ward, CO 7/00 11,000´

LOOK FOR white, domed umbels on plants in or near running water.

■ LIFE LIST Where _____ NUMBER _____

WHITE TOP
Cardaria draba
Mustard family   *Brassicaceae (Cruciferae)*

PERENNIAL to 2´ tall; STEMS erect and leafy, topped with a flat umbel; LEAVES wavy and ascending, petioled below and clasping above; FLOWERS white, tiny, 4-petaled and many.

ECOLOGY: Plains and foothills on disturbed ground – competitive.

LOCATION: Rt. 287 & 57 Rd., Loveland, CO 5/03 5000´

LOOK FOR uniform, wavy leaves and white tops.

■ **LIFE LIST**   Where _____ NUMBER _____

PERENNIAL PEPPERGRASS
Lepidium latifolium
Mustard family   *Brassicaceae (Cruciferae)*

PERENNIAL to 2´ high; STEMS erect and branched with alternate leaves; LEAVES elliptic, glossy and upward curled, to 1˝ long; FLOWERS white, 4-petaled, to ¼˝ wide in domed umbels; PODS egg shaped.

ECOLOGY: Plains in waste places.

LOCATION: Boulder Creek Trail, Boulder CO 9/91 5500´

LOOK FOR glossy, up-curled leaves and egg-shaped seed pods.

■ **LIFE LIST**   Where _____ NUMBER _____

BRANCHED PEPPERGRASS
Lepidium ramosissimum
Mustard family   *Brassicaceae (Cruciferae)*

ANNUAL or biennial to 18˝ tall; STEMS branched and leafy; stem LEAVES linear to ¾˝ with a long and short leaves alternating at each node, basal leaves spatulate and lobed to 2˝; FLOWERS white to ⅛˝ wide with 4 petals; PODS ⅛˝ wide, spoon-shaped and slightly notched.

ECOLOGY: Plains and foothills.

LOCATION: Timber Trail, Lory S.P., Ft. Collins, CO 6/05 5500´

LOOK FOR spoon-shaped pods.

■ **LIFE LIST**   Where _____ NUMBER _____

PEPPERGRASS

Lepidium virginicum

Mustard family *Brassicaceae (Cruciferae)*

ANNUAL, biennial, or perennial to 10″ high; STEMS slender, leafy and branched at the top; LEAVES linear and upright to ½″ long; FLOWERS white, tiny and 4-petaled; PODS spoon-like and glabrous.

ECOLOGY: Plains and foothills on dry slopes.

LOCATION: Homestead Trail, Hall Ranch, Lyons, CO 5/01 6000′

LOOK FOR a small, white-flowered plant with spoon-shaped pods.

■ **LIFE LIST** Where _____ NUMBER _____

WATERCRESS

Rorippa nasturtium-aquaticum
(Nasturtium officinale)

Mustard family *Brassicaceae (Cruciferae)*

PERENNIAL to 18″ tall; STEMS floating or ascending, rooting at nodes; LEAVES pinnate with 3–11 leaflets; FLOWERS white, 4-petaled, to ¼″ across.

ECOLOGY: Plains and foothills, in moving water.

LOCATION: Rolland Moore Park, Ft, Collins, CO 8/02 5000′

LOOK FOR an aquatic plant with white flowers and several leaflets per leaf.

■ **LIFE LIST** Where _____ NUMBER _____

PENNYCRESS

Thlaspi arvense

Mustard family *Brassicaceae (Cruciferae)*

ANNUAL to 2′ tall; STEMS erect and leafy; LEAVES lanceolate, toothed, with upper leaves ascending and sessile; FLOWERS white, 4-petaled and clustered at tips of stems; PODS flat, oval, winged, and notched at apex.

ECOLOGY: Plains to montane.

LOCATION: Eldorado Canyon S.P., Eldorado Springs, CO 5/01 6500′

LOOK FOR upright leaves and seed pods with winged margins.

■ **LIFE LIST** Where _____ NUMBER _____

WILD CANDYTUFT
Thlaspi montanum
Mustard family   *Brassicaceae (Cruciferae)*

PERENNIAL to 8″ tall; STEMS purplish, erect and leafy; basal LEAVES ovate to 1¾″ with slender petioles, stem leaves clasping; FLOWERS white, ¼″ across, 4-petaled, in rounded terminal clusters; PODS paddle-shaped.
ECOLOGY: Foothills to alpine.
LOCATION: Medicine Bow N.F., WY 6/02 10,500′
LOOK FOR slender stems topped with 1″ balls of white flowers.

■ **LIFE LIST**   Where _____ NUMBER _____

CLAMMY WEED
Polanisia dodecandra
Caper family   *Capparaceae*

ANNUAL to 2′ tall; STEMS erect, hairy and leafy; LEAVES trifoliate, sticky, hairy and petioled; leaflets to 1½″ long; FLOWERS white with exserted pink stamens; PODS to 3″ long, ascending from 1″, horizontal stalks.
ECOLOGY: Plains and foothills.
LOCATION: Orchard Cove, Lory S.P., Ft. Collins, CO 8/02 5500′
LOOK FOR a plant that resembles the garden spider plant (Cleome).

■ **LIFE LIST**   Where _____ NUMBER _____

MORROW'S HONEYSUCKLE
Lonicera morrowii
Honeysuckle family   *Caprifoliaceae*

SHRUB to 10′ tall; TWIGS gray; LEAVES dull gray-green and leathery to 1½″; FLOWERS white or pink in axils of leaves with stalks to ¾″; BERRIES orange to $^5/_{16}$″.
ECOLOGY: Plains and foothills – generally, an escapee from cultivation.
LOCATION: Legacy Park, Ft. Collins, CO 5/03 5000′
LOOK FOR dull gray-green leaves, white or pink flowers, and orange berries.

■ **LIFE LIST**   Where _____ NUMBER _____

ELDERBERRY

Sambucus canadensis
Honeysuckle family   *Caprifoliaceae*

SHRUB to 12´ tall; TWIGS brown; LEAVES pinnate to
10˝ long with 5–9 serrated leaflets to 3˝ long;
FLOWERS white, in a flat umbel to 6˝ wide;
BERRIES edible, black, to ¼˝.

ECOLOGY: Plains in moist places – usually, an
escapee from cultivation.

LOCATION: Spring Creek Trail, Ft. Collins, CO 9/02
5000´

LOOK FOR serrated leaflets, flat umbels, with tiny
white flowers or black berries.

■ **LIFE LIST** Where _____ NUMBER _____

RED-BERRIED ELDER

Sambucus racemosa (microbotrys)
Honeysuckle family   *Caprifoliaceae*

SHRUB to 12´ tall; LEAVES opposite, pinnate with
5–7 serrated leaflets to 4˝; FLOWERS white with
reflexed petals and exserted stamens, in domed
umbels; BERRIES scarlet and non-edible.

ECOLOGY: Montane and subalpine.

LOCATION: Hidden Valley, RMNP, CO 6/02 9500´

LOOK FOR an umbel with white flowers having
reflexed petals and prominent stamens.

■ **LIFE LIST** Where _____ NUMBER _____

HIGH BUSH CRANBERRY

Virburnum edule
Honeysuckle family   *Caprifoliaceae*

SHRUB to 4´ tall; LEAVES 3-lobed, 2˝ x 2˝; FLOWERS
white to ¼˝ across in clusters to 3˝ across; FRUIT red
or orange with a single seed.

ECOLOGY: Foothills to subalpine in moist forests.

LOCATION: Wild Basin, RMNP, CO 6/02 9000´

LOOK FOR tri-lobed leaves and 5-lobed, white
flowers in a cluster.

■ **LIFE LIST** Where _____ NUMBER _____

WAYFARING TREE
Viburnum lantana
Honeysuckle family   *Caprifoliaceae*

SHRUB to 5´ tall; LEAVES ovate to 3˝ long;
FLOWERS white, 5-lobed, to ¼˝ wide, in flat clusters
to 4˝ across; FRUIT red.
ECOLOGY: Plains and foothills – an escapee from
cultivation.
LOCATION: Alderfen Park, Evergreen, CO 9/99
7000´
LOOK FOR a white flowering shrub with oval leaves
and prominent veins that suggests inclusion in a
landscape plan.

■ LIFE LIST Where _____ NUMBER _____

CONGESTA SANDWORT
Arenaria (Eremogone) congesta
Pink family   *Caryophyllaceae*

PERENNIAL to 6˝ high; STEMS with grass-like
leaves; LEAVES linear to 1˝, paired or single;
FLOWER head to ⅜˝ wide having up to 5 white
flowers with 5 rectangular petals to ³/₁₆˝ long.
ECOLOGY: Plains to alpine on open slopes.
LOCATION: St. Alban's Chapel, Medicine Bow N.F.,
WY 7/02 10,500´
LOOK FOR tiny grass-like plants with white flowers.

■ LIFE LIST Where _____ NUMBER _____

FENDLER SANDWORT
Arenaria (Eremogone) fendleri
Pink family   *Caryophyllaceae*

PERENNIAL to 10˝ tall in clumps; STEMS slender
ascending and branched; LEAVES grass-like to 3˝;
FLOWERS white, to ½˝ across, with 5 petals and a
calyx with purple stripes.
ECOLOGY: Foothills to alpine
LOCATION: South Park Trail, Guanella Pass, CO 8/99
11,500´
LOOK FOR the purple stripes on the calyx.

■ LIFE LIST Where _____ NUMBER _____

FIELD MOUSE-EAR
Cerastium arvense
Pink family   *Caryophyllaceae*

PERENNIAL to 8″ tall; STEMS with tufts of leaves in leaf axils; LEAVES sessile, narrow-lanceolate, to 1″ long; FLOWERS to ¾″ across with 5 white, cleft petals.
ECOLOGY: Foothills and montane in open areas.
LOCATION: Rabbit Mt., Lyons CO 5/01 6000′
LOOK FOR a "mouse ear" flower with deeply cut petals at lower elevations.

■ **LIFE LIST**   Where _____ NUMBER _____

ALPINE MOUSE-EAR
Cerastium beeringianum
Pink family   *Caryophyllaceae*

PERENNIAL to 6″ and loosely matted; STEMS leafy and ascending; LEAVES opposite, sessile, narrow-lanceolate to 1″ long; FLOWERS white, to 1″ across with 5 cleft petals.
ECOLOGY: Alpine on tundra.
LOCATION: South Park Trail, Guanella Pass, CO 8/99 11,500′
LOOK FOR a flower with ″V″ notched petals on plants at high elevations.

■ **LIFE LIST**   Where _____ NUMBER _____

COMMON MOUSE-EAR
Cerastium fontanum
Pink family   *Caryophyllaceae*

BIENNIAL or perennial to 6″ tall; STEMS weak, trailing and branched at the top, often forming mats and rooting at nodes; LEAVES narrow-lanceolate, sessile to 1½″ long; FLOWERS to ¾″ across with 5 white notched petals.
ECOLOGY: Plains to montane in disturbed areas, lawns and gardens.
LOCATION: Arthur's Rock Trail, Lory S.P., CO 5/02 5500′
LOOK FOR a branching stem with opposite leaves at lower elevations.

■ **LIFE LIST**   Where _____ NUMBER _____

MOUSE-EAR CHICKWEED
Cerastium nutans
Pink family   *Caryophyllaceae*

PERENNIAL to 4″ tall; STEMS ascending or erect;
LEAVES thick, paired, pubescent, dark-green, sessile,
narrow-lanceolate to 1″ long; FLOWERS white, to ¾″
across with 5 cleft petals.
ECOLOGY: Foothills and montane in grassy moist
areas.
LOCATION: Cow Creek Trail, McGraw Ranch, RMNP,
CO 6/01 8000′
LOOK FOR a "mouse-eared" flower on a plant with
wavy, pubescent leaves.

■ **LIFE LIST** Where _____ NUMBER _____

ALPINE SANDWORT
Minuartia (Lidia) obtusiloba
Pink family   *Caryophyllaceae*

PERENNIAL to 2″ high, mat-forming; STEMS short,
green and leafless; LEAVES mainly basal, ¼″ long,
moss-like and in pairs; FLOWERS white, ⅜″ wide,
and single, with 5 white, separated petals with
indented tips.
ECOLOGY: Alpine on steep slopes.
LOCATION: Guanella Pass, CO 7/05 11,500′
LOOK FOR moss-like leaves and white, bowl-shaped
flowers with separated petals.

■ **LIFE LIST** Where _____ NUMBER _____

ALPINE CAMPION MOSS
Minuartia stricta
Pink family   *Caryophyllaceae*

ANNUAL to 1″ high; STEMS with a single flower;
LEAVES linear, fleshy, awl-like, to ¼″ long; FLOWERS
white, 5-petaled, to ⅜″ long with purple sepals.
ECOLOGY: Alpine on open slopes.
LOCATION: Guanella Pass, CO 7/05 11,500′
LOOK FOR a small patch of white flowers set in a
moss-like background.

■ **LIFE LIST** Where _____ NUMBER _____

BLUNT-LEAVED SANDWORT
Moehringia (Arenaria) lateriflora
Pink family   *Caryophyllaceae*

PERENNIAL to 7″ tall; STEMS delicate, succulent, leafy and terminating in a solitary flower; LEAVES opposite, sessile, lanceolate to spatulate, to 1″ long; FLOWERS white with white centers, to ¼″ across.
ECOLOGY: Foothills and montane.
LOCATION: Flower Rd., Stove Prairie, CO 6/04 7500′
LOOK FOR tiny white, solitary flowers on delicate, opposite-leafed plants.

◼ **LIFE LIST** Where _____ NUMBER _____

JAMES STARWORT
Pseudostellaria (Stellaria) jamesiana
Pink family   *Caryophyllaceae*

PERENNIAL to 8″ tall; STEMS fragile with spreading, thread-like branches; LEAVES opposite, sessile, narrow, to 3″; FLOWERS solitary to ½″ wide, with white ″V″ notched petals.
ECOLOGY: Foothills and montane.
LOCATION: Young Gulch, Poudre Canyon, CO 6/01 7000′
LOOK FOR a "mouse-eared" flower with separated petals and prominent anthers, at lower elevations.

◼ **LIFE LIST** Where _____ NUMBER _____

ARTIC PEARLWORT
Sagina saginoides
Pink family   *Caryophyllaceae*

BIENNIAL or perennial tufted plant to 3″ high; STEM numerous, leafy, to 4″ long, forming a compact tussock; LEAVES awl-like to ⅜″; FLOWERS white, bowl-shaped, 5-petaled, to ½″ wide.
ECOLOGY: Subalpine and alpine in wet areas, among rocks.
LOCATION: Rollins Pass, CO 9/99 11,500′
LOOK FOR a small tussock among rocks.

◼ **LIFE LIST** Where _____ NUMBER _____

SOAPWORT (BOUNCING BET)

Saponaria officinalis
Pink family   *Caryophyllaceae*

PERENNIAL to 3´ in dense stands; STEMS sturdy,
upright, leafy and branching; LEAVES opposite,
lanceolate, sessile, to 5″ long; FLOWERS white to 1½″
across with 5 separated petals and a tubular calyx to
1″ long.
ECOLOGY: Plains along stream banks.
LOCATION: Poudre R. Trail, Ft. Collins, CO 7/02
5000´
LOOK FOR a patch of white flowers on 3´ stems.

■ **LIFE LIST**   Where _____ NUMBER _____

NIGHT FLOWERING CATCH FLY

Silene antirrhina
Pink family   *Caryophlyyaceae*

ANNUAL to 2´ tall; STEMS hairy, slender and leafy;
LEAVES opposite, lanceolate to 3½″ long; FLOWERS
with 5 deeply cleft petals on long corolla tubes, calyx
inflated and has reddish stripes.
ECOLOGY: Foothills and montane – of European
origin.
LOCATION: Alderfen Park, Evergreen, CO 9/99
7000´
LOOK FOR slender, reddish stems and closed flowers
during the day.

■ **LIFE LIST**   Where _____ NUMBER _____

LYCHNIS CAMPION

Silene dioica
Pink family   *Caryophyllaceae*

PERENNIAL to 4´ tall; STEMS slender and upright;
LEAVES lanceolate, sessile, opposite and ascending to
4″ long; FLOWERS white with a raised center circle
and 5 cleft petals. Sexes on separate plants.
ECOLOGY: Plains to montane.
LOCATION: Young Gulch, Poudre Canyon, CO 6/01
7000´
LOOK FOR purple calyx stripes and a raised circle at
the flower center.

■ **LIFE LIST**   Where _____ NUMBER _____

WHITE CAMPION
Silene scouleri
Pink family   *Caryophyllaceae*

ANNUAL or biennial to 2´ tall; STEMS hairy and sticky; LEAVES elliptical, opposite, sessile and hairy, to 4˝; FLOWERS white, open in evening, male calyx ¾˝ long with 10 veins, female 1¼˝ with 20 veins, on separate plants.

ECOLOGY: Plains to montane.

LOCATION: Young Gulch, Poudre Canyon, CO 6/02 7000´

LOOK FOR multiple leaves per node and a lack of purple stripes on the calyx tube.

■ **LIFE LIST** Where _____ NUMBER _____

STARWORT
Stellaria longipes
Pink family   *Caryophyllaceae*

PERENNIAL to 6˝ tall; STEM erect and slender; LEAVES opposite to ½˝, narrow-lanceolate and sessile; FLOWERS white, single, terminal, with 5 cleft petals.

ECOLOGY: Foothills to alpine.

LOCATION: Boy Scout Rd. (68C), Elkhorn Ck., Larimer Cty., CO 7/04 8000´

LOOK FOR a white flower with separated petals.

■ **LIFE LIST** Where _____ NUMBER _____

CHICKWEED
Stellaria media
Pink family   *Caryophyllaceae*

ANNUAL or perennial to 4˝ high; STEMS succulent, reclining and leafy; LEAVES ovate, ½˝ wide with lower leaves petioled; FLOWERS white, tiny and inconspicuous.

ECOLOGY: Plains, as a lawn weed in shady, wet places.

LOCATION: Avery Park, Ft. Collins, CO 8/02 5000´

LOOK FOR a light green patch of broad leaved plants in a wet, shady area.

■ **LIFE LIST** Where _____ NUMBER _____

WILD MORNING GLORY
Calystegia sepium
Morning Glory family   *Convolvulaceae*

PERENNIAL vine to 5´ long; STEMS prostrate or climbing and leafy; LEAVES arrowhead-shaped to 1½″ wide with a 1¼″ petiole; FLOWERS white, funnel-shaped, to 2″ wide and 2″ deep.

ECOLOGY: Plains and foothills on moist disturbed sites.

LOCATION: Boyd Lake S.P., Loveland, CO 6/02 5000´

LOOK FOR large, white, funnel-shaped flowers.

■ **LIFE LIST**   Where _____ NUMBER _____

BINDWEED
Convolvulus arvensis
Morning Glory family   *Convolvulaceae*

PERENNIAL vine to 8´ long; STEMS leafy and climbing by twining; LEAVES arrowhead-shaped to 4″; FLOWERS white or pink and funnel-shaped to 1″ across.

ECOLOGY: Plains, almost anywhere – a noxious weed.

LOCATION: Rolland Moore Park, Ft. Collins, CO 8/02 5000´

LOOK FOR a twining vine with arrowhead leaves and funnel-shaped flowers.

■ **LIFE LIST**   Where _____ NUMBER _____

BUNCHBERRY
Cornus canadensis
Dogwood family   *Cornaceae*

PERENNIAL herb to 10″ tall, spreading by rhizomes; STEMS yellowish; LEAVES elliptical to 3″ long, evergreen and in whorls; FLOWER clusters are surrounded by 4 white, petal-like bracts.

ECOLOGY: Foothills and montane in partial shade.

LOCATION: Lion Gulch, Roosevelt N.F., US 36, CO 7/01 7500´

LOOK FOR shiny leaves, white bracts and green or red berries.

■ **LIFE LIST**   Where _____ NUMBER _____

RED OSIER DOGWOOD
Cornus sericea (stolonifera)
Dogwood family   *Cornaceae*

SHRUB to 8´ tall; STEMS smooth and mahogany
colored, twigs red; LEAVES elliptical, opposite with 2″
long blades and ½″ petioles; FLOWERS white to ¼″
across in flat topped umbels; BERRIES white turning
blue, to ¼″.

ECOLOGY: Plains to subalpine.

LOCATION: Spring Creek Trail, Ft. Collins, CO 8/02
5000´

LOOK FOR a shrub with opposite leaves and 4,
white, pointed petals (bracts).

■ **LIFE LIST** Where _____ NUMBER _____

THYME-LEAVED SPURGE
Chamaesyce (Euphorbia) serpyllifolia
Spurge family   *Euphorbiaceae*

ANNUAL to 1″ high spreading to form a small, round
mat; STEMS leafy, milky and branching as they
radiate out from the center; LEAVES opposite, oval to
½″; FLOWERS to ¹/₁₆″ wide with 4 petals.

ECOLOGY: Plains, in sidewalk cracks, etc.

LOCATION: Boyd Lake S.P., Loveland, CO 7/02
5000´

LOOK FOR a prostrate plant that suggests Purslane
but has milky sap.

■ **LIFE LIST** Where _____ NUMBER _____

SNOW ON THE MOUNTAIN
Euphorbia (Agaloma) marginata
Spurge family   *Euphorbiaceae*

ANNUAL to 2´ tall; STEMS erect, yellowish and
forking near the top; LEAVES ovate to 3″ long;
FLOWERS white and tiny.

ECOLOGY: Plains and foothills in dry open areas – a
native plant that has become a garden favorite.

LOCATION: Coyote Ridge Rec. Area, Ft. Collins, CO
7/01 5500´

LOOK FOR thick, leathery leaves with white margins
and milky sap.

■ **LIFE LIST** Where _____ NUMBER _____

STANDING MILKVETCH
Astragalus adsurgens
Pea family   *Fabaceae (Leguminosae)*

PERENNIAL to 14″ high; STEMS angular, smooth and creeping; LEAVES alternate, oddly pinnate with up to 12 pairs of leaflets; FLOWERS white to purple in oblong clusters; pods ⅜″ long.

ECOLOGY: Plains and foothills on prairies and gravely slopes.

LOCATION: Bitterbrush Trail, Hall Ranch, Lyons, CO 5/01 6000′

LOOK FOR in-rolled leaflets and a terminal cluster of white leguminous flowers.

■ **LIFE LIST** Where _____ NUMBER _____

ALPINE VETCH
Astragalus alpinus
Pea Family   *Fabaceae (Leguminosae)*

PERENNIAL; STEMS to 10″ long; LEAVES ALternate, pinnate with 6–11 pairs of hairy leaflets to ½″ long; FLOWERS white to purple, to ½″ long, in terminal clusters of 2–8.

ECOLOGY: Montane to alpine in moist, shady areas.

LOCATION: S. Park Trail, Guanella Pass, CO 8/99 11,500′

LOOK FOR a spindly plant with white flowers tinged with purple.

■ **LIFE LIST** Where _____ NUMBER _____

GROUND PLUM
Astragalus crassicarpus
Peas family   *Fabaceae (Leguminosae)*

PERENNIAL to 6″ high; SCAPE supporting a terminal flower cluster; LEAVES pinnate with many pairs of hairy leaflets to ⅜″ long; FLOWERS white, leguminous, in terminal clusters of 6–8 flowers; FRUIT resemble a miniature plum.

ECOLOGY: Plains and foothills.

LOCATION: Arthur's Rock Trail, Lory S.P., Ft. Collins, CO 5/00 5500′

LOOK FOR a tiny rosette with many pairs of hairy leaflets and scapes bearing white flowers.

■ **LIFE LIST** Where _____ NUMBER _____

DRUMMOND MILKVETCH
Astragalus drummondii
Pea family *Fabaceae (Leguminosae)*

PERENNIAL to 2´ tall; STEMS hairy, leafy and upright; LEAVES pinnate with hairy leaflets to ¾˝ long; FLOWERS white, curved upward, to 1˝ long, disarrayed in loose terminal racemes.

ECOLOGY: Plains to montane in open areas.

LOCATION: Nelson Loop, Hall Ranch, Lyons, CO 6/00 6500´

LOOK FOR a hairy leguminous plant with unruly, curved, white flowers.

■ **LIFE LIST** Where _____ NUMBER _____

WILD LICORICE
Glycyrrhiza lepidota
Pea family *Fabaceae (Leguminosae)*

PERENNIAL to 4´ tall in colonies; STEMS erect and leafy; LEAVES pinnately divided into paired, narrow, pointed leaflets to 1˝ long; FLOWERS white in 2˝ wide clusters on erect scapes, to 4˝ long; FRUIT are burs in elongated clusters.

ECOLOGY: Plains and foothills.

LOCATION: Dowdy Lake Rec. Area, Red Feathers, CO 7/01 8000´

LOOK FOR upright scapes in leaf axils, bearing white, leguminous flowers.

■ **LIFE LIST** Where _____ NUMBER _____

WHITE SWEET CLOVER
Melilotus altissimus (alba)
Pea family *Fabaceae (Leguminosae)*

PERENNIAL to 6´ tall; STEMS slender, wiry, and supple; LEAVES palmate with an irregular number of narrow leaflets of irregular length up to 1½˝ long; FLOWERS white on curved racemes to 4˝ long.

ECOLOGY: Plains to montane along road sides and streams.

LOCATION: Legacy Park, Ft. Collins, CO 6/01 5000´

LOOK FOR small, white, leguminous flowers on curved racemes.

■ **LIFE LIST** Where _____ NUMBER _____

WHITE LOCO

Oxytropis sericea
Pea family   *Fabaceae (Leguminoseae)*

PERENNIAL to 16″ tall in clumps; SCAPES silky-
gray; LEAVES pinnate to 12″ long; leaflets to 1½″
long; FLOWERS white, yellow or purple, to 1″ long,
with up to 27 on a raceme; PODS oblong to 1″ long,
leathery and erect.
ECOLOGY: Plains to subalpine.
LOCATION: Bitterbrush Trail, Hall Ranch, Lyons, CO
5/01 6000′
LOOK FOR a silvery gray plant with reclining leaves
and racemes with 10 or more flowers.

■ LIFE LIST   Where _____   NUMBER _____

WHIPROOT CLOVER

Trifolium dasyphyllum
Pea family   *Fabaceae*

PERENNIAL to 2″ tall; STEMS prostrate and
inconspicuous; LEAVES trifoliate with in-folded,
linear leaflets to ½″ long; FLOWERS ¾″ long, white
with pink tripped keels.
ECOLOGY: Subalpine to alpine.
LOCATION: Fall River Rd., RMNP, CO 7/04 10,500′
LOOK FOR a mat formed by a plant with trifoliate
leaves and in-folded leaflets.

■ LIFE LIST   Where _____   NUMBER _____

WHITE DUTCH CLOVER

Trifolium repens
Pea family   *Fabaceae (Leguminosae)*

PERENNIAL to 8″ tall; STEMS creeping and rooting
at nodes; LEAVES with long petioles and 3, oval,
serrated leaflets, to ¾″ wide; FLOWERS white in
loose, globose heads to ¾″, on scapes to 8″ high.
ECOLOGY: Plains to montane.
LOCATION: Gem Lake Trail, RMNP, CO 7/99 8500′
LOOK FOR a plant that resembles lawn clover; they
are the same.

■ LIFE LIST   Where _____   NUMBER _____

ARTIC GENTIAN
Gentiana (Gentianodes) algida
Gentian family *Gentianaceae*

PERENNIAL to 6″ high, in clumps; STEMS hidden by leaves; LEAVES narrow and infolded, to 4″ long; FLOWERS white, 3 per stem, barrel-shaped, to 2″ long, with purple steaks and spots.

ECOLOGY: Subalpine and alpine near water.

LOCATION: North Gap Lake Trail, Medicine Bow N.F., WY 8/00 10,500′

LOOK FOR little tubular flowers with pointed lobes and purple stripes and dots.

■ **LIFE LIST** Where _____ NUMBER _____

WHITE GERANIUM
Geranium richardsonii
Geranium family *Geraniaceae*

PERENNIAL to 18″ high; STEMS slender, branched and ascending; LEAVES palmately divided into 3–5 toothed lobes; FLOWERS 1″ across, with 5 white petals and red veins.

ECOLOGY: Foothills to subalpine in moist, shady areas.

LOCATION: Arthur's Rock Trail, Lory S.P., Ft. Collins, CO 5/00 5500′

LOOK FOR 5 horizontal, flat, white petals with pink anthers and veins.

■ **LIFE LIST** Where _____ NUMBER _____

WAXFLOWER
Jamesia americana
Hydrangea family *Hydrangeaceae*

SHRUB to 6′ high with flaking bark; LEAVES opposite, hairy, toothed, and rounded, to 2½″ long; FLOWERS waxy-white, ½″ across, 5-petaled and borne in clusters.

ECOLOGY: Foothills to subalpine on rocky slopes.

LOCATION: Well Gulch, Lory S.P., Ft. Collins, CO 5/01 5500′

LOOK FOR a shrub with dark green leaves, prominent veins, blunt teeth, and white, waxy flowers.

■ **LIFE LIST** Where _____ NUMBER _____

WATERLEAF
Hydrophyllum fendleri
Waterleaf family   *Hydrophyllaceae*

PERENNIAL to 3´ tall; STEMS brittle and watery; LEAVES thin, pinnate with 5–9 toothed leaflets; FLOWERS white with exserted stamens, resembling a pincushion; INFLORESCENCE consists of paired, globose clusters.

ECOLOGY: Plains to montane in moist, shady areas.

LOCATION: Shadow Canyon, Eldorado Canyon S.P., Eldorado Springs, CO 6/00 6500´

LOOK FOR twin globose flower heads and sharply toothed leaves.

█ **LIFE LIST** Where _____ NUMBER _____

SPEARSHAPED PHACELIA
Phacelia hastata
Waterleaf family   *Hydrophyllaceae*

PERENNIAL to 18˝ high; STEMS usually several, leafy and ascending; LEAVES hairy, alternate, clasping to 2˝ long, with parallel venation; FLOWERS white, with exserted stigmas on curved racemes.

ECOLOGY: Plains to alpine.

LOCATION: S. Mesa Trail, Eldorado Canyon S.P., Eldorado Springs, CO 6/00 6500´

LOOK FOR multiple stems and hairy, clasping leaves.

█ **LIFE LIST** Where _____ NUMBER _____

SCORPION WEED
Phacelia heterophylla
Waterleaf family   *Hydrophyllaceae*

BIENNIAL or perennial to 16˝ high; STEMS hairy and variable; LEAVES gray-green to 3˝ long, alternate and hairy with prominent veins; FLOWERS white or pink, tiny and crowded into tightly coiled clusters or on a one-sided, curved raceme.

ECOLOGY: Plains to montane on disturbed land.

LOCATION: Well Gulch, Lory S.P., Ft. Collins, CO 7/04 5500´

LOOK FOR curved flower clusters that resemble a scorpion's tail.

█ **LIFE LIST** Where _____ NUMBER _____

GIANT HYSSOP
Agastache foeniculum
Mint family   *Lamiaceae (Labiatae)*

PERENNIAL to 6´ tall; STEMS erect and branching from leaf axils; LEAVES cordate, toothed, to 3˝ long, with prominent veins; FLOWERS mainly white in crowded spikes with only a few open at a time.
ECOLOGY: Plains and foothills.
LOCATION: Well Gulch, Lory S.P., Ft. Collins, CO 8/01 5500´
LOOK FOR soft, velvety leaves and ascending side branches with terminal flower clusters.

■ **LIFE LIST** Where _____ NUMBER _____

COMMON HOREHOUND
Marrubium vulgare
Mint family   *Lamiaceae (Labiatae)*

PERENNIAL to 18˝ tall; STEMS square in cross section; LEAVES opposite, recurved, prominently-veined, ovate, to 2˝ long; FLOWERS white, small and clustered in whorls about the upper nodes.
ECOLOGY: Plains in open fields.
LOCATION: Watson Lake, Bellvue, CO 6/05 5000´
LOOK FOR clustered whorls of white flowers subtended by a pair of down-turned leaves.

■ **LIFE LIST** Where _____ NUMBER _____

HORSEMINT
Monarda pectinata
Mint family   *Lamiaceae (Labiatae)*

ANNUAL to 12˝ tall; STEMS square and curved with leaves and flowers in whorls at nodes; LEAVES to 2˝ long, sessile, linear and in-folded; FLOWERS white, hooded, to ¾˝ long, in whorls at nodes.
ECOLOGY: Plains and foothills on dry ground.
LOCATION: Shore Trail, Lory S.P., Ft. Collins, CO 6/03 5500´
LOOK FOR global flower cluster at nodes and inward folded leaves.

■ **LIFE LIST** Where _____ NUMBER _____

WILD ONION

Allium textile
Lily family *Liliaceae (Alliaceae)*

PERENNIAL to 10″ high, in clumps; LEAVES tubular
to 10″x ¼″; FLOWERS small, white, borne terminally
with 10–40 per umbel.
ECOLOGY: Plains and foothills in dry places.
LOCATION: Coyote Ridge Rec. Area, Ft. Collins, CO
5/02 5500´
LOOK FOR tubular leaves and tiny, urn-shaped,
white flowers.

■ **LIFE LIST** Where _____ NUMBER ____

MARIPOSE LILY

Calochortus gunnisonii
Lily family *Liliaceae*

PERENNIAL from a bulb, to 12″ tall; LEAVES linear
and grass-like to 6″ long; FLOWERS white, solitary
and bowl-shaped to 2″ across with 3 large petals and
3 small sepals
ECOLOGY: Foothills to subalpine in meadows and
open slopes.
LOCATION: Coyote Trail, Golden Gate S.P., Golden,
CO 7/00 8500´
LOOK FOR a bowl-shaped lily with brown spots and
a yellow center.

■ **LIFE LIST** Where _____ NUMBER ____

SANDLILY

Leucocrinum montanum
Lily family *Liliaceae*

PERENNIAL to 6″ high and stemless; LEAVES
narrowly linear, in-rolled, to 5″ long; FLOWERS
white, fragrant, to 1″ wide with 6 tepals
(undifferentiated petals and sepals).
ECOLOGY: Plains to foothills among sagebrush.
LOCATION: Pawnee National Grasslands, Keota, CO
5/99 5000´
LOOK FOR a tiny plant with 6 separated white
tepals.

■ **LIFE LIST** Where _____ NUMBER ____

FALSE SOLOMON'S SEAL
Maianthemum racemosum
(Smilacina racemosa)
Lily family   *Liliaceae*

PERENNIAL to 2′ tall; STEMS smooth, turning red in the fall; LEAVES alternate, sessile with parallel veins to 3″ long; FLOWERS white in a 4″ raceme; BERRIES red, to ¼″.
ECOLOGY: Plains to montane.
LOCATION: Mill Creek Trail, RMNP, CO 6/01 9000′
LOOK FOR two-dimensional leaf structure and exserted stamens.

■ **LIFE LIST** Where _____ NUMBER _____

STAR SOLOMON'S SEAL
Maianthemum (Smilacina) stellatum
Lily family   *Liliaceae*

PERENNIAL to 1′ high; STEMS erect with alternating leaves in 2 dimensions; LEAVES to 4″ long, elliptical, sessile, parallel veined and in-rolled; FLOWERS white, 6-petaled, in racemes to 2″ long; FRUIT round to ⅜″ with red stripes.
ECOLOGY: Foothills to subalpine.
LOCATION: Arthur's Rock Trail, Lory S.P., Ft. Collins, CO 5/02 5500′
LOOK FOR two-dimensional leaf structure, in-rolled, clasping leaves, and red striped fruit.

■ **LIFE LIST** Where _____ NUMBER _____

TWISTED STALK
Streptopus amplexifolius
Lily family   *Liliaceae*

PERENNIAL to 2′ long; LEAVES elliptical to 2″ long, alternate, sessile and parallel veined; FLOWERS white with reflexed petals, axillary, solitary and nodding at the end of slender stalks; BERRIES red to ¼″.
ECOLOGY: Foothills to subalpine.
LOCATION: Sheep Creek Trail, 44H Rd., Larimer Cty., CO 6/04 7500′
LOOK FOR two-dimensional leaf arrangement, elliptical leaves and a flower at each node.

■ **LIFE LIST** Where _____ NUMBER _____

MOUNTAIN DEATH CAMAS

Zigadenus (Anticlea) elegans
Lily family   *Liliaceae*

PERENNIAL to 18″ tall; LEAVES basal, narrow,
parallel veined to 10″ long; FLOWERS to ½″ across
with 6 white and green tepals in racemes to 10″ long
on tall scapes.

ECOLOGY: Montane to alpine in moist areas.

LOCATION: 4th of July Trail, Eldora, CO 7/01
11,500′

LOOK FOR upright basal leaves, a sturdy scape and
well-spaced flowers in a raceme.

◼ LIFE LIST Where _____ NUMBER _____

MEADOW DEATH CAMUS

Zigadenus (Anticlea) venenosus
Lily family   *Liliaceae*

PERENNIAL to 12″ high; STEMS solitary with 1 or 2
leaves; LEAVES in-folded, linear to 8″ long;
FLOWERS white to ¼″ wide with 6 petals, and
exserted flower parts on stalks ¼″ long in a cone
shaped raceme to 2″ long.

ECOLOGY: Plains and foothills on dry sunny slopes.

LOCATION: Coyote Ridge Rec. Area, Ft. Collins, CO
5/02 5500′

LOOK FOR a lily with a compact raceme and
greenish-white flowers.

◼ LIFE LIST Where _____ NUMBER _____

COMMON FLAX

Linum usitatissimum
Flax family   *Linaceae*

PERENNIAL to 2′ tall; STEMS erect, smooth and
wiry; LEAVES linear, soft, to 1¼″ long; FLOWERS 1″
across, white or blue with petals slightly overlapping.

ECOLOGY: Plains and foothills – the flax of
commerce.

LOCATION: Marshall Mesa, Boulder, CO 6/99 6000′

LOOK FOR a white saucer-shaped flower on a
slender stem, exserted style and berry-like seed pods.

◼ LIFE LIST Where _____ NUMBER _____

MANY-FLOWERED EVENING PRIMROSE
Mentzelia multiflora
Loasa family   *Loasaceae*

ANNUAL, biennial, or perennial to 4´ tall; STEM singular, upright with alternating leaves; LEAVES lanceolate to 4˝ and coarsely toothed; FLOWERS appear as white candles and open during the night; styles 4˝ and stamens 2˝ long.

ECOLOGY: Foothills on dry slopes.

LOCATION: Coyote Ridge Rec. Area, Ft. Collins, CO 7/01 5500´

LOOK FOR a small shrub that resembles a Christmas tree with white candles.

■ **LIFE LIST** Where _____ NUMBER _____

VENICE MALLOW (FLOWER OF AN HOUR)
Hibiscus trionum
Mallow family   *Malvaceae*

ANNUAL to 18˝ tall; STEMS ascending and leafy; LEAVES deeply lobed; FLOWERS white, to 1˝ across, with 5 overlapping petals, a dark red center and yellow flower parts.

ECOLOGY: Plains on disturbed ground.

LOCATION: Boyd Lake S.P., Loveland, CO 8/01 5000´

LOOK FOR a 5-lobed flower with a dark red center on a plant with deeply lobed leaves.

■ **LIFE LIST** Where _____ NUMBER _____

CHEESEWEED
Malva neglecta
Mallow family   *Malvaceae*

ANNUAL, biennial, or perennial to 10˝ high; STEMS ascending, viney, leafy and branching; LEAVES round to 1½˝ with petioles to 5˝ long; FLOWERS white, to ½˝ wide; FRUIT wheel-like, composed of a ring of seed.

ECOLOGY: Plains – a common weed.

LOCATION: Avery Park, Ft. Collins, CO 6/01 5000´

LOOK FOR round, lobed leaves and a white flower with a white center.

■ **LIFE LIST** Where _____ NUMBER _____

WHITE CHECKER MALLOW
Sidalcea candida
Mallow family   *Malvaceae*

PERENNIAL to 2′ tall; STEMS erect, smooth and topped with a raceme; basal LEAVES to 8″ wide and 5–7 lobed; stem leaves divided into 3–5 narrow segments; FLOWERS white to 1½″ wide in a raceme to 5″ long.

ECOLOGY: Subalpine in wet meadows.

LOCATION: Fern Lake Trail, RMNP, CO 6/00 9000′

LOOK FOR a flower with an exserted style and a flared stigma.

■ **LIFE LIST**   Where _____ NUMBER _____

BUCKBEAN
Menyanthes trifoliata
Buckbean family   *Menyanthaceae*

PERENNIAL aquatic plant to 1′ tall; STEMS leafless and succulent; LEAVES trifoliate, arising above the surface on succulent petioles; leaflets elliptic to 4″ long; FLOWERS white, bell-shaped, 5-lobed, to ⅝″ across.

ECOLOGY: Plains to montane in water.

LOCATION: Nymph Lake, RMNP, CO 7/99 9500′

LOOK FOR a white flowered raceme and upright, trifoliate leaves growing in shallow water.

■ **LIFE LIST**   Where _____ NUMBER _____

PRAIRIE SNOWBALL
Abronia fragrans
Four O'clock family   *Nyctaginaceae*

PERENNIAL to 3′ tall; STEMS erect and reddish; LEAVES opposite, ovate, pale beneath, to 3½″ long; FLOWERS white on stalks ¾″ long in loose, domed umbels to 2″ wide.

ECOLOGY: Plains and foothills in disturbed, sandy areas.

LOCATION: Cherry Creek Trail, Denver, CO 5/93 5000′

LOOK FOR red stalks bearing an umbel with little cup-like flowers.

■ **LIFE LIST**   Where _____ NUMBER _____

WILLOWHERB
Epilobium halleanum
Evening Primrose family   *Onagraceae*

PERENNIAL to 8″ tall; STEMS succulent, curved, leafy and branched; LEAVES lanceolate irregularly toothed to 1½″ long; FLOWERS white, 4-petaled to ¼″ wide in form of a cross; PODS to 3″ long.
ECOLOGY: Foothills to subalpine.
LOCATION: Well Gulch, Lory S.P., Ft. Collins, CO 8/99 5500′
LOOK FOR a tiny white flower with 4 notched petals, 4 white sepals and an elongated base.

■ **LIFE LIST** Where _____ NUMBER _____

WHITE FLOWER WILLOWHERB
Epilobium lactiflorum
Evening Primrose family   *Onagraceae*

PERENNIAL to 4′ tall; STEMS upright, leafy and reddish at maturity; LEAVES lanceolate and sessile, to 2″ long; FLOWERS white to ¼″ across with 4 notched petals; PODS upright, tubular, to 1½″, becoming curly, brown fibers after dehiscence.
ECOLOGY: Plains to montane in wet places.
LOCATION: Avery Park, Ft. Collins, CO 8/02 5000′
LOOK FOR a mass of curly brown fibers late in the season.

■ **LIFE LIST** Where _____ NUMBER _____

PRAIRIE EVENING PRIMROSE
Oenothera albicaulis
Evening Primrose family   *Onagraceae*

ANNUAL to 4″ high; LEAVES basal, to 4″ long and divided into many narrow lobes; FLOWERS are white to 3″ across, with 4 notched petals and exserted stamens.
ECOLOGY: Plains to montane
LOCATION: Devil's Backbone Rec. Area, Loveland, CO 5/00 5500′
LOOK FOR a large, white flowers and lobed, basal leaves.

■ **LIFE LIST** Where _____ NUMBER _____

STEMLESS EVENING PRIMROSE
Oenothera caespitosa
Evening Primrose family   *Onagraceae*

PERENNIAL to 4″ tall; SCAPES support a solitary
flower; LEAVES with irregular, wavy margins to 6″
long, in rosettes; FLOWERS to 4″ across with 4 white
petals turning pink with time.

ECOLOGY: Plains to montane in dry areas and on
sunny slopes.

LOCATION: Arthur's Rock Trail, Lory S.P., Ft. Collins,
CO 5/00 5500′

LOOK FOR a rosette of wavy lanceolate leaves and a
delicate, white, 4-petaled flower.

■ LIFE LIST Where _____ NUMBER _____

CUTLEAF EVENING PRIMROSE
Oenothera coronopifolia
Evening Primrose family   *Onagraceae*

PERENNIAL to 12″ high; STEMS yellowish and
leafy; LEAVES to 3″ long, divided into many string-
like lobes; FLOWERS white, 4-petaled, to 1½″ across.

ECOLOGY: Plains to foothills in dry areas.

LOCATION: Sheep Creek Trail, Rd. 44H, Larimer Cty.,
CO 6/04 7000′

LOOK FOR a string-like leaves and terminal, white
flower with exserted yellow stamens.

■ LIFE LIST Where _____ NUMBER _____

NUTTALL EVENING PRIMROSE
Oenthera nuttallii
Evening Primrose family   *Onagraceae*

PERENNIAL to 8″ tall; STEMS slender pink and
branchless; LEAVES linear, light green, to 3″ long
with deeply cut, toothed lobes; FLOWERS white, to
1½″ wide, 4 petaled, turning pink with time.

ECOLOGY: Plains and foothills.

LOCATION: Shore Trail, Lory S.P., Ft. Collins, CO
6/05 5500′

LOOK FOR white flowers on an upright stem with
deeply cut leaves.

■ LIFE LIST Where _____ NUMBER _____

SPOTTED CORALROOT
Corallorrhiza maculata
Orchid family   *Orchidaceae*

PERENNIAL saprophyte to 12″ tall; STEMS red and leafless with upper half a raceme; LEAVES absent; FLOWERS reddish to 1″ long with purple dots on the white, lower lobe.

ECOLOGY: Foothills to subalpine in decaying duff of conifers.

LOCATION: Wild Basin, Allenspark, CO 7/99 9000′

LOOK FOR red, succulent stems bearing little orchids with purple dots on the lower lobe.

■ **LIFE LIST**   Where _____ NUMBER _____

WHITE BOG ORCHID
Platanthera (Limnorchis) dilatata
Orchid family   *Orchidaceae*

PERENNIAL to 12″ tall; STEMS sturdy and leafy; LEAVES slender to 3″ long, alternate, clasping and ascending; FLOWERS white, waxy, fragrant, to ½″ across with a hood, 2 horizontal petals and a drooping lip.

ECOLOGY: Montane to alpine.

LOCATION: 4th of July Trail, Eldora, CO 7/00 11,500′

LOOK FOR a spike of tiny asymmetrical flowers.

■ **LIFE LIST**   Where _____ NUMBER _____

LADY'S TRESSES
Spiranthes romanzoffiana
Orchid family   *Orchidaceae*

PERENNIAL to 8″ tall; STEMS erect, stout and succulent; LEAVES few, linear to 6″ long and mostly basal; FLOWERS white and tubular to ½″ long in 3 spiraled ranks on a spike to 4″ long.

ECOLOGY: Subalpine in bogs.

LOCATION: Butler Gulch, Henderson Rd., Empire, CO 8/99 11,000′

LOOK FOR white flowers in spiraled ranks on a 4″ spike.

■ **LIFE LIST**   Where _____ NUMBER _____

PRICKLY POPPY

Argemone polyanthemos
Poppy family   *Papaveraceae*

ANNUAL, biennial, or perennial to 2´ tall; STEMS erect, leafy, stout and prickly; LEAVES to 5″ long with prickly margins, deeply lobed below and shallow lobed and reduced above; FLOWERS white to 3″ across; PODS ribbed and spiny.

ECOLOGY: Plains and foothills.

LOCATION: Bitterbrush Trail, Hall Ranch, Lyons, CO 6/00 6000´

LOOK FOR a white poppy with a yellow center on a prickly plant.

■ **LIFE LIST** Where _____ NUMBER ____

ENGLISH PLANTAIN

Plantago lanceolata
Plantain family   *Plantaginaceae*

ANNUAL, biennial, or perennial to 18″ high; SCAPES erect with 1″ terminal spikes; LEAVES narrow-lanceolate to 7″ long; FLOWERS crowded in cylindrical clusters; ANTHERS form a white collar that moves up the spike.

ECOLOGY: Plains and foothills.

LOCATION: Eldorado Canyon S.P., Eldorado Springs, CO 5/05 6500´

LOOK FOR a linear leafed rosette with wiry scapes and terminal spikes.

■ **LIFE LIST** Where _____ NUMBER ____

WHITE FAIRY TRUMPET

Ipomopsis aggregata candida
Phlox family   *Polemoniaceae*

BIENNIAL or perennial to 3´ tall; STEMS slender and leafy; LEAVES to 2″ long, alternate and pinnatifid with string-like lobes; FLOWERS 2″ long, white, trumpet-shaped, with recurved corolla lobes.

ECOLOGY: Foothills and montane in exposed areas near pine trees.

LOCATION: Coyote Trail, Golden Gate S.P., Golden, CO 7/00 8500´

LOOK FOR white trumpet flowers flaring into 5 lobes.

■ **LIFE LIST** Where _____ NUMBER ____

PRAIRIE PHLOX
Phlox andicola
Phlox family   *Polemoniaceae*

PERENNIAL to 3″ high, forming mats that spread by rhizomes; STEMS small and hidden by leaves and flowers; LEAVES linear, awl-shaped, to ¾″ long; FLOWERS white or purplish, ¾″ across, with 5 petals.

ECOLOGY: Plains to montane.

LOCATION: Pawnee National Grasslands, Keota, CO 5/99 5000′

LOOK FOR a tiny plant with needle-like leaves and white flowers with 5 petals.

■ LIFE LIST Where _____ NUMBER _____

ALPINE PHLOX
Phlox condensata
Phlox family   *Polemoniaceae*

PERENNIAL to 1″ high, forming cushions; STEMS inconspicuous; LEAVES hairy and awl-like, to ¼″ long; FLOWERS purplish-white to ½″ wide with 5 petals.

ECOLOGY: Subalpine and alpine on open slopes.

LOCATION: St. Alban's Chapel, Medicine Bow N.F., WY 6/02 10,500′

LOOK FOR green cushions with small purplish-white flowers having small, dark centers.

■ LIFE LIST Where _____ NUMBER _____

WHITE PHLOX
Phlox multiflora
Phlox family   *Polemoniaceae*

PERENNIAL to 4″ tall, forming mats; STEMS woody and prostrate to 12″ long; LEAVES linear to 1″ long, opposite and in-folded; FLOWERS purplish-white, to ¾″ across, 5-petaled, with a small purple center.

ECOLOGY: Foothills in dry areas.

LOCATION: Tenderfoot Trail, Walker Ranch, Boulder, CO 6/00 7500′

LOOK FOR a small purplish-white flower with grass-like leaves.

■ LIFE LIST Where _____ NUMBER _____

SUBALPINE BUCKWHEAT

Eriogonum umbellatum (subalpinum) majus
Buckwheat family *Polygonaceae*

PERENNIAL to 18˝ tall in mat-forming clumps; SCAPES supporting a compound umbel; LEAVES basal and spatulate; FLOWERS cream to rose, in umbels subtended by whorls of bracts.

ECOLOGY: Montane to alpine.

LOCATION: 4th of July Trail, Eldora, CO, 7/00 11,500´

LOOK FOR 10–20 small white umbels forming a head subtended by a whorl of bright green leaves.

■ **LIFE LIST** Where _____ NUMBER _____

KNOTWEED

Polygonum aviculare
Buckwheat family *Polygonaceae*

ANNUAL or perennial spreading in patches to 3´ in diameter; STEMS prostrate tough, viney, branching and leafy; LEAVES elliptical to 1˝ long; FLOWERS white with purple tinge, tiny, inconspicuous, and borne in leaf axils.

ECOLOGY: Plains, often as weeds in pavement cracks.

LOCATION: Spring Creek Trail, Ft. Collins, CO 8/02 5000´

LOOK FOR plants growing through pavement cracks, there is a good chance they are Knotweed.

■ **LIFE LIST** Where _____ NUMBER _____

BLACK BINDWEED (WILD BUCKWHEAT)

Polygonum convolvulus
Buckwheat family *Polygonaceae*

ANNUAL vine to 5´ long; STEMS slender, leafy and climbing by twining; LEAVES heart-shaped, alternate, to 2˝ wide; FLOWERS white, inconspicuous, to ¼˝ wide, with 5 spatulate petals; SEED singular, black and angular.

ECOLOGY: Plains and foothills.

LOCATION: Arthur's Rock Trail, Lory S.P., Ft. Collins, CO 6/03 5500´

LOOK FOR a twining plant with spade-like leaves.

■ **LIFE LIST** Where _____ NUMBER _____

MOUNTAIN KNOTWEED
Polygonum douglasii (sawatchense)
Buckwheat family   *Polygonaceae*

ANNUAL to 12″ high; STEMS wiry, branched, upright and leafy; LEAVES alternate, linear, bright green, to 1″ long; FLOWERS to 3/16″ wide with 5-pointed corolla lobes.
ECOLOGY: Plains to subalpine on open slopes.
LOCATION: Hidden Valley, RMNP, CO 8/01 9500′
LOOK FOR an upright version of the prostrate *P. aviculare.*

■ **LIFE LIST** Where _____ NUMBER _____

SMARTWEED
Polygonum (Persicaria) lapathifolium
Buckwheat family   *Polygonaceae*

ANNUAL to 3′ tall; STEMS slender, pale green, leafy and drooping; LEAVES lanceolate, and entire to 4″ long; FLOWERS white, tiny and crowded into spikes to 1½″ long.
ECOLOGY: Plains in moist, open areas.
LOCATION: Boyd Lake S.P., Loveland, CO 8/05 5000′
LOOK FOR alternating, lanceolate leaves and drooping white spikes.

■ **LIFE LIST** Where _____ NUMBER _____

SERPENT GRASS
Polygonum (Bistorta) viviparum
Buckwheat family   *Polygonaceae*

PERENNIAL to 6″ tall; STEMS erect and almost totally spikes; LEAVES alternate, narrow, mostly basal, to 2″ long; FLOWERS white to pinkish, tiny, crowded in spikes; bulblets are substituted for lowers flowers.
ECOLOGY: Subalpine and alpine.
LOCATION: St. Alban's Chapel, Medicine Bow N.F., WY 8/99 10,500′
LOOK FOR stems that are mostly spikes with flowers above and bulblets below.

■ **LIFE LIST** Where _____ NUMBER _____

SPRING BEAUTY
Claytonia lanceolata (rosea)
Purslane family   *Portulacaceae*

PERENNIAL to 5″ tall; STEMS erect, succulent and slender; LEAVES linear-lanceolate, opposite, to 3″ long; FLOWERS ¾″ across with 5 petals and pink anthers.

ECOLOGY: Foothills in moist areas. One of the earliest flowers.

LOCATION: Arthur's Rock Trail, Lory S.P., Ft. Collins, CO 5/01 5500′

LOOK FOR white flowers with pink anthers.

■ **LIFE LIST** Where _____ NUMBER _____

ALPINE SPRING BEAUTY
Montia chamissoi (Claytonia megarhiza)
Purslane family   *Portulacaceae*

PERENNIAL to 6″ tall, in patches; STEMS thick, succulent, short and leafy; basal LEAVES fleshy, glossy and spatulate; stem leaves opposite and oblanceolate; FLOWERS white to ⅜″ wide, 5-petaled and borne on 2–6 flowered panicles.

ECOLOGY: Montane to alpine.

LOCATION: Boy Scout Rd. (68C), at Elkhorn Creek, Larimer Cty., CO 7/04 8000′

LOOK FOR a small white flower and opposite, bright green, fleshy leaves.

■ **LIFE LIST** Where _____ NUMBER _____

NORTHERN ROCKJASMINE
Androsace occidentalis (septentrionalis)
Primrose family   *Primulaceae*

ANNUAL to 8″ high; STEMS slender, reddish, bearing loose umbels; LEAVES in a rosette, lanceolate to ¾″ long; FLOWERS white, to ¼″ wide, 5-petaled in loose clusters.

ECOLOGY: Foothills to alpine.

LOCATION: Cirque Meadow, Pingree Park, CO 6/01 9500′

LOOK FOR a tiny prostrate plant composed mostly of slender stems with tiny, white, terminal flowers.

■ **LIFE LIST** Where _____ NUMBER _____

WOOD NYMPH
Moneses (Pyrola) uniflora
Wintergreen family   *Pyrolaceae*

PERENNIAL to 5″ high from basal rosettes; SCAPES
fleshy and green, supporting a nodding flower;
LEAVES ovate-spatulate and finely toothed to 1″
long; FLOWERS white, singular, 5-petaled to 1″ wide.
ECOLOGY: Montane and subalpine.
LOCATION: Jean Lunning Trail, Brainard Lake Rec.
Area, Ward, CO 7/00 10,500′
LOOK FOR a tiny rosette of leaves with a nodding
white flower with a green stigma.

■ LIFE LIST   Where _____ NUMBER _____

LESSER WINTERGREEN
Pyrola minor
Wintergreen family   *Pyrolaceae*

PERENNIAL to 10″ high; SCAPES erect and green
with a raceme comprising the upper half; LEAVES
basal, petioled, round and glossy to 1½″ wide;
FLOWERS white to pink, sprially arranged, nearly
globose to ½″ wide with exserted styles and ½″
pedicles.
ECOLOGY: Montane to subalpine.
LOCATION: Cub Lake Trail, RMNP, CO 7/99 8500′
LOOK FOR a succulent, green scape with well-
spaced, nodding flowers and exserted styles.

■ LIFE LIST   Where _____ NUMBER _____

RED BANEBERRY
Actaea rubra
Buttercup family   *Ranunculaceae*

PERENNIAL to 2′ tall; STEMS slender, branched and
leafy; LEAVES twice pinnate with coarsely toothed
leaflets; FLOWERS tiny and white in terminal
clusters; BERRIES red to ¼″.
ECOLOGY: Montane in deep, shaded forests.
LOCATION: Cub Lake Trail, RMNP, CO 7/99 8500′
LOOK FOR a plant with toothed leaflets and clusters
of white flowers or red berries.

■ LIFE LIST   Where _____ NUMBER _____

MEADOW ANEMONE
Anemone canadensis
Buttercup family   *Ranunculaceae*

PERENNIAL to 10˝ tall; STEMS slender, leafy and branched; basal LEAVES long-petioled, incised and sharply toothed, stem leaves sessile, opposite and toothed; FLOWERS white, solitary, to 1½˝ across on stiff pedicles.

ECOLOGY: Plains to subalpine.

LOCATION: Young Gulch, Poudre Canyon, CO 6/02 7500´

LOOK FOR saucer-shaped flowers with yellow, brush-like centers subtended by a whorl of deeply toothed leaves.

■ LIFE LIST Where _____ NUMBER _____

THIMBLE WEED
Anemone cylindrica
Buttercup family   *Ranunculaceae*

PERENNIAL to 18˝ tall; STEMS erect with 2 whorls of leaves; LEAVES petioled, deeply cut into 5 segments; FLOWERS white, solitary, to ¾˝ across, on pedicles to 10˝ long, receptacle is fleshy and elongated, and sepals substitute for petals which are absent.

ECOLOGY: Plains to montane.

LOCATION: Crown Pt. Rd. (FR139), Larimer Cty., CO 6/04 8000´

LOOK FOR multiple flower stalks arising from a whorl of leaves near the top of the plant.

■ LIFE LIST Where _____ NUMBER _____

MARSH MARIGOLD
Caltha (Psychrophila) leptosepala
Buttercup family   *Ranunculaceae*

PERENNIAL to 8˝ tall; SCAPES erect and smooth bearing a solitary flower; LEAVES basal, heart-shaped, petioled, glossy and thick to 1¼˝ wide; FLOWERS white to 1¼˝ across with 8–10 showy sepals and no petals.

ECOLOGY: Subalpine and alpine in wet areas.

LOCATION: Eldora Ski Area, Eldora, CO 6/02 9500´

LOOK FOR patches of glossy leaves and white flowers with yellow centers.

■ LIFE LIST Where _____ NUMBER _____

WHITE CLEMATIS
Clematis ligusticifolia
Buttercup family   *Ranunculaceae*

VINE to 20´ long; LEAVES pinnate with 3–5 toothed
   leaflets to 1½˝ long; FLOWERS white with 4–5 petal-
   like sepals, sexes are on separate plants; FRUIT is a
   single seeded, silky haired fuzz ball.
ECOLOGY: Plains and foothills in moist areas.
LOCATION: Well Gulch, Lory S.P., Ft. Collins, CO
   8/01 5500´
LOOK FOR white flowers with exserted flower parts
   and unique sharp pointed leaves.

■ **LIFE LIST** Where _____ NUMBER _____

WHITE LARKSPUR
Delphinium carolinianum (virescens)
Buttercup family   *Ranunculaceae*

PERENNIAL to 3´ tall; STEMS erect, flexible and
   hairy; LEAVES palmately divided into narrow lobes;
   FLOWERS white, 1˝ wide with upward curved spurs;
   corolla lobes with purple spots; racemes to 10˝ long.
ECOLOGY: Plains and foothills on dry slopes.
LOCATION: Devil's Backbone Trail, Loveland, CO
   6/01 5500´
LOOK FOR a white larkspur with string-like leaves.

■ **LIFE LIST** Where _____ NUMBER _____

SPREADING GLOBEFLOWER
Trollius laxus
Buttercup family   *Ranunculaceae*

PERENNIAL to 8˝ high in clumps; STEMS erect,
   smooth and leafy; LEAVES alternate, petioled with
   5–7 parted leaf segments that are cleft and toothed;
   FLOWERS white, solitary, to 1½˝ wide with
   numerous yellow stamens.
ECOLOGY: montane to alpine.
LOCATION: Arapahoe Ski Area, CO 7/95 11,500´
LOOK FOR bright green, toothed foliage that
   distinguishes it from Marsh Marigold (*Caltha*).

■ **LIFE LIST** Where _____ NUMBER _____

BUCKBRUSH
Ceanothus fendleri
Buckthorn family   *Rhamnaceae*

SHRUB to 2′ high; STEMS becoming woody and
spiny; LEAVES alternate, petioled, lanceolate,
ascending, dark green above, silky beneath, to ¾″
long; FLOWERS white in loose racemes.
ECOLOGY: Foothills on dry hillsides.
LOCATION: Chautauqua Park, Boulder, CO 6/99
   6000′
LOOK FOR thorns and a raceme with white, nodding
flowers on white stalks.

■ **LIFE LIST** Where _____ NUMBER _____

MOUNTAIN BALM
Ceanothus herbaceus
Buckthorn family   *Rhamnaceae*

EVERGREEN shrub to 15″ tall; LEAVES alternate to
2½″ long, finely toothed and wavy with prominent
veins; FLOWERS white, in domed umbels to 2″
across.
ECOLOGY: Foothills to montane on hillsides, ravines
and burned areas.
LOCATION: Eldorado Canyon S.P., Eldorado Springs,
   CO 6/00 6500′
LOOK FOR prominent light green leaf veins and a
globular umbel with little white flowers held by white
pedicles.

■ **LIFE LIST** Where _____ NUMBER _____

STICKY LAUREL
Ceanothus velutinus
Buckthorn family   *Rhamnaceae*

EVERGREEN shrub to 5′ tall; STEMS reddish near
the terminals with smooth bark; LEAVES elliptic to
2½″ long, finely toothed, glossy above and pale
beneath; FLOWERS white in terminal clusters.
ECOLOGY: Foothills to subalpine.
LOCATION: Cirque Meadow, Pingree Park, CO 6/01
   9500′
LOOK FOR oval, thick, glossy leaves and a loose
raceme with little nodding flowers suspended by
white pedicles.

■ **LIFE LIST** Where _____ NUMBER _____

COMMON SHADBUSH
Amelanchier alnifolia (pumila)
Rose family   *Rosaceae*

SHRUB to 12´ tall; STEMS woody with smooth, gray bark, forming thickets; LEAVES oval, slightly toothed, petioled to 2½˝ long; FLOWERS to ¾˝ across with 5-white, separated petals.

ECOLOGY: Plains to subalpine.

LOCATION: Arthur's Rock Trail, Lory S.P., Ft. Collins, CO 5/01 5500´

LOOK FOR a shrub with white flowers having 5 well-spaced petals.

■ **LIFE LIST** Where _____ NUMBER _____

MOUNTAIN MAHOGANY
Cercocarpus montanus
Rose family   *Rosaceae*

SHRUB to 6´ high with gray-brown bark; LEAVES to 2˝ long, dark green above and pale beneath, with toothed margins and prominent veins; FLOWERS tubular with style exserted and anthers hanging over the edge of the corolla in a circle; FRUIT have a 4˝ fuzzy, twisted tail.

ECOLOGY: Foothills and montane.

LOCATION: Bitterbrush Trail, Hall Ranch, Lyons, CO 5/01 6000´

LOOK FOR bright green, toothed leaves and tubular flowers or fuzzy tails.

■ **LIFE LIST** Where _____ NUMBER _____

COTONEASTER
Cotoneaster franchetii
Rose family   *Rosaceae*

SHRUB to 10´ tall with long cane-like branches; STEMS slender, glossy-brown and studded with ½˝ spurs; LEAVES broad lanceolate with 1½˝ blades and ¼˝ petioles, in-rolled, alternate and ascending; FLOWERS white with pink tinge; fruit red, round, to ¼˝.

ECOLOGY: Plains – an escapee from cultivation.

LOCATION: Spring Creek Trail, Ft. Collins, CO 8/02 5000´

LOOK FOR clusters of white blossoms or red-orange fruit.

■ **LIFE LIST** Where _____ NUMBER _____

CERRO HAWTHORN
Crataegus erythropoda
Rose family   *Rosaceae*

TREE to 15´ tall; STEMS with smooth gray bark and
1″ thorns; LEAVES toothed, leathery and glossy, to
2″ long; FLOWERS to ¾″ across with white, rounded,
overlapping petals and pink anthers, found in clusters
on spurs; FRUIT red and round to ⅜″.
ECOLOGY: Foothills and mesas.
LOCATION: Legacy Park, Ft. Collins, CO 5/03 5000´
LOOK FOR white domed umbels and pink anthers or
red fruit.

■ **LIFE LIST**   Where _____ NUMBER _____

FLESHY HAWTHORN
Crataegus succulenta
Rose family   *Rosaceae*

SHRUB to 6´ tall; TWIGS reddish; THORNS purplish,
at nearly every node, to 2″ long; LEAVES ovate,
toothed to 2″ long; FLOWERS white to ¾″ across;
FRUIT dull red to ½″.
ECOLOGY: Plains and foothills in canyons and along
streams.
LOCATION: Well Gulch, Lory S.P., Ft. Collins, CO
5/05 5500´
LOOK FOR a bushy shrub with purple 2″ thorns.

■ **LIFE LIST**   Where _____ NUMBER _____

WOODLAND STRAWBERRY
Fragaria vesca
Rose family   *Rosaceae*

PERENNIAL to 10″ high; CAUDEX (stem) thick and
woody; STOLONS red, arching, to 12″ long; LEAVES
trifoliate, light green and petioled; leaflets obovate,
toothed, to 1″ long; FLOWERS to ¾″ across with 5
round, overlapping petals; FRUIT red to ¾″ wide.
ECOLOGY: Foothills to subalpine in meadows and
near forests.
LOCATION: Young Gulch, Poudre Canyon, CO 5/02
7000´
LOOK FOR a strawberry plant with thin, smooth
leaves.

■ **LIFE LIST**   Where _____ NUMBER _____

WILD STRAWBERRY
Fragaria virginiana
Rose family   *Rosaceae*

PERENNIAL to 4″ high; STOLONS red to 10″ long;
LEAVES trifoliate with reddish petioles; leaflets
broad-lanceolate, toothed, prominently veined, to
1¾″ long; FLOWERS white to ¾″ across; petals
rounded and overlapping; FRUIT to ¾″ wide, red and
seed in deep pits.

ECOLOGY: Foothills to subalpine.

LOCATION: Lion Gulch, Roosevelt N.F., US 36, CO
6/00 7500′

LOOK FOR a strawberry plant with dark, bright
green, toothed leaves and prominent veins.

■ **LIFE LIST** Where _____ NUMBER _____

APPLE
Malus pumila (domestica)
Rose family   *Rosaceae*

TREE to 25′ tall; TWIGS brown with a white bloom
that shines when rubbed; LEAVES elliptical, blade to
3″ with minute teeth, and pale beneath with a 1″
petiole; FLOWERS white, pink or red, to 1″ wide and
clustered on 2″ spurs; FRUIT are apples of various
sizes.

ECOLOGY: Plains and foothills – an escapee from
cultivation.

LOCATION: Well Gulch, Lory S.P., Ft. Collins, CO
8/02 5500′

LOOK FOR spurs bearing flowers or apples.

■ **LIFE LIST** Where _____ NUMBER _____

NINEBARK
Physocarpus monogynus
Rose family   *Rosaceae*

SHRUB to 6′ high; TWIGS red, lower stems shed bark
in strips; LEAVES have 3 major lobes with rounded
teeth and turn red in the fall; FLOWERS white to ⅜″
across forming umbels.

ECOLOGY: Foothills to subalpine on rocky slopes
and open woods.

LOCATION: Horsetooth Rock Trail, Horsetooth Park,
Ft. Collins, CO 6/99 5500′

LOOK FOR dark green, lobed leaves, shiny red twigs
and loose, white umbels.

■ **LIFE LIST** Where _____ NUMBER _____

VIBURNUM NINEBARK
Physocarpus opulifolius
Rose family   *Rosaceae*

SHRUB to 3´ tall, of commercial importance; TWIGS reddish near the tips; LEAVES tri-lobed like *Viburnum opulus* (Snowball Bush); FLOWERS white to ¼″ across and clustered in domed umbels to 2″ wide.

ECOLOGY: Plains and foothills – an escapee from cultivation.

LOCATION: Boulder Creek Trail, Boulder, CO 6/98 5500´

LOOK FOR this shrub in nurseries since it is quite rare in the wild.

■ **LIFE LIST** Where _____ NUMBER _____

WILD PLUM
Prunus americana
Rose family   *Rosaceae*

SHRUB to 8´ tall, in dense thickets; STEMS with grayish bark and stiff branches; LEAVES elliptical, petioled, acuminate and finely toothed, to 3″ long; FLOWERS fragrant, 5-petaled, to ¾″ across, in clusters of 3–5; fruit purple to ¾″.

ECOLOGY: Plains and foothills.

LOCATION: Timber Trail, Lory S.P., Ft. Collins, CO 5/00 5500´

LOOK FOR white flowers with exserted stamens borne profusely on branches.

■ **LIFE LIST** Where _____ NUMBER _____

WILD RED CHERRY
Prunus padus (pensylvanica)
Rose family   *Rosaceae*

TREE to 20´ tall with smooth, brown bark; LEAVES glossy, petioled, elliptical with pointed tips, to 2″ long; FLOWERS white and 5-petaled, to ½″ across; FRUIT red, to ¼″ on racemes.

ECOLOGY: Foothills and montane.

LOCATION: Roadside, Lory S.P., Ft. Collins, CO 7/05 5500´

LOOK FOR a tree with small, dark leaves and red cherries.

■ **LIFE LIST** Where _____ NUMBER _____

WESTERN CHOKECHERRY
Prunus virginiana
Rose family   *Rosaceae*

SHRUB or small tree to 15´ tall; TWIGS reddish-brown; LEAVES alternate, elliptical, to 4″ long, with pointed tips and finely toothed margins; FLOWERS white in drooping 2″ racemes; FRUIT black and round to ⅜″.

ECOLOGY: Plains to montane in gulches, canyons and moist places.

LOCATION: Nighthawk Trail, Hall Ranch, Lyons, CO 5/01 6000´

LOOK FOR a cylindrical raceme crowded with white flowers having exserted stamens.

■ **LIFE LIST** Where _____ NUMBER _____

ANTELOPE BRUSH
Purshia tridentata
Rose family   *Rosaceae*

SHRUB to 10´ tall; TWIGS reddish-gray; LEAVES to 1″ long, pale beneath and 3-lobed at the apex; FLOWERS solitary at the ends of ½″ spurs; male flowers white and 5-petaled, female flowers with an exserted cone-shaped style – sexes on separate plants.

ECOLOGY: Foothills and montane on rocky, southern slopes.

LOCATION: Gem Lake Trail, RMNP, CO 5/02 8500´

LOOK FOR leaves with 3 apex lobes.

■ **LIFE LIST** Where _____ NUMBER _____

BOULDER RASPBERRY
Rubus (Oreobatus) deliciosus
Rose family   *Rosaceae*

SHRUB to 4´ tall, spreading, arching and thornless; LEAVES bright green, crinkled, to 2″ long, with 3–5 lobes; FLOWERS white, mostly solitary, to 2″ across; FRUIT inedible, red to purple.

ECOLOGY: Plains to montane on sunny, rocky slopes.

LOCATION: Bitterbrush Trail, Hall Ranch, Lyons, CO 6/99 6000´

LOOK FOR crinkled leaves and large, flat, white flowers.

■ **LIFE LIST** Where _____ NUMBER _____

RED RASPBERRY
Rubus idaeus
Rose family   *Rosaceae*

SHRUB to 4´ tall; **STEMS** slender, thorny and leafy; **LEAVES** alternate, white beneath and divided into 3–7 toothed leaflets; **FLOWERS** white to ½″ wide with 5 petals; **BERRIES** red to ½″ wide formed by an aggregation of druplets.
ECOLOGY: Foothills to subalpine in moist places.
LOCATION: Hidden Valley, RMNP, CO 8/01 9500´
LOOK FOR thorns and raspberries.

■ LIFE LIST Where _____ NUMBER _____

MOUNTAIN ASH
Sorbus aucuparia
Rose family   *Rosaceae*

TREE to 20´ tall; **BRANCHES** bright tan extending laterally form a central leader; **LEAVES** to 5″ long with 9–13 leaflets, toothed near the tips; **FLOWERS** white, to ¼″ wide, in clusters to 4″ wide; **FRUIT** orange berries to ⅜″.
ECOLOGY: Plains, near water – an escapee from cultivation.
LOCATION: Prospect Ponds, Ft. Collins, CO 8/02 5000´
LOOK FOR white flower clusters, orange fruit and pinnate leaves.

■ LIFE LIST Where _____ NUMBER _____

NORTHERN BEDSTRAW
Galium boreale (septentrionale)
Madder family   *Rubiaceae*

PERENNIAL to 2´ high; **STEMS** erect, smooth and leafy; **LEAVES** narrow-lanceolate to 1½″ long, in whorls of 4; **FLOWERS** white, 4 & 5-petaled, to ⅜″ wide, forming clusters.
ECOLOGY: Plains to subalpine in open woods, meadows and slopes.
LOCATION: Young Gulch, Poudre Canyon, CO 6/01 7000´
LOOK FOR an inflorescence of slender axillary stalks with white terminal clusters.

■ LIFE LIST Where _____ NUMBER _____

STICKYWILLY
Galium spurium
Madder family   *Rubiaceae*

ANNUAL vine to 5′ long; STEMS slender with minute
hooks and leaves in whorls; LEAVES linear to 1″ long
with 5–6 per node; FLOWERS white, to ⅛″ wide, 4-
petaled, in clusters of 1–5.
ECOLOGY: Plains and foothills, often with *G.
boreale.*
LOCATION: Arthur's Rock Trail, Lory S.P., Ft. Collins,
CO 6/03 5500′
LOOK FOR a vining Bedstraw plant and feel for the
minute hooks.

■ **LIFE LIST** Where _____ NUMBER _____

BASTARD TOADFLAX
Comandra umbellata
Sandalwood family   *Santalaceae*

PERENNIAL to 10″ high; STEMS erect and leafy;
LEAVES upright, lanceolate, to 1″ long; FLOWERS
white, 5-lobed, in terminal clusters.
ECOLOGY: Plains and foothills.
LOCATION: Pine Ridge Nat. Area, Ft. Collins, CO
5/05 5000′
LOOK FOR a succulent plant with alternating,
upright leaves and a domed, terminal umbel of white
flowers.

■ **LIFE LIST** Where _____ NUMBER _____

STAR FLOWER
Lithophragma parviflorum
Saxifrage family   *Saxifragaceae*

PERENNIAL to 10″ tall; LEAVES basal, pinnatifid to
3″ long and incised into many pointed segments;
FLOWERS white to ½″ across with 4 petals, each cleft
into 3 segments, appearing as a 12 petaled flower.
ECOLOGY: Alpine on tundra slopes.
LOCATION: Trail Ridge Rd., RMNP, CO 8/99 12,000′
LOOK FOR incised leaves and white flowers with
petals cleft into 3 parts.

■ **LIFE LIST** Where _____ NUMBER _____

FRINGED GRASS OF PARNASSUS

Parnassia fimbriata
Saxifrage family   *Saxifragaceae*

PERENNIAL to 12″ high; SCAPES slender and erect
with a single flower; LEAVES basal, petioled, kidney-
shaped and glossy to 1½″ wide; FLOWERS white,
fringed, to 1″ wide, with 5 spaced petals and 5
anthers in the gaps between petals.
ECOLOGY: Subalpine in shaded bogs.
LOCATION: Herman Lake Trail, Bakerville, CO 8/99
11,000′
LOOK FOR round, thick, glossy, basal leaves and
slender scapes with a single white flower.

■ **LIFE LIST** Where _____ NUMBER _____

ROCK SAXIFRAGE

Saxifraga caespitosa
Saxifrage family   *Saxifragaceae*

PERENNIAL to 6″ tall, forming mats; STEMS reddish
and slender with tiny, red, awl-like leaves; basal
LEAVES crowded, awl-like, green, to ¼″ long;
FLOWERS white to ¾″ across, with exserted stamens
and 5 separated petals.
ECOLOGY: Montane to alpine.
LOCATION: Silver Dollar Lake Trail, Guanella Pass,
CO 8/99 11,000′
LOOK FOR moss-like patches with awl-like leaves
and little white flowers.

■ **LIFE LIST** Where _____ NUMBER _____

BROOK SAXIFRAGE

Saxifraga (Micranthes) odontoloma
Saxifrage family   *Saxifragaceae*

PERENNIAL to 20″ tall; SCAPES erect, red or green,
supporting a loose inflorescence; LEAVES basal,
petioled, glossy, rounded and toothed to 2″ wide;
FLOWERS to ⅜″ wide with 5 white petals and 10 red
anthers.
ECOLOGY: Montane to alpine in wet places.
LOCATION: Hassell Lake Trail, Urad Rd. Empire, CO
8/99 11,000′
LOOK FOR glossy, toothed, basal leaves, red stalks
and white flowers.

■ **LIFE LIST** Where _____ NUMBER _____

DIAMONDLEAF SAXIFRAGE
Saxifraga (Micranthes) rhomboidea
Saxifrage family *Saxifragaceae*

PERENNIAL to 10″ tall; SCAPES erect, green, supporting 2–3 clusters of flowers; LEAVES basal, diamond-shaped and slightly toothed; FLOWERS white with 5 lobes and 5 stamens in terminal clusters.
ECOLOGY: Foothills in shade and moisture.
LOCATION: Timber Trail, Lory S.P., Ft. Collins, CO 5/01 5500′
LOOK FOR a rosette of broad, leathery leaves and a slender scape bearing several small clusters of tiny flowers.

■ LIFE LIST Where _____ NUMBER _____

PARRY LOUSEWORT
Pedicularis parryi
Figwort family *Scrophulariaceae*

PERENNIAL to 10″ tall; STEMS erect, stiff and leafy; LEAVES pinnatafid to 5″ long with toothed lobes, reduced upward; FLOWERS white to pale yellow, to ¾″ long with downward pointing beaks.
ECOLOGY: Subalpine and alpine on dry hillsides.
LOCATION: Alban's Chapel, Medicine Bow N.F., WY 8/99 10,500′
LOOK FOR a clump of comb-like leaves with several stout stems ending in loose spikes.

■ LIFE LIST Where _____ NUMBER _____

SICKLE-TOP LOUSEWORT
Pedicularis racemosa
Figwort family *Scrophulariaceae*

PERENNIAL to 20″ tall, forming clumps; STEMS erect or ascending, slender and leafy; LEAVES all on stem, narrow-lanceolate to 3½″ long, alternate and finely toothed; FLOWERS white, in racemes, with downward curved corollas.
ECOLOGY: Montane and subalpine near conifers.
LOCATION: Sheep Lake Trail, Medicine Bow N.F., WY 7/01 10,500′
LOOK FOR linear leaves up into the spike, and downward curved corollas.

■ LIFE LIST Where _____ NUMBER _____

WHITE PENSTEMON
Penstemon albidus
Figwort family   *Scrophulariaceae*

PERENNIAL to 12″ tall; STEMS curved, succulent
and leafy; LEAVES opposite, gray-green, lanceolate
and clasping, to 1⅝″ long; FLOWERS white, to ⅝″
and crowded onto 3″ racemes.

ECOLOGY: Plains and foothills.

LOCATION: Horsetooth Trail, Lory S.P., Ft. Collins,
CO 5/02 5500′

LOOK FOR white flowers crowded into short
racemes and opposite, gray-green, succulent leaves.

■ **LIFE LIST**   Where _____ NUMBER _____

SNOWLOVER
Penstemon debilis
Figwort family   *Scrophulariaceae*

PERENNIAL to 6″ tall; STEMS ascending, leafy, and
slender; basal LEAVES lanceolate with 1″ blades and
1″ petioles, stem leaves opposite and sessile;
FLOWERS white, tubular, nodding to ¾″ long and in
pairs.

ECOLOGY: Alpine in wet areas.

LOCATION: Silver Dollar Lake, Guanella Pass, CO
8/99 11,000′

LOOK FOR a rosette of bright green leaves with
ascending stems bearing pairs of tubular flowers.

■ **LIFE LIST**   Where _____ NUMBER _____

BLACK NIGHTSHADE
Solanum nigrum
Potato family   *Solanaceae*

ANNUAL to 12″ high with a sprawling habit; STEMS
green, succulent, leafy and ascending; LEAVES fleshy,
broad-lanceolate and lobed, to 2″ long; FLOWERS
white to ⅜″ wide with recurved lobes and exserted
stigmas.

ECOLOGY: Plains, on disturbed land and in
cultivated fields.

LOCATION: Boyd Lake S.P., Loveland, CO 8/01
5000′

LOOK FOR soft, velvet leaves on green, succulent
stems.

■ **LIFE LIST**   Where _____ NUMBER _____

CANADIAN VIOLET

Viola canadensis
Violet family *Violaceae*

PERENNIAL to 6″ tall; STEMS inconspicuous; LEAVES basal, broadly cordate, finely toothed, to 2″ wide; FLOWERS white to ¾″ across, 5 petaled and bilaterally symmetrical.

ECOLOGY: Foothills to alpine in shade.

LOCATION: Timber Trail, Lory S.P., Ft. Collins, CO 5/01 5500′

LOOK FOR patches of bright green leaves and white, bi-symmetrical flowers in wet, shady areas.

■ **LIFE LIST** Where _____ NUMBER _____

WOODBINE

Parthenocissus quinquefolia
Grape family *Vitaceae*

WOODY VINE, deciduous, climbing with the aid of tendrils with suction-cup-like discs; LEAVES alternate, palmate, with 5 elliptical, coarse toothed and in-rolled leaflets; FLOWERS greenish-white in flat topped clusters; BERRIES to ¼″, dark blue with red stems.

ECOLOGY: Plains, climbing on trees – an escapee from cultivation.

LOCATION: Clear Creek Trail, Wheat Ridge, CO 9/92 5000′

LOOK FOR a woody vine with palmate leaves that turn red in the fall.

■ **LIFE LIST** Where _____ NUMBER _____

WILD GRAPES

Vitis riparia
Grape family *Vitaceae*

WOODY VINE to 12′ long; STEMS leafy and branched; LEAVES irregularly toothed with prominent veins, to 5″ wide; FLOWERS white in elongated clusters; FRUIT dark blue to ⅜″.

ECOLOGY: Plains and foothills along streams.

LOCATION: Boulder Creek Trail, Boulder, CO 8/05 5500′

LOOK FOR a vigorous vine climbing a tree, then observe the leaves.

■ **LIFE LIST** Where _____ NUMBER _____

ROCKY MOUNTAIN FLORA

Yellow Flowers

THREE-LEAF SUMAC
Rhus trilobata
Sumac family   *Anacardiaceae*

SHRUB to 6´ tall, forming thickets; STEMS gray with
   reddish terminals; LEAVES alternate and trifoliate;
   leaflets ovate with round lobes to 1˝ long; FLOWERS
   yellow, round to ⅛˝ appearing in clusters before
   leafing; FRUIT red, hairy, sticky, to ³⁄₁₆˝ wide.
ECOLOGY: Plains and foothills.
LOCATION: Young Gulch, Poudre Canyon, CO 7/02
   7000´
LOOK FOR leaflets that resemble little oak leaves.

■ **LIFE LIST**   Where _____ NUMBER _____

WHISKBROOM PARSLEY
Harbouria trachypleura
Celery family   *Apiaceae (Umbelliferae)*

PERENNIAL to 20˝ tall; STEMS flexible, slender and
   grooved; LEAVES twice divided into string-like
   segments; FLOWERS yellow, to ⅛˝ wide in long-
   stemmed, domed, umbels to 2˝ across.
ECOLOGY: Foothills and montane.
LOCATION: Cow Creek Trail, McGraw Ranch, RMNP,
   CO 6/01 8000´
LOOK FOR string-like foliage and an umbel
   composed of several smaller umbels.

■ **LIFE LIST**   Where _____ NUMBER _____

MUSINEON
Musineon divaricatum
Celery family   *Apicaeae (Umbelliferae)*

PERENNIAL to 6˝ high; STEMS curved and short;
   LEAVES to 4˝ long with deeply lobed leaflets;
   FLOWERS to ⅛˝ wide in flat, yellow umbels to 1˝
   wide, on leafless stalks (scapes).
ECOLOGY: Plains in dry open areas.
LOCATION: Coyote Ridge Rec. Area, Ft. Collins, CO
   4/02 5500´
LOOK FOR carrot-like leaves and several short stems
   bearing single umbels.

■ **LIFE LIST**   Where _____ NUMBER _____

MOUNTAIN CARAWAY
Musineon tenuifolium
Celery family   *Apiaceae (umbelliferae)*

PERENNIAL to 4″ high; SCAPES axillary with a
  terminal umbel; LEAVES to 6″ long, deeply cut into
  linear segments; FLOWERS yellow, tiny, in umbels to
  1¼″ wide.
ECOLOGY: Plains and foothills in dry areas.
LOCATION: Coyote Ridge Rec. Area, Ft. Collins, CO
  4/05 5500′
LOOK FOR a small rosette with several yellow
  umbels and string-like leaves.

■ **LIFE LIST** Where _____ NUMBER _____

ALPINE PARSLEY
Oreoxis alpina
Celery family   *Apiaceae (Umbelliferae)*

PERENNIAL to 1″ tall, forming mats; LEAVES to ½″,
  pinnately divided into narrow segments; FLOWERS
  yellow in umbels to ¾″ across on short scapes.
ECOLOGY: Alpine on tundra slopes.
LOCATION: Loveland Pass, CO 7/95 12,000′
LOOK FOR a dark green patch of very tiny, incised
  leaves and reddish scapes bearing tiny umbels.

■ **LIFE LIST** Where _____ NUMBER _____

MOUNTAIN PARSLEY
Pseudocymopterus montanus
Celery family   *Apiaceae (Umbelliferae)*

PERENNIAL to 2′ tall; STEMS slender, erect and
  nearly leafless; LEAVES pinnately divided sharp
  segments on petioles to 6″ long; FLOWERS yellow,
  ⅛″ across, in flat umbels to 2″ wide.
ECOLOGY: Foothills to alpine.
LOCATION: Berthoud Pass, CO 7/05 11,500′
LOOK FOR a reddish stalk, sharply incised leaves,
  and small yellow umbels.

■ **LIFE LIST** Where _____ NUMBER _____

FERNLEAF YARROW
Achillea filipendulina
Aster family   *Asteraceae (Compositae)*

PERENNIAL to 5´ tall; STEMS erect, stiff and leafy; LEAVES fern-like to 7″ long and deeply cut to the mid-rib, forming toothed segments; FLOWERS yellow, compressed into dense flat umbels to 6″ across.
ECOLOGY: Plains and foothills.
LOCATION: South Platte River Trail, Denver, CO 5/92 5000´
LOOK FOR fern-like leaves and large, yellow umbels.

■ LIFE LIST Where _____ NUMBER _____

FALSE DANDELION
Agoseris glauca dasycephala
Aster family   *Asteraceae (Compositae)*

PERENNIAL to 10″ high; SCAPE erect with milky sap; LEAVES variable, linear to oblanceolate with entire margins; FLOWER heads have only yellow ray flowers.
ECOLOGY: Foothills to alpine.
LOCATION: Berthoud Pass, CO 7/01 11,500´
LOOK FOR a flower resembling a dandelion with a rosette of narrow leaves.

■ LIFE LIST Where _____ NUMBER _____

CUTLEAF AGOSERIS
Agoseris glauca laciniata
Aster family   *Asteraceae (Compositae)*

PERENNIAL to 8″ tall; SCAPE bearing a solitary flower head; LEAVES to 5″ long, cut to the midrib to form sharp, wavy lobes; FLOWER heads yellow to 1″ across with purple tinged bracts.
ECOLOGY: Foothills to subalpine
LOCATION: Nighthawk Trail, Hall Ranch, Lyons, CO 5/01 6000´
LOOK FOR a dandelion-like flower and wavy, deeply cut leaves.

■ LIFE LIST Where _____ NUMBER _____

WESTERN RAGWEED

Ambrosia psilostachya
Aster family   *Asteraceae (Compositae)*

PERENNIAL to 5´ tall; STEMS upright and
yellowish; LEAVES deeply cut into narrow lobed
segments; FLOWERS yellow-green, berry-like, and
borne on spikes.

ECOLOGY: Plains to montane.

LOCATION: Eltuck Bay, Lory S.P., Ft. Collins, CO 8/01
5500´

LOOK FOR cut leaves and narrow, curved flower
spikes.

■ **LIFE LIST**   Where _____ NUMBER _____

GIANT RAGWEED

Ambrosia trifida
Aster family   *Asteraceae (Compositae)*

ANNUAL to 8´ tall; STEMS erect and sturdy,
branching in pairs from the upper nodes; LEAVES 3-
lobed, thin, drooping, to 5″ long; FLOWERS yellow-
green, berry-like and borne on spikes, rays absent
and anthers yellow.

ECOLOGY: Plains in neglected areas.

LOCATION: Boyd Lake S.P., Loveland, CO 8/01
5000´

LOOK FOR a tall plant with many slender green
spikes.

■ **LIFE LIST**   Where _____ NUMBER _____

HEART-LEAVED ARNICA

Arnica cordifolia
Aster family   *Asteraceae (Compositae)*

PERENNIAL to 14″ tall; STEMS slender, with a
solitary flower head; lower LEAVES petioled, cordate,
dull green to 2″ wide, stem leaves sessile and
opposite; FLOWER heads yellow to 2″ wide; rays
variable in number and length.

ECOLOGY: Foothills to subalpine in the shade of
conifers.

LOCATION: Timber Trail, Lory S.P., Ft. Collins, CO
5/01 5500´

LOOK FOR heart-shaped leaves.

■ **LIFE LIST**   Where _____ NUMBER _____

FOOTHILLS ARNICA
Arnica fulgens
Aster family   *Asteraceae (Compositae)*

PERENNIAL to 16" high; STEMS hairy with 2–3 pairs of leaves and a terminal flower; basal LEAVES spatulate, stem leaves sessile and lanceolate; FLOWER yellow to 1¼" wide.

ECOLOGY: Foothills

LOCATION: Timber Trail, Lory S.P., Ft. Collins, CO 5/04 5500´

LOOK FOR a solitary, daisy-like flower and hairy, paired leaves.

■ LIFE LIST Where _____ NUMBER _____

BROAD-LEAVED ARNICA
Arnica latifolia
Aster family   *Asteraceae (Compositae)*

PERENNIAL to 18" tall; STEMS slender, erect and leafy; basal LEAVES opposite, petioled and cordate; stem leaves ovate, and sessile to 2" long; FLOWER heads solitary, yellow, to 2" across.

ECOLOGY: Foothills to subalpine in moist shade.

LOCATION: Sheep Lake Trail, Medicine Bow N.F., WY 8/99 10,500´

LOOK FOR a single yellow flower with opposite, broad leaves, at high elevations.

■ LIFE LIST Where _____ NUMBER _____

SUBALPINE ARNICA
Arnica mollis
Aster family   *Asteraceae (Compositae)*

PERENNIAL to 2´ tall; STEMS erect, branching near the top; basal LEAVES to 5" long, ascending, lanceolate and petioled; stem leaves sessile and opposite; FLOWER heads yellow, to 2" wide.

ECOLOGY: Subalpine and alpine in moisture.

LOCATION: Medicine Bow N.F., WY 7/00 10,500´

LOOK FOR upright, hairy, paired leaves.

■ LIFE LIST Where _____ NUMBER _____

RAYLESS ARNICA
Arnica parryi
Aster family   *Asteraceae (Compositae)*

PERENNIAL to 2´ tall; STEMS erect with few leaves and branching near top; basal LEAVES lanceolate, opposite, petioled, and stem leaves sessile and reduced upward; FLOWER heads rayless, terminal and solitary to ⅜˝ wide.
ECOLOGY: Montane and subalpine.
LOCATION: 4th of July Trail, Eldora, CO 7/01 11,500´
LOOK FOR yellow, rayless flowers on a slender stem.

| ☐ **LIFE LIST** | Where _____ NUMBER _____ |

RYDBERG ARNICA
Arnica rydbergii
Aster family   *Asteraceae (Compositae)*

PERENNIAL to 12˝ tall; STEMS with 1 or 2 pair of opposite leaves and a solitary flower; LEAVES mostly basal, broad-linear and upright, to 6˝ long; FLOWERS yellow to 2˝ wide.
ECOLOGY: Foothills to subalpine.
LOCATION: Rabbit Mt. Rec. Area, Lyons, CO 5/02 6000´
LOOK FOR a solitary, yellow, daisy-like flower, facing upward.

| ☐ **LIFE LIST** | Where _____ NUMBER _____ |

TARRAGON
Artemisia (Oligosporus) campestris
Aster family   *Asteraceae (Compositae)*

PERENNIAL to 3´ tall; STEMS erect, reddish with alternating branches; LEAVES mostly on branches, linear, to 1˝ long; FLOWERS yellow, rayless and berry-like, to ⅛˝ wide, in racemes.
ECOLOGY: Foothills to subalpine.
LOCATION: Boyd Lake S.P., Loveland, CO 8/01 5000´
LOOK FOR columnar plant with reddish stem and many ascending branches.

| ☐ **LIFE LIST** | Where _____ NUMBER _____ |

FRINGED SAGE

Artemisia frigida
Aster family *Asteraceae (Compositae)*

PERENNIAL to 12″ tall; STEMS erect or leaning and leafy; LEAVES silvery-gray and cut into ½″ lobes; FLOWERS yellow, nodding, to ¼″ wide in 4″ spikes.
ECOLOGY: Plains to montane.
LOCATION: Parvin Lake Rec. Area, Red Feathers, CO, 8/01 8000′
LOOK FOR a silvery plant having racemes with nodding, button-like, rayless flowers.

■ **LIFE LIST** Where _____ NUMBER _____

BAHIA ASTER

Bahia dissecta
Aster family *Asteraceae (Compositae)*

ANNUAL, biennial, or perennial to 3′ tall; STEMS erect, slender and branched; LEAVES divided 1–3 times into narrow lobes; FLOWER heads yellow, to 1″ across, borne terminally on branches, in clusters of 1–3, each having 10–13 rays.
ECOLOGY: Foothills and montane.
LOCATION: Mill Creek Trail, RMNP, CO 8/05 9000′
LOOK FOR dissected basal leaves and sparsely leafed stems.

■ **LIFE LIST** Where _____ NUMBER _____

BEGGAR'S TICK

Bidens cernua
Aster family *Asteraceae (Compositae)*

ANNUAL to 16″ tall; STEMS erect, leafy, branched and turning reddish in fall; LEAVES opposite, to 2″ long, narrow-lanceolate and lightly toothed; FLOWERS yellow, rayless to ¾″ wide with a whorl of leaves under the head.
ECOLOGY: Plains and foothills.
LOCATION: Dixon Reservoir, Ft. Collins, CO 9/01 5000′
LOOK FOR flower heads subtended by a whorl of leaves, and seed that adhere to clothing.

■ **LIFE LIST** Where _____ NUMBER _____

SPANISH NEEDLES

Bidens frondosa
Aster family   *Asteraceae (Compositae)*

ANNUAL to 3´ tall; STEMS reddish, leafy and
branching in pairs at leaf nodes; LEAVES pinnate to
3˝ long, with 3–5 toothed, lanceolate leaflets;
FLOWERS yellow, to ¼˝ wide, subtended by a whorl
of bracts.

ECOLOGY: Plains, along stream banks.

LOCATION: Spring Creek Trail, Ft. Collins, CO 8/02
5000´

LOOK FOR opposite branching, pinnate leaves and
solitary flowers with long leaf-like bracts.

■ **LIFE LIST** Where _____ NUMBER _____

RABBITBRUSH

Chrysothamnus nauseosus
Aster family   *Asteraceae (Compositae)*

SHRUBS to 5´ tall; STEMS many, ascending and
branching; LEAVES linear to 3˝ long; FLOWER heads
in dense, rounded, yellow clusters, appearing in late
summer.

ECOLOGY: Plains and foothills on open slopes and
over-grazed pastures.

LOCATION: Highland Canal Trail, Denver, CO 5/92
5000´

LOOK FOR a dense flaring shrub, with clusters of
tiny, yellow flowers.

■ **LIFE LIST** Where _____ NUMBER _____

WESTERN GOLDENROD

Euthamia (Solidago) occidentalis
Aster family   *Asteraceae (Compositae)*

PERENNIAL to 5´ tall; STEMS leafy bearing loose
racemes; LEAVES narrow, to 4˝ long; FLOWERS
bright yellow to ¼˝ wide.

ECOLOGY: Plains and foothills.

LOCATION: Well Gulch, Lory S.P., Ft. Collins, CO
8/99 5500´

LOOK FOR a slender, upright stem, alternating linear
leaves and loose cluster of yellow flowers.

■ **LIFE LIST** Where _____ NUMBER _____

BLANKET FLOWER
Gaillardia aristata
Aster family *Asteraceae (Compositae)*

PERENNIAL to 20″ tall; STEMS erect, slender, and hairy with 3 or more alternate leaves; basal LEAVES lanceolate and stemmed to 5″ long; stem leaves sessile, wavy and hairy; FLOWER heads to 3″ across with reddish disc flowers and 3-lobed, yellow rays.
ECOLOGY: Plains to montane.
LOCATION: Bitterbrush Trail, Hall Ranch, Lyons, CO 6/00 6000′
LOOK FOR a large reddish disc surrounded by yellow rays.

☐ **LIFE LIST** Where _____ NUMBER _____

GUMWEED
Grindelia squarrosa
Aster family *Asteraceae (Compositae)*

ANNUAL, biennial, or perennial to 2′ tall; STEMS erect, leafy and branched; LEAVES alternate, stemless and toothed; FLOWER heads to 1¼″ across with yellow ray flowers and several rows of sticky, reflexed bracts.
ECOLOGY: Plains to montane.
LOCATION: Eltuck Bay, Lory S.P., Ft. Collins, CO 8/01 5500′
LOOK FOR sticky bracts beneath the flower heads.

☐ **LIFE LIST** Where _____ NUMBER _____

SUBALPINE GUMWEED
Grindelia subalpina
Aster family *Asteraceae (Compositae)*

BIENNIAL to 18″ tall; STEMS branched and flexible; LEAVES alternate, lanceolate, and toothed to 2″ long; FLOWER heads to 1″ across, subtended by sticky bracts.
ECOLOGY: Montane to subalpine.
LOCATION: Lawn Lake Trail, RMNP, CO 8/05 8500′
LOOK FOR gummy bracts and toothless, upper stem leaves.

☐ **LIFE LIST** Where _____ NUMBER _____

PARRY SUNFLOWER

Helianthella parryi
Aster family   *Asteraceae (Compositae)*

PERENNIAL to 12″ high; STEMS leafy and hairy
with a solitary terminal head; LEAVES hairy and
lanceolate, lower leaves petioled and opposite to 4″
long, stem leaves alternate and sessile; FLOWER
heads yellow to 2″ across.
ECOLOGY: Foothills and montane in ponderosa pine
forests.
LOCATION: Nature Trail, Lory S.P., Ft. Collins, CO
8/01 5500′
LOOK FOR a small sunflower with narrow, hairy
leaves and a solitary flower.

■ LIFE LIST Where _____ NUMBER _____

NODDING SUNFLOWER

Helianthella quinquenervis
Aster family   *Asteraceae (Compositae)*

PERENNIAL to 2′ tall; STEMS erect and leafy,
arising from under-ground rootstocks; LEAVES
lanceolate, upright and petioled below, and opposite,
sessile and reduced above; FLOWER heads to 3″
across, yellow, nodding and usually solitary.
ECOLOGY: Montane to subalpine.
LOCATION: Herman Gulch Trail, Bakerville, CO 8/00
11,000′
LOOK FOR narrow, opposite, glossy leaves and a 3″
sunflower.

■ LIFE LIST Where _____ NUMBER _____

LITTLE SUNFLOWER

Helianthella uniflora
Aster family   *Asteraceae (Compositae)*

PERENNIAL to 2′ tall; STEMS reddish, hairy and
leafy; LEAVES to 3″ long, leathery, lanceolate, petioled
and opposite; FLOWER heads to 2½″ wide, with
yellow rays and a disc that turns brown with time.
ECOLOGY: Plains to subalpine.
LOCATION: Mesa Trail, Eldorado Canyon S.P.,
Eldorado Springs, CO 6/99 6500′
LOOK FOR opposite, dark green leaves and a single
flower subtended by a pair of leaves.

■ LIFE LIST Where _____ NUMBER _____

COMMON SUNFLOWER
Helianthus annuus
Aster family   *Asteraceae (Compositae)*

ANNUAL to 6´ tall; STEMS rough, hairy, stout and reddish; LEAVES to 10˝ long, and hairy with toothed margins; FLOWERS to 4˝ across with yellow petals and brown centers.
ECOLOGY: Plains, along roadsides.
LOCATION: Boyd Lake S.P., Loveland, CO 6/01 5000´
LOOK FOR a tall plant with a large, nodding, terminal flower.

■ **LIFE LIST** Where _____ NUMBER _____

BLUEWEED
Helianthus ciliaris
Aster family   *Asteraceae (Compositae)*

PERENNIAL to 2´ high, in patches; STEMS slender and branched; LEAVES opposite, sessile, narrow, to 3˝ long with short, stiff bristles along wavy margins; FLOWER heads yellow to 1½˝ across with ½˝ disc.
ECOLOGY: Plains and foothills in wet places.
LOCATION: Avery Park, Ft. Collins, CO 8/01 5000´
LOOK FOR a tangle of slender stems, narrow, pointed leaves and yellow flowers with 6–10 rays.

■ **LIFE LIST** Where _____ NUMBER _____

TALL MARSH SUNFLOWER
Helianthus nuttallii
Aster family   *Asteraceae (Compositae)*

PERENNIAL to 8´ tall; STEMS reddish, slender and leafy; LEAVES narrow, to 6˝ long, upper leaves alternate and lower leaves opposite with finely serrated margins; FLOWER heads yellow to 2½˝ across, discs yellow, going to brown and developing stiff bristles.
ECOLOGY: Plains and foothills in wet sites.
LOCATION: Boulder Creek Trail, Boulder, CO 8/97 5500´
LOOK FOR tiny spines on leaf margins.

■ **LIFE LIST** Where _____ NUMBER _____

YELLOW FLOWERS

BUSH SUNFLOWER
Helianthus pumilus
Aster family   *Asteraceae (Compositae)*

PERENNIAL to 30″ tall, bushy with several rough, hairy stems; **LEAVES** opposite, hairy, short-stalked and broadly lanceolate; **FLOWER** heads to 3″ across with yellow rays and a tan disc.
ECOLOGY: Foothills and montane.
LOCATION: Timber Trail, Lory S.P., Ft. Collins, CO 5/04 5500′
LOOK FOR gray-green, hairy, lanceolate leaves that are unusually uniform.

■ **LIFE LIST**   Where _____ NUMBER _____

PRAIRIE SUNFLOWER
Heliomeris multiflora
Aster family   *Asteraceae (Compositae)*

PERENNIAL to 2′ tall; **STEMS** erect, hairy, reddish and leafy; **LEAVES** narrow-lanceolate, petioled and may be both alternate and opposite on the same plant; **FLOWER** heads yellow, to 2″ wide, solitary on terminals with discs turning brown.
ECOLOGY: Plains to montane.
LOCATION: Parvin Lake Rec. Area, Red Feathers, CO 8/01 8000′
LOOK FOR a sprawling sunflower with slender stems.

■ **LIFE LIST**   Where _____ NUMBER _____

GOLDEN ASTER FULCRATA
Heterotheca fulcrata
Aster family   *Asteraceae (Compositae)*

PERENNIAL to 1′ tall, in clumps; **STEMS** slender reddish and leafy; **LEAVES** oblong, in-rolled, light green, sessile, alternate, to 1½″ long; **FLOWER** heads yellow to 1¼″ wide in leafy clusters, with discs turning brown.
ECOLOGY: Montane to alpine.
LOCATION: Guanella Pass, CO 8/99 11,500′
LOOK FOR curved stems, yellow daisy-type flowers and leaves that are abundant, in-rolled and quite uniform.

■ **LIFE LIST**   Where _____ NUMBER _____

GOLDEN ASTER VILLOSA
Heterotheca (Chrysopsis) villosa
Aster family   *Asteraceae (Compositae)*

PERENNIAL to 10″ tall, covered with hairs; STEMS ascending, purplish, branched and leafy; LEAVES hairy, wavy, lanceolate and petioled on lower stem, with upper leaves sessile and narrow; FLOWER heads yellow to 1½″ wide with 20–30 rays.
ECOLOGY: Foothills and montane.
LOCATION: Rabbit Mt. Rec. Area, Lyons, CO 5/02 6000′
LOOK FOR small, hairy, twisted, sessile leaves and a terminal cluster of flowers.

■ **LIFE LIST** Where _____ NUMBER ____

DWARF GOLDEN ASTER
Heterotheca villosa hispida
Aster family   *Asteraceae (Compositae)*

PERENNIAL to 10″ high, forming clumps; STEMS erect, stiff, purplish, leafy and top-branched; LEAVES grayish, sticky, thick, spatulate, sessile and twisted to 1″ long; FLOWER heads solitary on terminals, yellow, to ¾″ wide with sticky bracts.
ECOLOGY: Foothills and montane.
LOCATION: South Platte River Trail, Denver, CO 5/92 5000′
LOOK FOR multiple branches at the top, each one with a solitary flower.

■ **LIFE LIST** Where _____ NUMBER ____

SLENDER HAWKWEED
Hieracium gracile
Aster family   *Asteraceae (Compositae)*

PERENNIAL to 18″ tall; STEMS slender, erect, nearly leafless and top-branched; LEAVES basal, mostly spatulate, petioled, to 4″ long; FLOWER heads to ½″ long on 2″ stalks with yellow disc flowers extending beyond the involucre by ⅛″; rays absent.
ECOLOGY: Subalpine in spruce forests.
LOCATION: Sheep Lake Trail, Medicine Bow N.F., WY 7/00 10,500′
LOOK FOR a rosette with slender, branching stems bearing bulb-shaped, rayless flowers.

■ **LIFE LIST** Where _____ NUMBER ____

CREAM TIPS
Hymenopappus filifolius (cinereus)
Aster family   *Asteraceae (Compositae)*

PERENNIAL to 2´ tall; STEMS wiry, leafless and branched at the top; LEAVES basal and dissected into linear segments; FLOWER heads composed of singular yellow disc flowers on branch tips.
ECOLOGY: Plains and foothills.
LOCATION: Bitterbrush Trail, Hall Ranch, Lyons, CO 6/99 6000´
LOOK FOR string-like foliage, a slender, branched stalk and rayless flowers with exserted stamens.

■ **LIFE LIST** Where _____ NUMBER _____

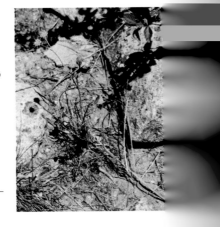

CANADIAN WILD LETTUCE
Lactuca canadensis
Aster family   *Asteraceae (Compositae)*

ANNUAL or biennial to 6´ tall; STEMS erect, succulent and leafy; LEAVES deeply lobed and toothed to 8″ long; FLOWERS yellow to ½″ wide with separated, rectangular rays in terminal clusters.
ECOLOGY: Plains in moist places.
LOCATION: Poudre River Trail, Ft. Collins, CO 7/02 5000´
LOOK FOR a plant resembling Prickly Lettuce, but larger with tighter flower clusters.

■ **LIFE LIST** Where _____ NUMBER _____

PRICKLY LETTUCE
Lactuca serriola
Aster family   *Asteraceae (Compositae)*

ANNUAL to 5´ tall; STEMS upright, leafy and branching at the top; LEAVES deeply lobed, to 10″ long with spines along midribs and margins; FLOWERS yellow, to ½″ wide and borne in a loose panicle, opening only briefly, in early morning.
ECOLOGY: Plains and foothills.
LOCATION: Ft. Collins, CO 8/01 5000´
LOOK FOR large irregularly lobed leaves with milky sap.

■ **LIFE LIST** Where _____ NUMBER _____

PINEAPPLE WEED
Matricaria discoidea (matricariodes)
(Chamomilla suaveolens)
Aster family   *Asteraceae (Compositae)*

ANNUAL to 1´ high; STEMS erect, smooth, aromatic and leafy; LEAVES to 2″ long, dissected into linear segments; FLOWER heads to ¼″ wide, conical with papery bracts; disc flowers greenish-yellow, ray flowers absent.

ECOLOGY: Foothills and montane.

LOCATION: Sheep Creek Trail, 44H Rd., Larimer Cty., CO 6/04 7000´

LOOK FOR conical flower heads resembling pineapples.

■ **LIFE LIST** Where _____ NUMBER _____

NODDING MICROCERIS
Microseris nutans
Aster family   *Asteraceae (Compositae)*

PERENNIAL to 18″ tall; STEMS slender and branching at the top; LEAVES mostly basal to 4″ long, narrow and irregularly toothed; FLOWER heads yellow to ¾″ across with only ray flowers; stigmas protruding above the heads.

ECOLOGY: Montane and subalpine.

LOCATION: Horseshoe Trail, Golden Gate S.P., Golden CO 7/99 8500´

LOOK FOR a dandelion with a wiry stem and multiple heads.

■ **LIFE LIST** Where _____ NUMBER _____

WAVYLEAF DANDELION
Nothocalais cuspidata
Aster family   *Asteraceae (Compositae)*

PERENNIAL to 4″ tall; STEMS leafless and pubescent; LEAVES are linear, in-folded and wavy, to 5″ long, forming a basal rosette; FLOWER heads to 1½″ across, solitary, terminal and yellow; petals toothed, with blunt tips; stamens forked at the tips.

ECOLOGY: Plains and foothills.

LOCATION: Timber Trail, Lory S.P., Ft. Collins, CO 4/01 5500´

LOOK FOR leaves with whitish margins and midribs.

■ **LIFE LIST** Where _____ NUMBER _____

MEXICAN HAT
Ratibida columnifera
Aster family   *Asteraceae (Compositae)*

PERENNIAL or biennial to 2′ tall; **STEMS** wiry, with a few leaves and a single ternimal flower; **LEAVES** alternate, pinnatifid with linear segments; disc **FLOWERS** on domed column; rays yellow and reflexed to 1″ long.

ECOLOGY: Plains and foothills.

LOCATION: Pavilion Garden, Westminster, CO 6/99 5000′

LOOK FOR the column of disc flowers and the whorl of rays that form a hat.

■ **LIFE LIST**   Where _____ NUMBER _____

BLACKEYED SUSAN
Rudbeckia hirta
Aster family   *Asteraceae (Compositae)*

ANNUAL, biennial, or perennial to 2′ tall; **STEMS** erect, hairy and purple-tinged; **LEAVES** linear, alternate and hairy, to 6″ long, lower leaves petioled, upper leaves sessile; **FLOWERS** to 3″ across, disc raised and turning brown, rays yellow to 1″ long.

ECOLOGY: Foothills to montane.

LOCATION: Young Gulch, Poudre Canyon, CO 6/02 7000′

LOOK FOR dark brown, flat, raised discs.

■ **LIFE LIST**   Where _____ NUMBER _____

TALL CONEFLOWER
Rudbeckia laciniata (ampla)
Aster family   *Asteraceae (Compositae)*

PERENNIAL to 6′ tall; **STEMS** erect, slender and stiff; **LEAVES** smooth, pinnately divided into 3–5 toothed lobes; **FLOWERS** yellow, to 4″ wide, with a domed receptacle and twisted, separated rays.

ECOLOGY: Foothills to montane in wet, shady places.

LOCATION: Young Gulch, Poudre Canyon, CO 7/02 7500′

LOOK FOR a domed receptacle and 5–15 rays on a 3″ yellow flower.

■ **LIFE LIST**   Where _____ NUMBER _____

FALSE SALSIFY

Scorzonera (Podospermum) laciniata
Aster family *Asteraceae (Compositae)*

PERENNIAL to 18˝ high; STEMS upright and
sparingly branched; LEAVES to 6˝ long with lateral
linear lobes; FLOWERS yellow, with disc flowers
having shorter rays than the peripheral flowers.

ECOLOGY: Plains and foothills.

LOCATION: Nighthawk Trail, Hall Ranch, Lyons, CO
5/01 6000´

LOOK FOR dandelion-type flower and pitchfork-like
leaves.

☐ **LIFE LIST** Where _____ NUMBER _____

ALPINE GROUNDSEL

Senecio (Ligularia) amplectens
Aster family *Asteraceae (Compositae)*

PERENNIAL to 2´ tall; STEMS smooth, erect and
branching near the top; basal LEAVES toothed,
narrow-lanceolate to 8˝ long with winged petioles,
stem leaves sessile and reduced upward; FLOWER
heads yellow, to 3˝ across with separated and unruly
rays.

ECOLOGY: Subalpine and alpine.

LOCATION: Berthoud Pass, CO 7/01 11,500´

LOOK FOR toothed leaves, a branching, upright
stem, and twisted, unruly rays.

☐ **LIFE LIST** Where _____ NUMBER _____

BLACK TIPPED SENECIO

Senecio atratus
Aster family *Asteraceae (Compositae)*

PERENNIAL to 2´ tall in clumps; STEMS hairy with
ascending, alternate leaves; LEAVES narrow-
lanceolate, petioled below and sessile above;
FLOWERS yellow, ¼˝ across, in umbel-like panicles
of up to 50 flowers.

ECOLOGY: Montane to alpine in scree and rock
slides.

LOCATION: Boreas Pass, CO 8/99 11,500´

LOOK FOR brown tips on the bracts under the
flower heads.

☐ **LIFE LIST** Where _____ NUMBER _____

BIGELOW SENECIO
Senecio (Ligularia) bigelovii
Aster family   *Asteraceae (Compositae)*

PERENNIAL to 18″ tall; STEMS erect, fleshy, green,
with alternate leaves and 1 terminal and 2 or 3
axillary flower heads; LEAVES narrow-lanceolate,
clasping, wavy, with toothed margins, to 9″ long;
FLOWER heads rayless, nodding, to 1½″ long.
ECOLOGY: Montane and subalpine.
LOCATION: Herman Gulch Trail, Bakerville, CO 8/00
11,000′
LOOK FOR a raceme of 3 or 4, yellow or red, rayless,
nodding flower heads.

■ LIFE LIST Where _____ NUMBER _____

WOOLLY GROUNDSEL
Senecio canus (Packera cana)
Aster family   *Asteraceae (Compositae)*

PERENNIAL to 12″ tall; STEMS several and slender;
basal LEAVES to 4″ long, spoon-shaped, in loose
rosettes, stem leaves reduced and sessile; FLOWER
heads yellow, to ½″ wide, with 5–13 rays and woolly
bracts, in terminal clusters of 20 or more.
ECOLOGY: Foothills.
LOCATION: Timber Trail, Lory S.P., Ft. Collins, CO
5/02 5500′
LOOK FOR white pubescence on upper leaves and
stems, and separated rays.

■ LIFE LIST Where _____ NUMBER _____

THICK-BRACTED SENECIO
Senecio crassulus
Aster family   *Asteraceae (Compositae)*

PERENNIAL to 16″ tall; STEMS erect, smooth, leafy
and branching into a panicle; LEAVES thick, fleshy,
wavy, lanceolate, stemmed at the base and clasping
above; FLOWER heads yellow, involucre encasing
most of head, rays ¼″ long, radiating and separated.
ECOLOGY: Subalpine and alpine.
LOCATION: 4th of July Trail, Eldora, CO 7/00
11,500′
LOOK FOR clasping, finely-toothed leaves.

■ LIFE LIST Where _____ NUMBER _____

WESTERN GOLDEN RAGWORT
Senecio eremophilus
Aster family   *Asteraceae (Compositae)*

PERENNIAL to 2′ tall; STEMS reddish, leafy, slender and erect; LEAVES to 4″ long, pinnatifid with toothed lobes, stemmed at the base and sessile above; FLOWER heads yellow to 1″ across with spaced rays, in panicles with up to 15 heads.
ECOLOGY: Montane and subalpine.
LOCATION: Cub Lake Trail, RMNP, CO 7/93 8500′
LOOK FOR irregularly lobed leaves and flowers with unruly rays.

■ **LIFE LIST** Where _____ NUMBER _____

FENDLER GROUNDSEL
Senecio (Packera) fendleri
Aster family   *Asteraceae (Compositae)*

PERENNIAL to 12″ tall; STEMS slender and erect with alternate leaves; LEAVES narrow-lanceolate, ascending, toothed, to 3½″ long, petioled below and sessile above; FLOWER heads to ¾″ wide, yellow and clustered in a small, tight panicle with 3–10 heads.
ECOLOGY: Foothills and montane in clearings.
LOCATION: Arthur's Rock Trail, Lory S.P., Ft. Collins 5/00 5500′
LOOK FOR blunt teeth on stem leaves.

■ **LIFE LIST** Where _____ NUMBER _____

ROCK RAGWORT
Senecio fremontii
Aster family   *Asteraceae (Compositae)*

PERENNIAL to 12″ high; STEMS leafy, smooth, upright, topped with 1–5 flowers; LEAVES oval, glossy, smooth, thick, toothed, to 1″ wide, stemmed at the base and sessile above; FLOWER heads yellow, to 1″ across with spaced rays.
ECOLOGY: Subalpine and alpine.
LOCATION: Loveland Pass, CO 8/00 12,000′
LOOK FOR 8 ray flowers and glossy, thick leaves with sharp pointed teeth.

■ **LIFE LIST** Where _____ NUMBER _____

LAMB'S TONGUE GROUNDSEL

Senecio integerrimus
Aster family *Asteraceae (Compositae)*

BIENNIAL or perennial to 30″ tall; STEMS erect and light green; basal LEAVES narrow to 6″ long, stem leaves reduced, upright and sessile; FLOWER heads to ⅝″ wide, yellow and borne in a loose panicle.
ECOLOGY: Foothills to subalpine in dry sites.
LOCATION: Rabbit Mt., Lyons, CO 5/01 6000′
LOOK FOR ascending, wavy leaves and an erect, sparsely leafed stem with 10–15 flower heads.

■ **LIFE LIST** Where _____ NUMBER _____

PLATTE SENECIO

Senecio (Packera) plattensis
Aster family   *Asteraceae (Compositae)*

BIENNIAL or perennial to 12″ tall; STEMS erect, sparcely leafed, supporting a loose panicle; basal LEAVES to 3″ long, petioled, ovate and irregularly lobed, stem leaves reduced and sessile; FLOWER heads yellow, with 10–15 in a panicle.
ECOLOGY: Foothills – named for the Platte River.
LOCATION: Eagle Wind Trail, Rabbit Mt., Lyons, CO 5/00 6000′
LOOK FOR thick oval leaves with irregular lobes.

■ **LIFE LIST** Where _____ NUMBER _____

RIDDELL GROUNDSEL

Senecio riddellii
Aster family   *Asteraceae (Compositae)*

PERENNIAL to 3′ tall; STEMS several from a woody crown; LEAVES to 6″ long resembling a pitchfork; FLOWER heads with unruly, spaced, yellow rays, in clusters of 15–20 heads.
ECOLOGY: Foothills.
LOCATION: Horsetooth Rock Trail, Ft. Collins, CO 6/99 5500′
LOOK FOR a leaf that resembles a pitchfork.

■ **LIFE LIST** Where _____ NUMBER _____

ALPINE SENECIO
Senecio soldanella
Aster family *Asteraceae (Compositae)*

PERENNIAL to 4″ tall; STEMS short, leafless with solitary heads; LEAVES smooth glossy, basal, thick, oval and petioled to 1″ wide; FLOWER heads yellow to 1″ across with spaced rays.
ECOLOGY: Subalpine and alpine.
LOCATION: Herman Lake Trail, Bakerville, CO 8/99 11,000′
LOOK FOR a group of low growing plants with glossy leaves and yellow flowers with spaced rays.

■ **LIFE LIST** Where _____ NUMBER ____

BROOM SENECIO
Senecio spartioides
Aster family *Asteraceae (Compositae)*

PERENNIAL to 30″ tall in clumps; STEMS erect, slender, reddish and top branched; LEAVES grass-like to 3″ long, alternating upward with little size reduction; FLOWER heads to 1½″ across, yellow, with 5–10 narrow, spaced rays, in terminal panicles.
ECOLOGY: Plains and foothills.
LOCATION: Prospect Ponds, Ft. Collins, CO 9/04 5000′
LOOK FOR grass-like leaves alternately arranged, unreduced, up to the top.

■ **LIFE LIST** Where _____ NUMBER ____

ARROWLEAF SENECIO
Senecio triangularis
Aster family *Asteraceae (Compositae)*

PERENNIAL to 3′ tall in clumps; STEMS tough, erect and leafy; LEAVES arrow-shaped to 6″ long, alternate and toothed; FLOWER heads yellow to 1″ wide with spaced rays, in panicles of 5–15 heads.
ECOLOGY: Subalpine in moist forests.
LOCATION: Niwot Trail, Brainard Lake Rec. Area, Ward, CO 7/00 10,500′
LOOK FOR glossy, arrowhead leaves with sharp-toothed margins.

■ **LIFE LIST** Where _____ NUMBER ____

WERNER SENECIO
Senecio werneriifolius
Aster family   *Asteraceae (Compositae)*

PERENNIAL to 6″ tall; STEMS hairy and leafy;
  LEAVES upright, spatulate, hairy to 2″ long and
  mostly basal, stem leaves sessile and reduced;
  FLOWERS yellow, to 1″ wide with 8 or fewer
  drooping rays.
ECOLOGY: Subalpine and alpine on rocky ridges.
LOCATION: Boreas Pass, CO 8/99 11,500′
LOOK FOR a small clump of upright, hairy, gray-
  green leaves and yellow flowers with spaced rays.

■ LIFE LIST Where _____ NUMBER _____

CANADIAN GOLDENROD
Solidago canadensis
Aster family   *Asteraceae (Compositae)*

PERENNIAL to 16″ tall; STEMS erect with several
  reduced leaves; LEAVES to 4″ long, mostly basal,
  elliptical and toothed; FLOWER heads yellow and
  tiny in an upright panicle.
ECOLOGY: Foothills to montane along rivers, in
  gravel and among rocks.
LOCATION: Dowdy Lake Rec. Area, Red Feathers, CO
  8/02 8000′
LOOK FOR a golden rod with coarsely toothed basal
  leaves.

■ LIFE LIST Where _____ NUMBER _____

LATE GOLDENROD
Solidago gigantea
Aster family   *Asteraceae (Compositae)*

PERENNIAL to 7′ tall; STEMS erect and leafy;
  LEAVES lanceolate to 6″ long, sharp tipped and
  toothed; FLOWER heads yellow and many, to ⅜″
  across in an upright panicle.
ECOLOGY: Plains and foothills in moist sites.
LOCATION: Poudre River Trail, Ft. Collins, CO 7/02
  5000′
LOOK FOR a robust goldenrod with closely spaced,
  stiff leaves.

■ LIFE LIST Where _____ NUMBER _____

SMOOTH GOLDENROD
Solidago missouriensis
Aster family   *Asteraceae (Compositae)*

PERENNIAL to 2½´ tall; STEMS erect unbranched and reddish at the base; upper LEAVES linear, sessile and alternate; FLOWER heads yellow and clustered on axillary racemes.

ECOLOGY: Plains to montane on rocky slopes and forest openings.

LOCATION: Carter Lake Rec. Area, Loveland, CO 8/01 6000´

LOOK FOR alternate, linear leaves extending up to the inflorescence.

■ **LIFE LIST**   Where _____ NUMBER _____

MOLLIS GOLDENROD
Solidago mollis
Aster family   *Asteraceae (Compositae)*

PERENNIAL to 2´ tall; STEMS erect and leafy; LEAVES alternate, broad-lanceolate and gray-green, to 1¼˝ long; FLOWER heads yellow to ¼˝ wide in multiple racemes to 3˝ long.

ECOLOGY: Plains in open fields.

LOCATION: Pine Ridge Nat. Area, Ft. Collins, CO 8/02 5000´

LOOK FOR a short goldenrod with closely spaced, broad, alternate leaves.

■ **LIFE LIST**   Where _____ NUMBER _____

ALPINE GOLDENROD
Solidago multiradiata
Aster family   *Asteraceae (Compositae)*

PERENNIAL to 1½´ tall; STEMS reddish, erect or ascending, unbranched and leafy; LEAVES oblanceolate to 4˝ long, smooth, alternate, petioled at the base and sessile and reduced above; FLOWER heads yellow in solitary racemes to 6˝ long.

ECOLOGY: Montane to alpine in sunny exposed areas.

LOCATION: Horse Trail, Wild Basin, RMNP, CO 7/00 9000´

LOOK FOR a short goldenrod with well-spaced stem leaves, at high elevations.

■ **LIFE LIST**   Where _____ NUMBER _____

DWARF GOLDENROD

Solidago nana
Aster family   *Asteraceae (Compositae)*

PERENNIAL to 6″ high; STEMS reddish and leaning; LEAVES spatulate to 2½″ long, smooth and glossy; FLOWER heads yellow in rounded clusters with about 12 heads each.
ECOLOGY: Subalpine to alpine on scree in exposed areas.
LOCATION: Trail Ridge Rd., RMNP, CO 7/05 12,500′
LOOK FOR glossy, upright leaves and loose, yellow clusters, at high elevations.

■ LIFE LIST Where _____ NUMBER _____

THREENERVE GOLDENROD

Solidago velutina (sparsiflora)
Aster family   *Asteraceae (Compositae)*

PERENNIAL to 2′ tall; STEMS erect, slender, green and leafy; LEAVES elliptical to 4″ long with basal leaves petioled and stem leaves narrow and sessile; FLOWER heads yellow in loose racemes to 8″ long.
ECOLOGY: Plains and foothills in meadows.
LOCATION: Roxborough S.P., Littleton, CO 9/00 6000′
LOOK FOR a slender goldenrod with elliptical leaves, reduced upward, at low elevations.

■ LIFE LIST Where _____ NUMBER _____

SPINY SOWTHISTLE

Sonchus arvensis
Aster family   *Asteraceae (Compositae)*

PERENNIAL to 4′ tall; STEMS erect, leafy and branched; LEAVES to 6″ long with spine tipped lobes; FLOWERS yellow to 1″ across with onion-shaped buds.
ECOLOGY: Plains in open, damp areas.
LOCATION: Boyd Lake S.P., Loveland, CO 8/01 5000′
LOOK FOR onion-shaped flower buds and leaves similar to Prickly Lettuce (*Lactuca serriola*).

■ LIFE LIST Where _____ NUMBER _____

COMMON DANDELION
Taraxacum officinale
Aster family   *Asteraceae (Compositae)*

PERENNIAL to 15″ tall; SCAPES hollow, milky and may be reddish; LEAVES rosetted and pinnatifid with terminal lobe the largest; FLOWER heads to 2″ across, yellow, with only ray flowers.
ECOLOGY: Plains to alpine, almost anywhere.
LOCATION: Berthoud Pass, CO 7/05 11,500′
LOOK FOR a common, lawn-type dandelion.

☐ **LIFE LIST** Where _____ NUMBER _____

TUNDRA DANDELION
Taraxacum officinale ceratophorum
Aster family   *Asteraceae (Compositae)*

PERENNIAL to 12″ tall; SCAPES hollow and hairy, and may be reddish; LEAVES rosetted, spatulate, wavy and upright, to 6″ long; FLOWER heads yellow to 2″ wide with only ray flowers.
ECOLOGY: Subalpine and alpine in open areas, meadows and tundra slopes.
LOCATION: Herman Lake Trail, Bakerville, CO 8/00 11,000′
LOOK FOR a dandelion with smooth (entire) leaf margins, at high elevations.

☐ **LIFE LIST** Where _____ NUMBER _____

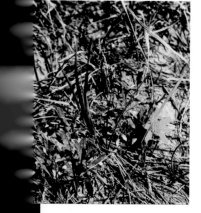

BUTTE MARIGOLD
Tetraneuris (Hymenoxys) acaulis
Aster family   *Asteraceae (Compositae)*

PERENNIAL to 2″ high; STEMS inconspicuous; LEAVES tiny, oblanceolate with soft, silvery hairs; FLOWERS yellow to 1″ wide with up to 10 petals.
ECOLOGY: Plains in dry, open areas.
LOCATION: Pawnee National Grasslands, Keota, CO 5/99 5000′
LOOK FOR a tiny clump of gray-green leaves covered with soft, silvery hairs and, perhaps, 1–2 yellow flowers with 5–10 petals.

☐ **LIFE LIST** Where _____ NUMBER _____

WOOLLY TETRANEURIS

Tetraneuris (Hymenoxys) acaulis caespitosa
Aster family   *Asteraceae (Compositae)*

PERENNIAL to 3″ high; STEMS woolly bearing a
single flower; LEAVES linear, woolly and pitchforking
near the tip, to 1½″ long; FLOWER disc to 1″ wide
with ½″ long rays having 3-lobed tips.
ECOLOGY: Alpine in open areas.
LOCATION: Sheep Lake Trail, Medicine Bow N.F.,
WY 6/02 10,500′
LOOK FOR a tiny woolly plant bearing a
proportionally large flower with a large disc.

■ **LIFE LIST** Where _____ NUMBER _____

ALPINE SUNFLOWER

Tetraneuris (Hymenoxys) grandiflora
Aster family   *Asteraceae (Compositae)*

PERENNIAL to 8″ tall; STEMS woolly, stout and
nearly leafless; LEAVES pinnatafid with well-spaced
linear lobes; FLOWER heads yellow and solitary to 2″
across with rays notched at the tips.
ECOLOGY: Alpine slopes among rocks.
LOCATION: Berthoud Pass, CO 7/01 11,500′
LOOK FOR string-like leaves and a proportionally
large flower with a domed center.

■ **LIFE LIST** Where _____ NUMBER _____

GREENTHREAD

Thelesperma filifolium
Aster family   *Asteraceae (Compositae)*

ANNUAL or perennial to 2′ tall; STEMS slender, wiry,
sparsely leafed and branching; LEAVES linear and
string-like; FLOWER heads yellow and tube-like with
some rays that drop early; involucre has fused
phyllaries forming a cup.
ECOLOGY: Foothills on dry slopes.
LOCATION: Coyote Ridge Rec. Area, Ft. Collins, CO
7/02 5500′
LOOK FOR a skeleton-like plant and yellow rayless
flowers contained in little cups.

■ **LIFE LIST** Where _____ NUMBER _____

FIELD COREOPSIS
Thelesperma megapotamicum
Aster family   *Asteraceae (Compositae)*

PERENNIAL to 2´ tall; STEMS upright, branching, slender and sparsely leafed; LEAVES string-like to 2″ long; FLOWER heads yellow and rayless to ½″ wide.
ECOLOGY: Plains and foothills, on dry sites.
LOCATION: Hall Ranch, Lyons, CO 7/01 6000´
LOOK FOR a skeleton-like plant, rayless yellow flowers and an involucre with 5 points.

■ **LIFE LIST** Where _____ NUMBER _____

PYGMY GOLDENWEED
Tonestus pygmaeus
Aster family   *Asteraceae (Compositae)*

PERENNIAL to 3″ tall; STEMS pale green and leafy; LEAVES spatulate, wavy and hairy to 2″ long; FLOWERS heads yellow to ¾″ wide.
ECOLOGY: Subalpine and alpine on open slopes.
LOCATION: Mt. Evans, CO 6/05 11,000´
LOOK FOR wavy, dull-green, clasping leaves and yellow flowers.

■ **LIFE LIST** Where _____ NUMBER _____

YELLOW SALSIFY
Tragopogon dubius
Aster family   *Asteraceae (Compositae)*

ANNUAL or biennial to 3´ tall; STEMS erect and hollow with milky sap; LEAVES mostly on stems, linear, clasping and infolded, to 10″ long; FLOWER heads yellow, bowl-shaped, to 2″ across with pointed bracts.
ECOLOGY: Plains to montane in waste areas.
LOCATION: Boyd Lake S.P., Loveland, CO 5/03 5000´
LOOK FOR narrow, upright, clasping, sharply pointed, grass-like leaves and yellow flower heads with needle-like bracts.

■ **LIFE LIST** Where _____ NUMBER _____

HOLLYGRAPE

Mahonia repens
Barberry family *Berberidaceae*

SHRUB to 1′ tall; LEAVES with 2–3 pairs of leaflets plus a terminal leaflet that is ovate and wavy with 5–9 spiny teeth; FLOWERS yellow, barrel-shaped, to ¼″ wide and clustered; FRUIT is a dark blue berry.

ECOLOGY: Foothills and montane on hillsides, often in association with conifers and oaks.

LOCATION: Wild Basin, RMNP, CO 7/99 9000′

LOOK FOR leaves that have a papery texture.

■ LIFE LIST Where _____ NUMBER _____

NARROW-LEAVED PUCCOON

Lithospermum incisum
Borage family *Boraginaceae*

PERENNIAL to 10″ tall; STEMS erect, bristly and leafy; LEAVES alternate, narrow, fleshy, hairy, sessile, to 1″ long; FLOWERS yellow, ¾″ wide with a flaring, tubular corolla and 5 fringed lobes.

ECOLOGY: Plains and foothills in open dry areas.

LOCATION: Pine Ridge Nat. Area, Ft. Collins, CO 5/05 5000′

LOOK FOR succulent, linear leaves and trumpet-like flowers.

■ LIFE LIST Where _____ NUMBER _____

MANY FLOWERED PUCCOON

Lithospermum multiflorum
Borage family *Boraginaceae*

PERENNIAL to 18″ tall; STEMS erect, many, alternate-leafed with ½″ or more between nodes; LEAVES narrow, sessile, often twisted, to 2″ long; FLOWERS yellow in terminal clusters of 2–6, with flaring, tubular corollas and 5 lobes.

ECOLOGY: Foothills and montane.

LOCATION: S. Mesa Trail, Eldorado Canyon S.P., Eldorado Springs, CO 6/02 6500′

LOOK FOR uniform, linear leaves, and yellow, trumpet-like flowers in terminal clusters.

■ LIFE LIST Where _____ NUMBER _____

YELLOW ALYSSUM
Alyssum alyssoides
Mustard family *Brassicaceae (Cruciferae)*

ANNUAL or biennial to 16″ tall; STEMS curved, bristly and leafy; LEAVES yellow-green, oblanceolate, sessile and bristly; FLOWERS yellow, 4-petaled to ⅛″ across; PODS disc-shaped, winged, bristly, to ¼″ across, with style attached.
ECOLOGY: Plains and foothills.
LOCATION: Lower Narrows Campground, Poudre Canyon, CO 6/00 6500′
LOOK FOR curved stems with 1″ leaves, yellow flowers and disc-like pods with marginal wings.

■ LIFE LIST Where _____ NUMBER _____

FIELD ALYSSUM
Alyssum parviflorum (minus)
Mustard family *Brassicaceae (Cruciferae)*

ANNUAL to 10″ tall; STEMS leafy, bristly and decumbent; LEAVES hairy to 1¼″ long; FLOWERS yellow, 4-petaled, to 1/32″ across, cluster in a tight terminal head that advances with growth.
ECOLOGY: Plains and foothills.
LOCATION: Horsetooth Trail, Lory S.P., Ft. Collins, CO 5/04 5500′
LOOK FOR a small, spreading plant with creeping stems, each terminating in a green and yellow cluster.

■ LIFE LIST Where _____ NUMBER _____

AMERICAN WINTERCRESS
Barbarea orthoceras
Mustard family *Brassicaceae (Cruciferae)*

ANNUAL, biennial, or perennial to 20″ tall; STEMS erect and leafy; LEAVES pinnatifid with the terminal lobe largest; FLOWERS yellow, 4-petaled, to ¼″ wide, in terminal clusters; pods upright, wire-like to 1¼″ long.
ECOLOGY: Plains to subalpine.
LOCATION: Jefferson County Fair Ground, Golden, CO 5/02 6500′
LOOK FOR terminal clusters of yellow flowers, lobed, leathery leaves and ascending cylindrical pods.

■ LIFE LIST Where _____ NUMBER _____

FALSE FLAX
Camelina microcarpa
Mustard family   *Brassicaceae (Cruciferae)*

ANNUAL or biennial to 30″ tall; STEMS erect, leafy
and slender; LEAVES clasping and linear with bristly
margins; FLOWERS tiny with 4 yellow petals; PODS
rounded to ⅛″ with ½″ stalks and attached styles.
ECOLOGY: Plains and foothills.
LOCATION: Eldorado Canyon S.P., Eldorado Springs,
CO 5/01 6500′
LOOK FOR teardrop-shaped pods with styles
attached, held away form the stem by a ½″ stalk.

■ **LIFE LIST** Where _____ NUMBER _____

TANSY MUSTARD
Descurainia sophia
Mustard family   *Brassicaceae (Cruciferae)*

ANNUAL or biennial to 3′ high; STEMS erect, leafy,
green and slender; LEAVES bipinnatifid to 6″ long
with linear lobes; FLOWERS yellow, clustered
terminally and progressing with stem growth.
ECOLOGY: Plains and foothills.
LOCATION: Legacy Park, Ft. Collins, CO 5/02 5000′
LOOK FOR yellow flowers, slender stems with string-
like leaves and slender, red, up-curved pods.

■ **LIFE LIST** Where _____ NUMBER _____

GOLDEN DRABA
Draba aurea
Mustard family   *Brassicaceae (Cruciferae)*

PERENNIAL to 6″ tall; STEMS leafy and erect; basal
LEAVES broad-lanceolate and petioled to 1″ long,
stem leaves lanceolate, sessile and upward reduced;
FLOWERS yellow, tiny, in 1″ long terminal clusters;
PODS twisted and ascending to 1″ long.
ECOLOGY: Montane to alpine.
LOCATION: Brown Lake Trail, Crown Pt. Rd.,
Larimer Cty., CO 7/04 11,000′
LOOK FOR twisted pods. These are diagnostic.

■ **LIFE LIST** Where _____ NUMBER _____

WESTERN WALLFLOWER

Erysimum asperum
Mustard family   *Brassicaceae (Cruciferae)*

BIENNIAL or perennial to 18″ tall; STEMS erect,
stout and leafy; LEAVES linear, in-folded, pointed,
sessile, hairy, dull green, to 4″ long; FLOWERS in
terminal clusters, yellow or orange, with 4, spaced
petals to ½″ long.

ECOLOGY: Plains to subalpine.

LOCATION: Timber Trail, Lory S.P., Ft. Collins, CO
5/03 5500′

LOOK FOR linear leaves with a few sharp marginal
teeth and an inflorescence of bright 4-petaled flowers.

■ **LIFE LIST** Where _____ NUMBER _____

DWARF WALLFLOWER

Erysimum capitatum
Mustard family   *Brassicaceae (Cruciferae)*

BIENNIAL or perennial to 6″ tall; STEMS ascending
leafy and few; LEAVES gray-green, downward curved
and in-rolled to 1″ long; FLOWERS yellow, 4-petaled
to ½″ across in terminal clusters.

ECOLOGY: Foothills on dry hillsides.

LOCATION: Pawnee Nat. Grasslands, Keota, CO 5/99
5000′

LOOK FOR a tuft of hairy, grayish, 1″ leaves and a
terminal cluster of 4-petaled, yellow flowers.

■ **LIFE LIST** Where _____ NUMBER _____

DYER'S WOAD

Isatis tinctoria
Mustard family   *Brassicaceae (Cruciferae)*

PERENNIAL to 20″ tall; STEMS erect, pubescent and
leafy; basal LEAVES dull green and spatulate, stem
leaves lanceolate, sessile and ascending; FLOWERS
yellow on branched racemes with petals ⅛″ long.

ECOLOGY: Montane and subalpine.

LOCATION: Vail Pass Trail, Vail, CO 8/91 10,500′

LOOK FOR a rosette of gray-green, spatulate leaves
and leafy stems supporting loose clusters of yellow,
4-petaled flowers.

■ **LIFE LIST** Where _____ NUMBER _____

PEPPER WEED

Lepidium densiflorum
Mustard family   *Brassicaceae (Cruciferae)*

ANNUAL or biennial to 10″ tall; STEMS leafy and
   hairy with upper half given to raceme; LEAVES
   ascending, in-folded and hairy to ½″ long; FLOWERS
   yellow, to ¹⁄₁₆″ wide; PODS stalked, flat, round and
   hairy, to ¼″.
ECOLOGY: Plains and foothills.
LOCATION: Jefferson County Fair Ground, Golden,
   CO 5/02 6500′
LOOK FOR a stalk with upright, leaves, tiny yellow
   flowers and disc-like pods.

■ LIFE LIST Where _____ NUMBER _____

MOUNTAIN BLADDERPOD

Lesquerella montana
Mustard family   *Brassicaceae (Cruciferae)*

PERENNIAL to 12″ tall; STEMS slender, pubescent
   and leafy; basal LEAVES petioled, to 2″ long, stem
   leaves to ¾″ long, sessile and ascending; FLOWERS
   yellow, 4-petaled, ½″ wide, on racemes; PODS egg-
   shaped, held upright by right-angled pedicles.
ECOLOGY: Plains to montane on dry slopes.
LOCATION: Bitterbrush Trail, Hall Ranch, Lyons, CO
   5/01 6000′
LOOK FOR egg-shaped pods held up like lamps.

■ LIFE LIST Where _____ NUMBER _____

PICEANCE BLADDERPOD

Lesquerella parviflora
Mustard family   *Brassicaceae (Cruciferae)*

PERENNIAL to 2″ high, prostrate plant forming a
   mat; STEMS reddish to 12″ long; LEAVES toothed,
   glossy and leathery, to 1″ long; FLOWERS yellow,
   very tiny, in terminal clusters; PODS are terminal
   swellings on stalks.
ECOLOGY: Montane to subalpine.
LOCATION: Mirror Lake Campground, Medicine
   Bow N.F., WY 8/00 10,500′
LOOK FOR a succulent prostrate plant with a variety
   of leaf shapes.

■ LIFE LIST Where _____ NUMBER _____

DOUBLE BLADDER POD
Physaria bellii
Mustard family *Brassicaceae (Cruciferae)*

PERENNIAL to 7″ tall; STEMS ascending and leafy; basal LEAVES spatulate to 2″ long, forming a rosette, stem leaves alternate and reduced; FLOWERS yellow, 4-petaled to ½″ across in terminal clusters; PODS doubled to ¼″.

ECOLOGY: Foothills and montane.

LOCATION: Coyote Ridge Rec. Area, Ft. Collins, CO 4/02 5500′

LOOK FOR a rosette of gray-green leaves, ascending stems and yellow clusters of 4-petaled flowers.

■ **LIFE LIST** Where _____ NUMBER _____

SPREADING YELLOWCRESS
Rorippa sinuata
Mustard family *Brassicaceae (Cruciferae)*

PERENNIAL to 10″ tall; STEMS unbranched, succulent, pubescent and leafy; LEAVES deeply and irregularly lobed, to 3″ long; FLOWERS yellow, tiny, 4-petaled, in terminal clusters.

ECOLOGY: Plains and foothills.

LOCATION: Boyd Lake S.P., Loveland, CO 5/04 5000′

LOOK FOR deeply lobed leaves and yellow petals that remain mostly inside the bud.

■ **LIFE LIST** Where _____ NUMBER _____

TUMBLE MUSTARD
Sisymbrium altissimum
Mustard family *Brassicaceae (Cruciferae)*

ANNUAL or biennial to 4′ tall; STEMS smooth, branched and slender; basal LEAVES fern-like to 6″ long; upper leaves string-like; FLOWERS light yellow and 4-petaled in terminal clusters on axillary branches.

ECOLOGY: Plains and foothills.

LOCATION: Cherry Creek Trail, Denver, CO 5/93 5000′

LOOK FOR a large, sprawling plant with minimal leaf area that seems insufficient for such a large plant.

■ **LIFE LIST** Where _____ NUMBER _____

GOLDEN PRINCE'S PLUME
Stanleya pinnata
Mustard family   *Brassicaceae (Cruciferae)*

PERENNIAL to 3′ tall; STEMS stout, leafy, and
branching to form several plumes; LEAVES to 6″ long
and deeply lobed; FLOWERS yellow, 4-petaled with
exserted stamens in a spike-like 10″ raceme.
ECOLOGY: Plains and foothills.
LOCATION: Coyote Ridge Rec. Area, Ft. Collins, CO
7/01 5500′
LOOK FOR yellow flowers in a raceme that resembles
a bottlebrush.

■ **LIFE LIST**   Where _____ NUMBER _____

NIPPLE CACTUS
Escobaria (Coryphantha) vivipara
Cactus family   *Cactaceae*

PERENNIAL to 3″ high; STEMS round to 4″ wide,
slightly flattened on top and covered with little
nipples, each topped by radial spines; FLOWERS
yellow to orange and 1½″ wide.
ECOLOGY: Foothills on dry southern slopes.
LOCATION: Eldorado Canyon S.P., Eldorado Springs,
CO 5/01 6500′
LOOK FOR a round cactus with nipples, radiating
spines and orange flowers.

■ **LIFE LIST**   Where _____ NUMBER _____

PRICKLY PEAR CACTUS
Opuntia macrorhiza
Cactus family   *Cactaceae*

PERENNIAL to 8″ high, with a woody root; PADS to
8″ long with spiny warts spaced about ½″ apart over
the surface; FLOWERS yellow, tinged with pink, to 3″
across; FRUIT is club-shaped, fleshy and red to 2″
long.
ECOLOGY: Plains and foothills in dry areas.
LOCATION: Hall Ranch, Lyons, CO 6/99 6000′
LOOK FOR a spiny, green, oval, upright pad with 1 or
more rose-like flowers.

■ **LIFE LIST**   Where _____ NUMBER _____

BUSH HONEYSUCKLE

Lonicera (Distegia) involucrata
Honeysuckle family   *Caprifoliaceae*

SHRUB to 6´ tall; STEMS erect or ascending, leafy
with gray bark; LEAVES opposite, ovate, to 5˝ long;
FLOWERS in pairs at nodes with yellow tubular
corollas; FRUIT paired, shiny and purple-black, with
red bracts.

ECOLOGY: Foothills to subalpine.

LOCATION: Wild Basin, RMNP, CO 7/99 9000´

LOOK FOR a shrub with opposite leaves, prominent
veins, twin yellow flowers and twin black fruit with
red bracts.

■ **LIFE LIST**   Where _____ NUMBER _____

YELLOW STONECROP

Sedum (Amerosedum) lanceolatum
Stonecrop family   *Crassulaceae*

PERENNIAL to 8˝ tall and tufted; STEMS erect,
reddish, fleshy and leafy; basal LEAVES ½˝ long,
forming many tiny, round rosettes; stem leaves red,
narrow, upright, overlapping to ¼˝ long; FLOWERS
yellow to ½˝ wide, borne in terminal clusters.

ECOLOGY: Plains to alpine.

LOCATION: Cub Lake Trail, RMNP, CO 7/99 8500´

LOOK FOR moss-like rosettes, red stems, and
terminal clusters of 3–6 yellow flowers.

■ **LIFE LIST**   Where _____ NUMBER _____

RUSSIAN OLIVE

Elaeagnus angustifolia
Oleaster family   *Elaeagnaceae*

TREE to 30´ high; young TWIGS twigs with silvery
bloom, older twigs mahogany; LEAVES lanceolate
and glaucous to 2˝ long; FLOWERS pale yellow to ¼"
wide.

ECOLOGY: Plains – a lawn tree that has naturalized
along streams and wet places.

LOCATION: Boyd Lake S.P., Loveland, CO 6/02
5000´

LOOK FOR gray-green leaves with a white bloom.

■ **LIFE LIST**   Where _____ NUMBER _____

LEAFY SPURGE
Euphorbia (Tithymalus) esula
Spurge family   *Euphorbiaceae*

PERENNIAL to 4´ tall in dense patches; STEMS
   erect, slender, milky and leafy; LEAVES linear, sessile
   and pointed to 2½˝ long; FLOWERS yellow, attended
   by 2 leaf-like bracts.
ECOLOGY: Plains to montane – listed as a noxious
   weed.
LOCATION: Legacy Park, Ft. Collins, CO 5/02 5000´
LOOK FOR a pair of twin yellow flowers subtended
   by a pair of green bracts.

■ LIFE LIST   Where _____ NUMBER _____

BIRDFOOT TREFOIL
Lotus corniculatus
Pea family   *Fabaceae (Leguminosae)*

PERENNIAL to 12˝ tall with sprawling habit; STEMS
   weak, branched and leafy; LEAVES trifoliate with
   oblong leaflets to ½˝ long; FLOWERS yellow,
   leguminous, to ½˝ across, in terminal umbels of 3–4
   flowers.
ECOLOGY: Plains to foothills.
LOCATION: Prospect Ponds, Ft. Collins, CO 5/04
   5000´
LOOK FOR bright, yellow flowers on a plant that
   resembles alfalfa.

■ LIFE LIST   Where _____ NUMBER _____

BLACK MEDIC
Medicago lupulina
Pea family   *Fabaceae (Leguminosae)*

ANNUAL or perennial creeping vine to 2˝ tall,
   forming mats; STEMS creeping, ascending and
   branching; LEAVES trifoliate with ¼˝ leaflets,
   minutely toothed; FLOWERS yellow, ⅛˝ wide in ½˝
   globose, terminal clusters.
ECOLOGY: Plains and foothills in lawns and waste
   places.
LOCATION: Young Gulch, Poudre Canyon, CO 9/04
   7000´
LOOK FOR a green mat with little, clover-like leaves
   and clusters of tiny flowers.

■ LIFE LIST   Where _____ NUMBER _____

YELLOW SWEET CLOVER
Melilotus officinalis
Pea family   *Fabaceae (Leguminosae)*

ANNUAL, biennial, or perennial to 5´ tall; STEMS branched, slender and erect; LEAVES trifoliate with oval leaflets to 1″ long with minute teeth; FLOWERS yellow and drooping in 4″, upright racemes.
ECOLOGY: Plains to montane.
LOCATION: Legacy Park, Ft. Collins, CO 6/01 5000´
LOOK FOR a tall plant with trifoliate leaves and racemes of yellow, drooping flowers.

■ LIFE LIST Where _____ NUMBER _____

GOLDEN BANNER
Thermopsis rhombifolia (divaricarpa)
Pea family   *Fabaceae (Leguminosae)*

PERENNIAL to 2´ tall; STEMS erect and leafy; LEAVES trifoliate, alternate with paired, leaf-like stipules at bases of leaves; leaflets lanceolate to 2″ long; FLOWERS yellow to 1″ across in racemes to 6″ long.
ECOLOGY: Foothills to subalpine.
LOCATION: Bierstadt Lake Trail, RMNP, CO 7/99 9500´
LOOK FOR a single stem with trifoliate leaves and an upright raceme of bright yellow flowers.

■ LIFE LIST Where _____ NUMBER _____

GOLDEN CORYDALIS
Corydalis aurea
Bleeding Heart family   *Fumariaceae*

ANNUAL or biennial to 12″ tall; STEMS erect or ascending and fleshy; LEAVES to 2″ long, alternate with spaced, incised lobes; FLOWERS yellow, 2-lipped, 1″ long with a prominent spur.
ECOLOGY: Foothills and montane.
LOCATION: Nighthawk Trail, Hall Ranch, Lyons, CO 5/01 6000´
LOOK FOR a small plant with twice-pinnatifid leaves and yellow, spurred flowers.

■ LIFE LIST Where _____ NUMBER _____

GOLDEN CURRANT
Ribes aureum
Gooseberry family   *Grossulariaceae*

SHRUB to 8´ tall; STEMS brown with gray spots
(lenticles), new growth red; LEAVES fan-shaped to
1″ wide with 3 apex lobes; FLOWERS yellow,
½″ wide, tubular, with 5 lobes and 3–5 flowers per
spur; BERRIES red to ¼″.
ECOLOGY: Plains and foothills near water.
LOCATION: Highland Canal Trail, Denver, CO 5/92
5000´
LOOK FOR fan-shaped leaves and yellow trumpet
flowers with red centers.

■ LIFE LIST   Where _____ NUMBER _____

ASPARAGUS
Asparagus officinalis
Lily family   *Liliaceae (Asparagaceae)*

PERENNIAL to 6´ tall and harvested at 8–12″ as a
vegetable, but produces a fern if uncut; LEAVES are
fern-like, soft and turn brilliant yellow in fall;
FLOWERS yellow-green, to ⅛″ wide, bell-shaped
with 5 lobes; berries red.
ECOLOGY: Plains along streams – an escapee from
cultivation.
LOCATION: Poudre River Trail, Ft. Collins, CO 7/02
5000´
LOOK FOR succulent stalks; soft, willowy, ferns or
red, ¼″ berries.

■ LIFE LIST   Where _____ NUMBER _____

AVALANCHE LILY
Erythronium grandiflorum
Lily family   *Liliaceae*

PERENNIAL to 12″ high STEMS slender and crook-
necked; LEAVES elliptic to 6″ long and sheathed at
bases; FLOWERS solitary, yellow, nodding with
recurved petals and exserted anthers and style;
PODS reddish and club-shaped.
ECOLOGY: Montane to alpine in bogs.
LOCATION: Sheep Lake Trail, Medicine Bow N.F.,
WY 6/02 10,500´
LOOK FOR a leafless stalk bearing a single, yellow,
nodding lily.

■ LIFE LIST   Where _____ NUMBER _____

WHITE-STEM BLAZING STAR
Mentzelia albicaulis
Loasa family   *Loasaceae*

ANNUAL to 10″ tall; STEMS succulent, pale-green, leafy and branched; LEAVES to 6″ long, pinnatifid with irregular lobes, bearing tiny hooks; FLOWERS yellow, to ½″ across, 5-petaled, bowl-shaped with numerous anthers.

ECOLOGY: Plains and foothills on dry sites.

LOCATION: Horsetooth Trail, Lory S.P., Ft. Collins, CO 5/02 5500′

LOOK FOR irregularly lobed leaves, yellow flowers and whitish stems.

■ LIFE LIST Where _____ NUMBER _____

YELLOW POND LILY
Nuphar polysepala
Waterlily family   *Nymphaeaceae*

PERENNIAL aquatic plant; STEMS erect, smooth and fleshy; LEAVES floating, cordate, to 12″ wide; FLOWERS yellow, bowl-shaped, to 2¼″ across with overlapping petals and held above the water by long stems, arising from the bottom.

ECOLOGY: Subalpine in shallow water.

LOCATION: Bear Lake, RMNP, CO 7/97 9500′

LOOK FOR a yellow, bowl-shaped flower with a large raised disc.

■ LIFE LIST Where _____ NUMBER _____

TOOTHED EVENING PRIMROSE
Calylophus serrulatus
Evening Primrose family   *Onagraceae*

PERENNIAL to 10″ tall; STEMS branching and very leafy; LEAVES alternate, linear, in-folded, and toothed, to 1½″ long; FLOWERS yellow to 1″ wide with 4 overlapping petals, a 4-lobed stigma and 8 stamen.

ECOLOGY: Prairie and foothills in dry open areas.

LOCATION: Marshall Mesa, Boulder, CO 6/99 6000′

LOOK FOR a yellow evening primrose with in-folded, curved, linear leaves.

■ LIFE LIST Where _____ NUMBER _____

HOWARD EVENING PRIMROSE
Oenothera howardii
Evening Primrose family *Onagraceae*

PERENNIAL to 6″ tall; STEMS prostrate and hidden by leaves; LEAVES narrow-lanceolate, dark green, to 3″ long; FLOWERS saucer-shaped to 3″ wide with 4 yellow, overlapping petals.
ECOLOGY: Plains and foothills.
LOCATION: Coyote Ridge Rec. Area, Ft. Collins, CO 5/02 5500′
LOOK FOR a small clump of dark green leaves and large yellow flowers.

■ **LIFE LIST** Where _____ NUMBER _____

HAIRY EVENING PRIMROSE
Oenothera villosa strigosa
Evening primrose family *Onagraceae*

BIENNIAL or perennial to 16″ high; STEMS curved, leafy and light green to reddish; LEAVES lanceolate, alternate, to 2″ long with a pale green mid-rib; FLOWERS yellow, to 1½″ across, bowl-shaped with 4 overlapping petals.
ECOLOGY: Plains to montane on hillsides.
LOCATION: Dowdy Lake Rec. Area, Red Feathers, CO 7/01 8000′
LOOK FOR ascending, leafy stems and yellow flowers arising from leaf axils.

■ **LIFE LIST** Where _____ NUMBER _____

COMMON EVENING PRIMROSE
Oenothera villosa villosa
Evening Primrose family *Onagraceae*

BIENNIAL or perennial to 6′ tall; STEMS erect, unbranched, hairy and reddish; LEAVES lanceolate to 5″ long, alternate and ascending; FLOWERS yellow, to 2″ across with 4 overlapping petals that turn red on aging.
ECOLOGY: Plains and foothills.
LOCATION: Eltuck Bay, Lory S.P., Ft. Collins, CO 8/01 5500′
LOOK FOR a sturdy, upright stalk with a progression of axillary flowers.

■ **LIFE LIST** Where _____ NUMBER _____

WOOD SORREL

Oxalis stricta
Wood Sorrel family   *Oxalidaceae*

PERENNIAL to 2″ high; SCAPES to 3″ long; LEAVES trifoliate, green or red, with ¼″ leaflets, in-folded and notched at the tips; FLOWERS yellow, funnel-shaped, to ½″ across with 5 flaring lobes.

ECOLOGY: Plains to montane in lawns, gardens and woods.

LOCATION: Nighthawk Trail, Hall Ranch, Lyons, CO 5/01 6000′

LOOK FOR a trifoliate leaf with in-folded leaflets notched at the apex.

■ **LIFE LIST** Where _____ NUMBER _____

ALPINE SULPHUR FLOWER

Eriogonum jamesii
Buckwheat family   *Polygonaceae*

PERENNIAL to 3″ tall, forming mats; STEMS prostrate, arising from root crowns; LEAVES spatulate and woolly to 1″ long; FLOWERS yellow, to ¼″ wide, in clusters, with styles and stamens exserted.

ECOLOGY: Alpine, on tundra, among rocks.

LOCATION: S. Park Trail, Guanella Pass, CO 8/99 11,500′

LOOK FOR a clump of gray-green, upright, spatulate leaves and interspersed clusters of yellow flowers.

■ **LIFE LIST** Where _____ NUMBER _____

SULPHUR FLOWER

Eriogonum umbellatum
Buckwheat family   *Polygonaceae*

PERENNIAL to 12″ tall forming loose mats; STEMS (scapes) leafless, supporting umbels subtended by a whorl of spatulate bracts; LEAVES are basal, spatulate, pubescent, to ⅜″ wide; FLOWERS yellow, in 2″ umbels made up of ½″ umbels.

ECOLOGY: Foothills to subalpine.

LOCATION: Young Gulch, Poudre Canyon, CO 6/01 7500′

LOOK FOR a rosette of spatulate leaves and an umbel formed by 3–10 smaller umbels.

■ **LIFE LIST** Where _____ NUMBER _____

PURSLANE

Portulaca oleracea
Purslane family   *Portulacaceae*

ANNUAL, forming mats to 2´x2´; STEMS prostrate, reddish, branching, leafy and succulent; LEAVES fleshy, reddish beneath and green above to 1˝ long; FLOWERS yellow to ¼˝ wide at branch tips.
ECOLOGY: Plains, as a weed in crops.
LOCATION: Boyd Lake S.P., Loveland, CO 8/01 5000´
LOOK FOR a succulent mat of red stems and rounded leaves.

■ LIFE LIST Where _____ NUMBER _____

MEADOW BUTTERCUP

Ranunculus acris (repens)
Buttercup family   *Ranunculaceae*

PERENNIAL to 30˝ tall; STEMS hollow, erect and branched; LEAVES palmately divided into 3–5, many toothed lobes, basal leaves petioled, stem leaves sessile; FLOWERS yellow, glossy and bowl-shaped to ¾˝ wide.
ECOLOGY: Plains and foothills in bogs.
LOCATION: Marshall Mesa, Boulder, CO 6/99 6000´
LOOK FOR leaves that are palmately cut into many sharp lobes and glossy, yellow flowers.

■ LIFE LIST Where _____ NUMBER _____

CALTHA FLOWERED BUTTERCUP

Ranunculus alismaefolius
Buttercup family   *Ranunculaceae*

PERENNIAL to 4˝ high; SCAPES bearing a single flower; LEAVES glossy, lanceolate, to 3˝ long; FLOWERS yellow to ⅝˝ wide with ⅜˝ centers
ECOLOGY: Subalpine and alpine in bogs.
LOCATION: St. Alban's Chapel, Medicine Bow N.F., WY 6/02 10,500´
LOOK FOR a Marsh Marigold (*Caltha leptosepala*) with yellow flowers.

■ LIFE LIST Where _____ NUMBER _____

SHORE BUTTERCUP
Ranunculus cymbalaria
Buttercup family   *Ranunculaceae*

PERENNIAL to 1″ high; STEMS prostrate, rooting at nodes; LEAVES rosetted, spoon-shaped, leathery and lobed to ¼″ wide with ½″ petiole; FLOWERS yellow, 5-petaled, to ⅜″ wide with a ⅛″ center.

ECOLOGY: Foothills and montane on drying mud flats.

LOCATION: Dowdy Lake Rec. Area, Red Feathers, CO 6/02 8000′

LOOK FOR tiny yellow buttercup flowers on miniature plants along the shore.

■ **LIFE LIST**   Where _____ NUMBER _____

SUBALPINE BUTTERCUP
Ranunculus eschscholtzii
Buttercup family   *Ranunculaceae*

PERENNIAL to 8″ tall; STEMS 1 to 5 succulent and leafy; LEAVES palmately divided into 3–5 narrow segments to 1″ long; basal leaves petioled, upper leaves sessile; FLOWERS yellow to ¾″ across with 5 petals, and subtended by a whorl of leaves.

ECOLOGY: Montane to alpine in bogs.

LOCATION: Mitchell Lake Trail, Brainard Lake Rec Area, Ward, CO 7/00 11,000′

LOOK FOR whorled leaves cut into narrow, irregular segments and a little buttercup.

■ **LIFE LIST**   Where _____ NUMBER _____

SNOW BUTTERCUP
Ranunculus eschscholtzii adoneus
Buttercup family   *Ranunculaceae*

PERENNIAL to 6″ tall; STEMS with a whorl of string-like leaves below solitary flower; LEAVES, mainly basal, string-like to 2″ long; FLOWERS saucer-shaped to 1″ across with 4 overlapping, corrugated, yellow petals.

ECOLOGY: Subalpine and alpine in bogs.

LOCATION: Jean Lunning Trail, Brainard Lake Rec. Area, Ward, CO 7/01 10,500′

LOOK FOR a patch of buttercups with light green, string-like leaves and yellow flowers with corrugated petals.

■ **LIFE LIST**   Where _____ NUMBER _____

SPEARWORT
Ranunculus flammula (reptans)
Buttercup family   *Ranunculaceae*

PERENNIAL to 2″ tall; STEMS stolon-like, rooting
at the joints; LEAVES basal, linear, to 1″ long;
FLOWERS solitary, yellow, saucer-shaped to ⅜″ wide
with 5 petals.
ECOLOGY: Montane and subalpine in mud.
LOCATION: Moraine Park, RMNP, CO 6/02 9000′
LOOK FOR linear leaves and rooting at nodes. These
traits identify this species.

■ LIFE LIST Where _____ NUMBER _____

SAGEBRUSH BUTTERCUP
Ranunculus glaberrimus
Buttercup family   *Ranunculaceae*

PERENNIAL to 5″ tall; STEMS succulent, reddish,
leafy and unbranched; LEAVES succulent, irregular,
rounded with an occasional mitten leaf; FLOWERS
yellow with ½″ global center and ¼″ long petals.
ECOLOGY: Foothills in shady places.
LOCATION: Timber Trail, Lory S.P., Ft. Collins, CO
4/01 5500′
LOOK FOR a rosette of rounded leaves and the
globe-shaped flower center.

■ LIFE LIST Where _____ NUMBER _____

ALPINE BUTTERCUP
Ranunculus inamoenus
Buttercup family   *Ranunculuaceae*

PERENNIAL to 2″ tall; STEMS inconspicuous;
LEAVES twice pinnatifid with very regular dissecting,
fleshy to 2″ long; FLOWERS yellow with 12 separated
tepals, 6 of which are petals and 6 are sepals.
ECOLOGY: Alpine, rarely found.
LOCATION: Boreas Pass, CO 8/99 11,500′
LOOK FOR an aster-type flower and foliage that is
dissected very regularly.

■ LIFE LIST Where _____ NUMBER _____

NUTTALL BUTTERCUP
Ranunculus ranunculinus
(Cyrtorhyncha ranunculina)
Buttercup family   *Ranunculaceae*

PERENNIAL to 20″ high; STEMS ascending, slender, sparsely leafed with a terminal flower; LEAVES dissected into many leaf-like lobes to ½″ long; FLOWERS yellow with 5 petals and 5 slightly different sepals.

ECOLOGY: Foothills and montane in moisture and shade.

LOCATION: Horsetooth Trail, Lory S.P., Ft. Collins, CO 5/02 5500′

LOOK FOR a mass of delicately cut leaves and ascending stem with yellow flowers.

■ **LIFE LIST**   Where _____ NUMBER _____

BLISTER BUTTERCUP
Ranunculus sceleratus
Buttercup family   *Ranunculaceae*

ANNUAL or perennial to 10″ tall; STEMS branched, succulent, yellow-green and leafy; LEAVES succulent and irregularly lobed, and petioles, reddish to 3″ long; FLOWERS yellow buttercups to ½″ wide with a ¼″ domed center.

ECOLOGY: Foothills and montane along shores or near water.

LOCATION: Dowdy Lake Rec. Area, Red Feathers, CO 6/02 8000′

LOOK FOR a succulent, yellow-green plant with buttercup flowers.

■ **LIFE LIST**   Where _____ NUMBER _____

AGRIMONY
Agrimonia striata
Rose family   *Rosaceae*

ANNUAL to 5′ tall; STEMS upright, stiff, branched and leafy; LEAVES pinnate with alternating pairs of small and large leaflets, terminating in a trifoliate set of equal sized, serrated leaflets; FLOWERS yellow, 5-petaled to ¼″ wide, borne on racemes; FRUIT a hanging, corrugated bell to ⅜″ wide.

ECOLOGY: Foothills in canyons on moist ground.

LOCATION: Well Gulch, Lory S.P., Ft. Collins, CO 8/01 5500′

LOOK FOR pairs of alternating large and small leaflets.

■ **LIFE LIST**   Where _____ NUMBER _____

SILVERWEED

Argentina (Potentilla) anserina
Rose family   *Rosaceae*

PERENNIAL to 8″ high with creeping runners;
STEMS prostrate, leafy to 3′ long and rooting at
nodes; LEAVES pinnate with 5 or more pairs of
toothed leaflets; FLOWERS bright yellow and solitary
to ½″ wide.

ECOLOGY: Plains to montane near water.

LOCATION: Dowdy Lake Rec. Area, Red Feathers, CO
7/01 8000′

LOOK FOR a mat of creeping stems with rose-like
leaves and bright yellow flowers.

■ LIFE LIST   Where _____ NUMBER _____

YELLOW AVENS

Geum aleppicum
Rose family   *Rosaceae*

PERENNIAL to 2′ tall; STEMS upright and leafy;
LEAVES trifoliate with leaflets sharp toothed to 2″
long; FLOWERS yellow to ½″ across forming a soft
bur at maturity.

ECOLOGY: Foothills to montane in ravines.

LOCATION: Young Gulch, Poudre Canyon, CO 6/02
7000′

LOOK FOR 3 leafy inflorescences pointing in all
directions.

■ LIFE LIST   Where _____ NUMBER _____

BUR AVENS

Geum macrophyllum
Rose family   *Rosaceae*

PERENNIAL to 3′ tall; STEMS upright, slender, and
branching near top; LEAVES alternate, sessile,
trisected into narrow lanceolate lobes that are
coarsely toothed; FLOWERS with white or yellow
petals; FRUIT round, soft burs.

ECOLOGY: Foothills to subalpine in moist areas.

LOCATION: Horseshoe Trail, Golden Gate S.P.,
Golden, CO 7/00 8500′

LOOK FOR round fuzzy seed balls and yellow flowers
with domed centers.

■ LIFE LIST   Where _____ NUMBER _____

ROSS AVENS
Geum rossii
Rose family *Rosaceae*

PERENNIAL to 12″ tall; STEMS slender with few leaves and branching at the top; LEAVES to 5″ long, pinnately divided into many irregular and deeply cut leaflets; FLOWERS bright yellow and saucer-shaped.
ECOLOGY: Subalpine and alpine in bogs.
LOCATION: Silver Dollar Lake Trail, Guanella Pass, CO 8/99 11,000′
LOOK FOR fern-like foliage, slender stems, and a loose inflorescence of yellow flowers.

■ **LIFE LIST** Where _____ NUMBER _____

ALPINE AVENS
Geum (Acomostylis) rossii turbinatum
Rose family *Rosaceae*

PERENNIAL to 6″ tall in dense clumps; STEMS erect, reddish with 1–4 blooms; LEAVES numerous, basal, pinnately-divided into ½″ long, overlapping leaflets; FLOWERS yellow, to 1″ across with red sepals, and a cone shape.
ECOLOGY: Alpine on sunny slopes.
LOCATION: St. Alban's Chapel, Medicine Bow N.F., WY 8/99 10,500′
LOOK FOR a plant having leaves with up to 20 pairs of over-lapping, toothed leaflets.

■ **LIFE LIST** Where _____ NUMBER _____

SHRUBBY CINQUEFOIL
Pentaphylloides floribunda
(Potentilla fruticosa)
Rose family *Rosaceae*

SHRUB to 4′ tall; STEMS much branched; LEAVES palmate, with 5 lanceolate leaflets to ¾″ long; FLOWERS yellow to 1″ across.
ECOLOGY: Foothills to alpine.
LOCATION: Clear Creek, Berthoud Falls, CO 7/02 10,000′
LOOK FOR palmate leaves with 5 leaflets and an abundance of yellow flowers. A cultivated version is commonly used in McDonald's landscapes.

■ **LIFE LIST** Where _____ NUMBER _____

DIVERSE LEAVED CINQUEFOIL
Potentilla diversifolia
Rose family *Rosaceae*

PERENNIAL to 12″ tall; STEMS slender curved and
branching above; LEAVES mainly basal, palmate with
5 leaflets, toothed, to 1″ long; FLOWERS bright
yellow, saucer-shaped to 1″ wide, in open clusters.
ECOLOGY: Montane and subalpine meadows.
LOCATION: Butler Gulch, Henderson Mine Rd.,
Berthoud Pass, CO 7/00 11,000′
LOOK FOR palmate leaves with 5 leaflets and yellow
flowers with overlapping petals.

LIFE LIST Where _____ NUMBER _____

BLUELEAF CINQUEFOIL
Potentilla effusa
Rose family *Rosaceae*

PERENNIAL, tufted to 18″ tall; STEMS slender, erect,
pubescent, sparsely leafed and branched at the top;
LEAVES bluish-green above, silky-gray beneath and
divided into 5–7, toothed leaflets; FLOWERS to ½″
across, yellow, with 5 rounded, serrated petals.
ECOLOGY: Foothills to alpine.
LOCATION: Parvin Lake Rec. Area, Red Feathers, CO
6/02 8000′
LOOK FOR a cinquefoil with blue-green, pubescent
foliage.

LIFE LIST Where _____ NUMBER _____

LEAFY CINQUEFOIL
Potentilla (Drymocallis) fissa
Rose family *Rosaceae*

PERENNIAL to 18″ tall; STEMS reddish and leafy;
LEAVES pinnate with 7 or more broad, toothed
leaflets; FLOWERS creamy-yellow to ¾″ across.
ECOLOGY: Foothills to subalpine.
LOCATION: Cub Lake Trail, RMNP, CO 7/99 9000′
LOOK FOR a cinquefoil with an abundance of broad,
bright green leaflets and pale yellow flowers.

LIFE LIST Where _____ NUMBER _____

BUSHY CINQUEFOIL
Potentilla glandulosa
Rose family   *Rosaceae*

PERENNIAL to 10″ high with sprawling habit; STEMS slender, reddish and branched in all directions; LEAVES trifoliate, coarsely serrated with the longest leaflet 1½″ and a pair of clasping leaflets at the stem; FLOWERS yellow, to ½″ wide with spaced petals.

ECOLOGY: Plains and foothills.

LOCATION: Eltuck Bay, Lory S.P., Ft. Collins, CO 8/01 5500′

LOOK FOR a cinquefoil with leaves, buds, flowers and fruit all crowded into terminal clusters.

 ■ **LIFE LIST** Where _____ NUMBER _____

GRACEFUL CINQUEFOIL
Potentilla gracilis
Rose family   *Rosaceae*

PERENNIAL to 20″ tall; STEMS erect and slender; LEAVES alternate and palmate with 7 toothed leaflets to 2½″ long; FLOWERS saucer-shaped with 5 pale-yellow petals and a bright yellow center, borne in clusters with many buds but few open flowers.

ECOLOGY: Foothills to subalpine.

LOCATION: Pingree Park Rd. (63E), Larimer Cty., CO 6/04 7500′

LOOK FOR a cinquefoil with pale-yellow petals and bright yellow centers.

■ **LIFE LIST** Where _____ NUMBER _____

WOOLLY CINQUEFOIL
Potentillla hippiana
Rose family   *Rosaceae*

PERENNIAL sprawling plant to 10″ tall in clumps; STEMS slender, woolly and branching at top; LEAVES pinnate with up to 13 leaflets, coarsely toothed, pubescent above and white-wooly beneath; FLOWERS yellow, ½″ wide with exserted stamens.

ECOLOGY: Foothills to subalpine.

LOCATION: Wild Basin, RMNP, CO 7/99 9000′

LOOK FOR flowers with separated petals, extending in an almost flat plane.

■ **LIFE LIST** Where _____ NUMBER _____

REDSTEM CINQUEFOIL
Potentilla rubricaulis
Rose family   *Rosaceae*

PERENNIAL to 8″ tall; STEMS red and slender, with
few leaves and some branching; LEAVES palmate,
dark green with 5 coarse-toothed leaflets and another
pair on the petiole; stem leaves are sessile; FLOWERS
are bright yellow and saucer-shaped.
ECOLOGY: Subalpine and alpine.
LOCATION: Mt. Evans, CO 6/05 11,000′
LOOK FOR red stems and dark green palmate leaves.

■ LIFE LIST   Where _____ NUMBER _____

ONE FLOWERED CINQUEFOIL
Potentilla uniflora
Rose family   *Rosaceae*

PERENNIAL to 3″ tall; STEMS reclining, reddish,
and leafy, bearing a flower; LEAVES pinnate with 5
sharply-toothed leaflets to ½″ long; FLOWERS yellow
to ⅝″ wide with 5 overlapping petals.
ECOLOGY: Subalpine and alpine on rocky, open
slopes.
LOCATION: Brainard Lake Rec. Area, Ward, CO 6/02
10,500′
LOOK FOR yellow flowers on a tiny plant with
pinnate leaves.

■ LIFE LIST   Where _____ NUMBER _____

CLOVERLEAF ROSE
Sibbaldia procumbens
Rose family   *Rosaceae*

PERENNIAL to 4″ tall in small patches; STEMS
ascending and leafy; LEAVES trifoliate with leaflets to
1″ long and 3-lobed at the tip; FLOWERS in clusters
of 3–4 with 5 yellow petals to ⅛″ and 5 sepals to ¼″.
ECOLOGY: Subalpine and alpine.
LOCATION: Berthoud Pass, CO 7/01 11,500′
LOOK FOR a small tuft of clover with lobed leaflet
tips and non-leguminous flowers.

■ LIFE LIST   Where _____ NUMBER _____

COMMON ALUMROOT
Heuchera parvifolia
Saxifrage family   *Saxifragaceae*

PERENNIAL to 15″ high; SCAPES bearing sparsely flowered racemes; LEAVES kidney shaped to 1½″ wide with 7–9 shallow lobes; FLOWERS tiny, yellow and bell-shaped.

ECOLOGY: Plains to subalpine in rocky soils.

LOCATION: Timber Trail, Lory S.P., Ft. Collins, CO 5/01 5500′

LOOK FOR a rosette of blunt-toothed kidney shaped leaves and 1–3 stalks bearing loose racemes of yellow, bell-shaped flowers.

■ **LIFE LIST** Where _____ NUMBER _____

YELLOW MARSH SAXIFRAGE
Saxifraga hirculus
Saxifrage family   *Saxifragaceae*

PERENNIAL to 4″ tall; STEMS succulent, reddish, with tiny linear leaves; LEAVES mostly basal, lanceolate to ¾″ long; FLOWERS yellow, 5 petaled and bowl-shaped to ¾″ wide.

ECOLOGY: Alpine in wet areas.

LOCATION: Mt. Evans, CO 8/96 13,000′

LOOK FOR tiny little buttercups at alpine and check leaf type.

■ **LIFE LIST** Where _____ NUMBER _____

WESTERN YELLOW PAINTBRUSH
Castilleja occidentalis
Figwort family   *Scrophulariaceae*

PERENNIAL to 8″ high; STEMS leafy and unbranched; terminal LEAVES (bracts) yellow, ovate, to 1″ long, stem leaves, alternate, narrow, to 1½″ long; FLOWERS are enfolded in yellow bracts.

ECOLOGY: Subalpine and alpine in open areas.

LOCATION: Mt. Evans, CO 8/96 13,000′

LOOK FOR overlapping yellow bracts and stemless leaves.

■ **LIFE LIST** Where _____ NUMBER _____

YELLOW PAINTBRUSH

Castilleja sulphurea
Figwort family   *Scrophulariaceae*

PERENNIAL to 16″ tall; STEMS erect and
  unbranched; lower stem LEAVES sessile, ascending,
  alternate and narrow-lanceolate, to 3″ long; upper
  leaves (bracts) yellow, cleft and overlapping;
  FLOWERS hidden in terminal bracts.
ECOLOGY: Montane and subalpine.
LOCATION: Hassell Lake Trail, Urad Rd., Berthoud
  Pass, CO 7/01 11,000′
LOOK FOR a loose terminal head of yellow, oval
  bracts and lanceolate stem leaves.

■ LIFE LIST Where _____ NUMBER ____

DALMATION TOADFLAX

Linaria dalmatica
Figwort family   *Scrophulariaceae*

PERENNIAL to 4′ tall; STEMS erect, leafy and
  branching at the top; LEAVES opposite, stiff, clasping
  and broad-lanceolate to 1½″ long; FLOWERS yellow
  to 2″ long including the spur.
ECOLOGY: Plains and foothills in disturbed areas.
LOCATION: Eagle Wind Trail, Rabbit Mt., Lyons, CO
  5/00 6000′
LOOK FOR yellow flowers with a long spur and
  orange flower buds.

■ LIFE LIST Where _____ NUMBER ____

BUTTER AND EGGS

Linaria vulgaris
Figwort family   *Scrophulariaceae*

PERENNIAL to 3′ tall; STEMS erect, leafy, slender
  and unbranched; LEAVES linear, alternate, ascending
  to 4″ long; FLOWERS light and dark yellow, 2-lipped
  and spurred, to 1″ long, in dense racemes.
ECOLOGY: Plains to montane in disturbed areas.
LOCATION: Copper Mt. Trail, Copper Mt., CO 8/91
  10,000′
LOOK FOR yellow, spurred flowers and linear leaves
  on a stiff, unbranched stem.

■ LIFE LIST Where _____ NUMBER ____

YELLOW MONKEY FLOWER
Mimulus guttatus
Figwort family *Scrophulariaceae*

ANNUAL or perennial to 2´ tall; STEMS square, erect or reclining; LEAVES opposite, ovate, toothed and clasping, to 3˝ long; FLOWERS yellow, tubular, with 2 upper lobes and 3 lower ones.

ECOLOGY: Foothills to subalpine in moist areas.

LOCATION: Hassell Lake, Urad Rd., Berthoud Pass, CO 8/99 11,000´

LOOK FOR opposite, clasping leaves and a yellow, 5-lobed, tubular flower.

■ **LIFE LIST** Where _____ NUMBER _____

YELLOW OWLCLOVER
Orthocarpus luteus
Figwort family *Scrophulariaceae*

ANNUAL to 20˝ tall; STEMS reddish, erect, sticky, leafy with ascending branches; LEAVES narrow, alternate and sessile to 1˝ long; FLOWERS yellow and tubular to ½˝ long.

ECOLOGY: Montane in exposed areas.

LOCATION: Mill Creek Trail, RMNP, CO 8/05 9000´

LOOK FOR a leafy raceme with yellow tubular flowers and linear leaves.

■ **LIFE LIST** Where _____ NUMBER _____

FERNLEAF LOUSEWORT
Pedicularis bracteosa
Figwort family *Scrophulariaceae*

PERENNIAL to 2´ tall; STEMS erect, stiff, leafy and unbranched; LEAVES pinnately compound with toothed lanceolate leaflets to 2˝ long; FLOWERS pale yellow, beaked, to ¾˝ long, in spikes to 5˝ long.

ECOLOGY: Montane to alpine in moist areas.

LOCATION: Mitchell Lake Trail, Brainard Lake Rec. Area, Ward, CO 7/00 11,000´

LOOK FOR pale yellow, ascending, beaked flowers in a terminal spike.

■ **LIFE LIST** Where _____ NUMBER _____

COMMON MULLEIN
Verbascum thapsus
Figwort family   *Scrophulariaceae*

BIENNNIAL to 6´ tall; STEMS stout, woolly, leafy and
unbranched; LEAVES to 16″ long, soft, woolly and
gray-green; FLOWERS yellow, sessile, to 1″ across
and clustered in dense spikes.

ECOLOGY: Plains to montane in disturbed areas and
over-grazed pastures.

LOCATION: Lower Elk Trail, Golden Gate S.P.,
Golden, CO 7/99 8500´

LOOK FOR a raceme tightly packed with yellow
flowers on a large woolly plant.

■ LIFE LIST   Where _____ NUMBER _____

GROUND CHERRY
Physalis virginiana
Potato family   *Solanaceae*

PERENNIAL to 2´ tall with a bushy habit; STEMS
branching, grooved and leafy; LEAVES in-folded,
lanceolate to 2″ long plus a ¾″ petiole; FLOWERS
saucer-shaped, pale yellow with a purple center to 1″
wide; fruit to 1″ deep resembling a hanging lantern.

ECOLOGY: Plains along stream banks.

LOCATION: Spring Creek Trail, Ft. Collins, CO 8/02
5000´

LOOK FOR pale yellow and purple flowers and
lantern-like fruit.

■ LIFE LIST   Where _____ NUMBER _____

BUFFALO BUR
Solanum rostratum
Potato family   *Solanaceae*

ANNUAL to 12″ high; STEMS spiny and leafy;
LEAVES pinnatifid to 5″ long with a spiny midrib
and rounded lobes; FLOWERS yellow to 1″ wide with
5 petals.

ECOLOGY: Plains and foothills.

LOCATION: Coyote Ridge Rec. Area, Ft. Collins, CO
7/01 5500´

LOOK FOR a low growing potato plant with yellow
flowers, spiny leaves and burs.

■ LIFE LIST   Where _____ NUMBER _____

WESTERN VALERIAN
Valeriana edulis
Valerian family   *Valerianaceae*

PERENNIAL to 30″ tall; STEMS erect, nearly leafless and top branched; basal LEAVES thick, narrow and in-rolled to 6″ long; stem leaves opposite with paired linear lobes; FLOWERS pale yellow to ¼″ wide in small clusters on a loose panicle.

ECOLOGY: Foothills to alpine in wet areas.

LOCATION: Roadside, Medicine Bow N.F., WY 7/00 10,500′

LOOK FOR wiry stems and a sparse inflorescence.

■ **LIFE LIST**   Where _____ NUMBER _____

YELLOW VIOLET
Viola nuttallii
Violet family   *Violaceae*

PERENNIAL to 6″ tall; SCAPES fleshy, erect with a solitary nodding flower; LEAVES basal and lanceolate to 3″ long; FLOWERS yellow to ½″ wide with brown streaks on the petals.

ECOLOGY: Plains to subalpine.

LOCATION: Shadow Canyon, Eldorado Canyon S.P., Eldorado Springs, CO 6/02 6500′

LOOK FOR a tiny yellow violet with brown streaks on the petals.

■ **LIFE LIST**   Where _____ NUMBER _____

PUNCTURE VINE
Tribulus terrestris
Caltop family   *Zygophyllaceae*

ANNUAL prostrate weed forming mats; STEMS reddish, hairy, leafy and branched; LEAVES pinnate with 4 or more pairs of leaflets to ½″ long; FLOWERS yellow to ½″ wide; FRUIT segmented into 5 parts, each armed with a pair of sturdy thorns.

ECOLOGY: Plains, often with crops.

LOCATION: Vacant area, Wheat Ridge, CO 7/02 5000′

LOOK FOR a green mat bearing thorns known to puncture bicycle tires.

■ **LIFE LIST**   Where _____ NUMBER _____

ROCKY MOUNTAIN FLORA

Red
Flowers

SMOOTH SUMAC
Rhus glabra
Sumac family *Anacardiaaceae*

SHRUB to 8´ tall in thickets; TWIGS smooth and blue-gray; LEAVES to 12˝ long with up to 13 leaflets to 2˝ long; FLOWER sexes on separate shrubs, male flowers in an 8˝ loose panicle, female flowers in a tighter, 6˝ panicle; BERRIES red-orange to ⅛˝

ECOLOGY: Plains and foothills.

LOCATION: Spring Creek Trail, Ft. Collins, CO 9/02 5000´

LOOK FOR bluish petioles.

☐ **LIFE LIST** Where _____ NUMBER ____

SPREADING DOGBANE
Apocynum androsaemifolium
Dogbane family *Apocynaceae*

PERENNIAL to 2´ tall; STEMS reddish, slender and willowy; LEAVES opposite, broad-lanceolate and thin to 2˝ long; FLOWERS pink, bell-shaped to ⅜˝ wide with recurved lobes, in clusters of 3–12 blooms.

ECOLOGY: Foothills and montane.

LOCATION: Gem Lake Trail, RMNP, CO 6/00 8500´

LOOK FOR a patch of red-stemmed plants with opposite leaves and pink and white flowers.

☐ **LIFE LIST** Where _____ NUMBER ____

SHOWY MILKWEED
Asclepias speciosa
Milkweed family *Asclepiadaceae*

PERENNIAL to 5´ tall; STEMS erect stout and leafy; LEAVES opposite, to 12˝ long with milky sap; FLOWERS purple-rose in spherical clusters of up to 30 blooms; PODS spiny and fat to 4˝ long.

ECOLOGY: Plains and foothills near water.

LOCATION: Pavilion Gardens, Westminster, CO 6/99 5000´

LOOK FOR a pink cluster of star-shaped flowers, shiny leaves and milky sap.

☐ **LIFE LIST** Where _____ NUMBER ____

ORANGE AGOSERIS

Agoseris aurantiaca
Aster family   *Asteraceae (Compositae)*

PERENNIAL to 12″ with milky sap; SCAPES erect,
curved and unbranched; LEAVES basal, variable,
spatulate to grass-like, with or without lobes, to 8″
long; FLOWER heads orange, ray flowers only, to 1″
across with phyllaries tiered, some of which may be
purple.

ECOLOGY: Foothills to alpine in the open.

LOCATION: Crown Pt. Rd. (FR139), Larimer Cty., CO
6/04 9000′

LOOK FOR an orange dandelion.

■ **LIFE LIST**   Where _____ NUMBER _____

PINK PUSSYTOES

Antennaria rosea
Aster family   *Asteraceae (Compositae)*

PERENNIAL to 10″, forming mats; STEMS erect,
white and woolly; rosette LEAVES spatulate to 1″
long, stem leaves linear to ½″ long; FLOWERS
composed of white bracts with pink tips and crowded
into tiny terminal clusters.

ECOLOGY: Foothills to alpine.

LOCATION: 4th of July Trail, Eldora, CO 7/00
11,500′

LOOK FOR a tiny woolly plant with several pink
flower heads resembling a kitten's toes.

■ **LIFE LIST**   Where _____ NUMBER _____

BRISTLE THISTLE

Carduus nutans
Aster family   *Asteraceae (Compositae)*

BIENNIAL or perennial to 6′ tall; STEMS erect, spiny
and leafy; LEAVES alternate, pinnatifid, shiny and
spiny to 16″ long; FLOWER heads purple-rose, disc
flowers only, solitary, nodding, on long stalks with
spine tipped bracts.

ECOLOGY: Plains to montane in open sites.

LOCATION: Dowdy Lake Rec. Area, Red Feathers, CO
7/01 8000′

LOOK FOR a dense, pink furry flower head,
subtended by several rows of spiny bracts.

■ **LIFE LIST**   Where _____ NUMBER _____

WAVYLEAF THISTLE
Cirsium undulatum
Aster family   *Asteraceae (Compositae)*

BIENNIAL or perennial to 2´ tall; STEMS erect, pale green and branching; LEAVES to 10˝ long, and reduced upward, toothed and hairy with spines to ½˝ long; FLOWER heads pink, purple or creamy with an urn-shaped, spiny involucre.
ECOLOGY: Plains and foothills.
LOCATION: Eltuck Bay, Lory S.P., Ft. Collins, CO 6/02 5500´
LOOK FOR incised leaves with spiny, up-turned lobes.

■ **LIFE LIST** Where _____ NUMBER _____

BULL THISTLE
Cirsium vulgare
Aster family   *Asteraceae (Compositae)*

BIENNIAL to 6´ tall; STEMS stout, spiny, leafy and branched; LEAVES pinnatifid with pointed, spine-tipped lobes; FLOWER heads to 2½˝ across, ray flowers absent, disc flowers rose-purple and involucre bracts spiny.
ECOLOGY: Plains and foothills.
LOCATION: Boulder Creek Trail, Boulder, CO 6/92 5500´
LOOK FOR a pink, fluffy flower head on an urn-shaped flower base.

■ **LIFE LIST** Where _____ NUMBER _____

SHOWY DAISY
Erigeron speciosus
Aster family   *Asteraceae (Compositae)*

PERENNIAL to 2½´ tall; STEMS several, leafy with woody crown; lower LEAVES spatulate; upper leaves lanceolate and sessile; FLOWER heads to 1½˝ across with pink rays
ECOLOGY: Foothills to subalpine.
LOCATION: Medicine Bow N.F., WY 7/00 10,500´
LOOK FOR saucer-shaped, terminal flower heads and great beauty.

■ **LIFE LIST** Where _____ NUMBER _____

HOUNDS TONGUE

Cynoglossum officinale
Borage family   *Boraginaceae*

BIENNIAL or perennial to 3´ tall; STEMS fleshy, erect
and leafy; LEAVES lanceolate, alternate, hairy, to 12˝
long with winged petioles at the base and sessile
above; FLOWERS rose colored, bowl-shaped, to ⅜˝
wide with 5 overlapping, oval petals.
ECOLOGY: Plains and foothills.
LOCATION: Arthur's Rock Trail, Lory S.P., Ft. Collins,
CO 6/99 5500´
LOOK FOR rose colored flowers interspersed with
leaves, on dense racemes.

LIFE LIST   Where _____ NUMBER _____

DAME'S ROCKET

Hesperis matronalis
Mustard family   *Brassicaceae (Cruciferae)*

BIENNIAL or perennial to 4´ tall; STEMS leafy, erect,
branching and succulent; LEAVES sessile, lanceolate
to 4˝ long; FLOWERS pink to purple, 4-petaled to ¾˝
across; PODS cylindrical, slender and ascending.
ECOLOGY: Plains and foothills near water.
LOCATION: St. Vrain Canyon, Lyons, CO 6/02 6500´
LOOK FOR tall, slender plants with racemes of red
flowers.

LIFE LIST   Where _____ NUMBER _____

HUNGER CACTUS

Opuntia polyacantha
Cactus family   *Cactaceae*

PERENNIAL to 4˝ high; PADS oval, fleshy to 6˝,
patterned with spiny warts at ½˝ intervals;
FLOWERS to 3˝ across, pink to red with several
whorls of showy petals; FRUIT fleshy and edible.
ECOLOGY: Plains and foothills under dessert-like
conditions.
LOCATION: Pavilion Nature Garden, Westminster, CO
6/99 5000´
LOOK FOR a disc-shaped cactus plant with large, red
flowers.

LIFE LIST   Where _____ NUMBER _____

TWINFLOWER
Linnaea borealis
Honeysuckle family *Caprifoliaceae*

PERENNIAL to 6″ high forming mats; STEMS producing erect branches that appear as separate plants; LEAVES evergreen, opposite, shiny, rounded to ¾″ wide; FLOWERS paired, pink, nodding and bell-shaped on 4″ stalks.

ECOLOGY: Montane to subalpine. Named for renowned botanist, Carolus Linnaeus.

LOCATION: Ouzel Falls Trail, Wild Basin, RMNP, CO 7/99 9000′

LOOK FOR little flowers hanging like twin lanterns on a lamp pole.

■ **LIFE LIST** Where _____ NUMBER _____

MORROW'S HONEYSUCKLE
Lonicera morrowii
Honeysuckle family *Caprifoliaceae*

SHRUB, woody, to 10′ tall; STEMS smooth with light brown bark, turning darker with age; LEAVES paired and dark green, to 2″ long; FLOWERS white, yellow or red, in pairs, arising from leaf axils.

ECOLOGY: Plains and foothills

LOCATION: Dixon Reservoir, Ft. Collins, CO 5/03 5000′

LOOK FOR a shrub with pink flowers.

■ **LIFE LIST** Where _____ NUMBER _____

COMMON SNOWBERRY
Symphoricarpos albus
Honeysuckle family *Caprifoliaceae*

SHRUB to 2′ tall; STEMS woody, slender, gray and weeping; LEAVES opposite, oval, to 1½″ long, thin and dark green; FLOWERS pinkish, paired, saucer-shaped to ¼″ across; FRUIT white, paired berries to ½″.

ECOLOGY: Foothills and montane in shade.

LOCATION: Well Gulch, Lory S.P., Ft. Collins, CO 8/01 5500′

LOOK FOR slender stems, opposite leaves and paired, pink flowers or white berries.

■ **LIFE LIST** Where _____ NUMBER _____

WESTERN SNOWBERRY
Symphoricarpos occidentalis
Honeysuckle family   *Caprifolicaeae*

SHRUB to 5´ tall; TWIGS reddish, slender and
willowy; LEAVES thick, leathery, oval and dull gray-
green to 1½˝ long; FLOWERS pinkish, to ½˝ wide, in
axillary clusters; BERRIES white, to ½˝ in clusters or
8 or more.

ECOLOGY: Plains to montane – often used in
landscaping.

LOCATION: Shore Trail, Lory S.P., Ft. Collins, CO
7/04 5500´

LOOK FOR clusters of pink flowers or white berries.

■ **LIFE LIST**   Where _____ NUMBER _____

MAIDEN PINK
Dianthus deltoides
Pink family   *Caryophyllaceae*

PERENNIAL to 18˝ tall; STEMS slender and
branched; LEAVES linear, opposite with hairy
margins, to ¾˝ long; FLOWERS to ½˝ across, tubular
with 5 radiating pink or white lobes that may be
fringed; calyx to ¾˝ long.

ECOLOGY: Plains to montane.

LOCATION: Shore Trail, Lory S.P., Ft. Collins, CO
7/04 5500´

LOOK FOR a slender stem, linear leaves and clusters
of upright flowers in all stages of development.

■ **LIFE LIST**   Where _____ NUMBER _____

MOSS CAMPION
Silene acaulis
Pink family   *Caryophyllaceae*

PERENNIAL to 2˝ high forming mats; LEAVES linear
to 1½˝ long, bright green and grass-like; FLOWERS
single, tubular, pink and white, to ⅜˝ long with 5,
notched lobes.

ECOLOGY: Alpine, on exposed slopes.

LOCATION: Mitchell Lake Trail, Brainard Lake Rec.
Area, Ward CO 7/00 11,000´

LOOK FOR 5-lobed pink flowers springing up from
what appears to be a patch of bright green turf.

■ **LIFE LIST**   Where _____ NUMBER _____

MEDIA SPURRY
Spergularia maritima (media)
Pink family   *Caryophyllaceae*

ANNUAL or perennial, prostrate, to 3″ high; STEMS creeping, hairy and branching to 12″ long; LEAVES opposite, linear to 1″ long; FLOWERS pink, to ½″ across with elliptical petals.

ECOLOGY: Plains and foothills near water.

LOCATION: Boyd Lake S.P., Loveland, CO 7/02 5000′

LOOK FOR a prostrate plant, often in drying mud, with linear leaves and pink flowers.

☐ LIFE LIST Where _____ NUMBER _____

RED SPURRY
Spergularia rubra
Pink family   *Caryophyllaceae*

ANNUAL or perennial to 3″ high forming mats; STEMS branching and leafy to 6″ long; LEAVES linear in whorls at nodes, to ½″ long; FLOWERS pink, 5-petaled to ¼″ wide.

ECOLOGY: Montane to alpine in open sites.

LOCATION: Berthoud Pass, CO 7/02 11,500′

LOOK FOR a circular matted plant to 12″ across with tiny pink flowers.

☐ LIFE LIST Where _____ NUMBER _____

STRAWBERRY BLITE
Chenopodium capitatum
Goosefoot family   *Chenopodiaceae*

ANNUAL to 12″ tall; STEMS upright or ascending, unbranched and leafy; LEAVES delta-shaped with coarse teeth and blade to 1½″ with a ¾″ petiole; FLOWERS forming red balls on spikes.

ECOLOGY: Montane to subalpine on open, moist slopes.

LOCATION: Devil′s Gulch Rd., Estes Park, CO 7/04 7500′

LOOK FOR bright red, raspberry-like balls.

☐ LIFE LIST Where _____ NUMBER _____

GOOSEFOOT
Chenopodium simplex
Goosefoot family *Chenopodiaceae*

ANNUAL to 4´ tall; STEMS slender and leafy with
several long, slender branches; LEAVES delta-shaped
to 2″ long with 5 to 7 sharp lobes; FLOWERS tiny,
pink, in spikes to ½″ long.
ECOLOGY: Plains, near water.
LOCATION: Young Gulch, Poudre River Canyon, CO
9/04 7000´
LOOK FOR tiny pink flower clusters on a slender
plant with deltoid leaves.

■ **LIFE LIST** Where _____ NUMBER _____

KING'S CROWN
Sedum (Rhodiola) integrifolium
Stonecrop family *Crassulaceae*

PERENNIAL to 12″ tall; STEMS fleshy, erect and
leafy with a terminal umbel; LEAVES fleshy, sessile,
spoon-shaped to 1″ long; FLOWERS to ¼″ wide with
4 dark red or purple petals in terminal umbels.
ECOLOGY: Subalpine and alpine in moisture.
LOCATION: Mt. Evans, CO 8/96 13,000´
LOOK FOR a short, succulent plant with a dark red
terminal umbel.

■ **LIFE LIST** Where _____ NUMBER _____

QUEEN'S (ROSE) CROWN
Sedum (Clementsia) rhodanthum
Stonecrop family *Crassulaceae*

PERENNIAL to 12″ tall; STEMS succulent, fleshy,
leafy and topped with a globose inflorescence;
LEAVES stem, linear, alternate, fleshy and sessile to 1″
long; FLOWERS pink, ½″ long, 5-petaled in terminal
clusters.
ECOLOGY: Subalpine and alpine in moisture.
LOCATION: Copper Mt. bike trail, CO 8/91 10,000´
LOOK FOR red, thickly leafed stems and rose colored
umbels.

■ **LIFE LIST** Where _____ NUMBER _____

KINNIKINNIK (BEARBERRY)
Arctostaphylos uva-ursi
Heath family   *Ericaceae*

EVERGREEN shrub to 6″ high, prostrate and creeping; STEMS prostrate producing upright branches bearing leaves and flowers; LEAVES glossy, alternate, spatulate to 1″ long with short petioles; FLOWERS white or pink; berries red to ¼″.

ECOLOGY: Foothills to subalpine.

LOCATION: Cherokee Park, CO 8/02 8000′

LOOK FOR red berries on an evergreen plant in association with pine trees.

■ **LIFE LIST**   Where _____ NUMBER _____

MOUNTAIN LAUREL
Kalmia microphylla
Heath family   *Ericaceae*

EVERGREEN shrub to 6″ tall; STEMS creeping and producing red, upright flower stalks; LEAVES opposite, sessile, lanceolate, leathery to 1″; FLOWERS pink, 5-lobed, bowl-shaped, nodding, to ½″ across, in loose clusters.

ECOLOGY: Subalpine and alpine in moisture.

LOCATION: Mitchell Lake Trail, Brainard Lake Rec. Area, Ward, CO 7/00 11,000′

LOOK FOR pink flowers with out-rolled petals and exserted styles and stamens.

■ **LIFE LIST**   Where _____ NUMBER _____

FIELD MILKVETCH
Astragalus agrestis (dasyglottis)
Pea family   *Fabaceae (Leguminosae)*

PERENNIAL to 12″ tall, in clumps; STEMS erect, slender, 1–3 nodes, leafed and branched; LEAVES alternate, pinnate with up to 21 elliptical leaflets to ¾″ long; FLOWERS pink to ¾″ in compact racemes; calyx with black hairs.

ECOLOGY: Plains to montane in moisture.

LOCATION: S. Platte River Pathway, Denver, CO 5/92 5000′

LOOK FOR pink leguminous flowers in dense racemes on 6″ axillary, leafless stalks.

■ **LIFE LIST**   Where _____ NUMBER _____

LIMBER VETCH
Astragalus flexuosus
Pea family   *Fabaceae (Leguminosae)*

PERENNIAL vine to 20″ long; STEMS sprawling,
wiry and hairy; LEAVES pinnate with hairy, in-folded
leaflets to ½″ long; FLOWERS pink to ½″ long;
PODS to 1″ long.

ECOLOGY: Foothills and montane.

LOCATION: Marshall Mesa, Boulder, CO 6/99 6000′

LOOK FOR a sprawling plant with loose racemes of
pink, leguminous flowers.

◻ **LIFE LIST**   Where _____ NUMBER _____

CROWN VETCH
Coronilla varia
Pea family   *Fabaceae (Leguminosae)*

PERENNIAL vine to 2′ tall; STEMS to 4′ long,
trailing, angular and branching; LEAVES pinnate
with up to 25 oblong leaflets to ½″ long; FLOWERS
pink and white to ½″ long in globose clusters; PODS
erect, beaked and constricted into 1-seeded sections.

ECOLOGY: Plains – often planted to stabilize a bank.

LOCATION: Edora Park, Ft. Collins, CO 9/02 5000′

LOOK FOR globose clusters of pink flowers.

◻ **LIFE LIST**   Where _____ NUMBER _____

PRAIRIE CLOVER
Dalea purpurea
Pea family   *Fabaceae (Leguminosae)*

PERENNIAL to 18″ tall in clumps; STEMS erect,
leafy and unbranched; LEAVES pinnately divided
into 5, 1″ linear leaflets; FLOWERS pink, borne on a
cylindrical head to 1½″ long and ⅝″ wide.

ECOLOGY: Foothills on dry hillsides.

LOCATION: Coyote Ridge Rec. Area, Ft. Collins, CO
6/03 5500′

LOOK FOR straight, yellowish stems; linear leaflets
and pink flowers with exserted styles and stamens.

◻ **LIFE LIST**   Where _____ NUMBER _____

PERENNIAL SWEET PEA
Lathyrus latifolius
Pea family *Fabaceae (Leguminosae)*

PERENNIAL vine to 8´ long; STEMS winged and trailing; LEAVES alternate to 4˝ long with winged petioles and 2 lanceolate leaflets plus a forked tendril; FLOWERS rose or white to 1˝ across in loose, globose clusters.

ECOLOGY: Plains and foothills – an escapee from cultivation.

LOCATION: Chautauqua Park, Boulder, CO 6/99 6000´

LOOK FOR a vine with winged stems and forked tendrils.

■ **LIFE LIST** Where _____ NUMBER _____

COLORADO LOCO
Oxytropis lambertii
Pea family *Fabaceae (Leguminosae)*

PERENNIAL to 16˝ tall, in clumps; SCAPES to 10˝ including a raceme to 4˝; LEAVES basal, oddly pinnate with up to 15 leaflets per leaf; leaflets narrow-lanceolate, pubescent, to ½˝ long; FLOWERS pink to purple with a white striped patch on the banner.

ECOLOGY: Plains and foothills.

LOCATION: Homestead Trail, Hall Ranch, Lyons, CO 5/01 6000´

LOOK FOR a white striped patch on a pink leguminous flower.

■ **LIFE LIST** Where _____ NUMBER _____

FEW FLOWERED LOCO
Oxytropis multiceps
Pea family *Fabaceae (Leguminosae)*

PERENNIAL to 1˝ tall; SCAPES pubescent and bearing twin flowers; LEAVES basal, oddly pinnate, with hairy, in-folded leaflets to ¼˝ long; FLOWERS hairy, red to purple, to ½˝ long.

ECOLOGY: Montane to alpine in open areas.

LOCATION: Brainard Lake Rec. Area, Ward, CO 6/02 10,500´

LOOK FOR a tiny, hairy plant with pinnate leaves and pink, leguminous flowers.

■ **LIFE LIST** Where _____ NUMBER _____

SHOWY LOCOWEED
Oxytropis splendens
Pea family   *Fabaceae (Leguminosae)*

PERENNIAL to 16″ tall; SCAPES pubescent,
ascending with a fleecy raceme to 6″ long; LEAVES
pinnate to 6″ long, crowded with leaflets to ½″ long;
FLOWERS pink to purple, packed in a raceme with
woolly fleece.
ECOLOGY: Montane and subalpine.
LOCATION: I-80 at Exit 323, WY   7/05 8500′
LOOK FOR pink leguminous flowers on a raceme
packed with fleece.

■ LIFE LIST   Where _____ NUMBER ____

STRAWBERRY CLOVER
Trifolium fragiferum
Pea family   *Fabaceae (Leguminosae)*

PERENNIAL to 4″ high and creeping; STEMS
prostrate producing leaves and scapes; LEAVES
trifoliate with leaflets to ⅝″ long; FLOWERS pink, in
½″ globose clusters supported by 6″ scapes; SEED
heads globose, to ⅝″, composed of papery, inflated
calyxes.
ECOLOGY: Plains and foothills.
LOCATION: Rolland Moore Park, Ft. Collins, CO 8/02
5000′
LOOK FOR a round inflated seed ball.

■ LIFE LIST   Where _____ NUMBER ____

ASLIKE CLOVER
Trifolium hybridum
Pea family   *Fabaceae (Leguminosae)*

ANNUAL or perennial vine to 2′ long; STEMS leafy,
willowy and non-rooting at nodes; LEAVES trifoliate
with ovate leaflets, finely toothed to 1″ long;
FLOWERS in globose, terminal clusters to ¾″;
corollas white at top of cluster and pink at the
bottom.
ECOLOGY: Plains to montane – an escapee from
cultivation.
LOCATION: Gem Lake Trail, RMNP, CO 7/99 8500′
LOOK FOR a clover head with white and pink
flowers.

■ LIFE LIST   Where _____ NUMBER ____

DWARF CLOVER
Trifolium nanum
Pea family   *Fabaceae (Leguminosae)*

PERENNIAL to 2″ high forming mats; STEMS inconspicuous; LEAVES trifoliate with ½″ petioles and in-folded, lanceolate leaflets to ½″ long; FLOWERS pink, to ⅜″ long and never fully opening.

ECOLOGY: Subalpine and alpine on scree in open sites.

LOCATION: Loveland Pass, CO 7/95 12,000′

LOOK FOR tiny, pink upright flowers and tiny trifoliate leaves, growing in gravel.

■ LIFE LIST   Where _____ NUMBER _____

PARRY CLOVER
Trifolium parryi
Pea family   *Fabaceae (Leguminosae)*

PERENNIAL to 6″ tall forming tufts; SCAPES to 4″ tall bearing a single flower head; LEAVES basal, trifoliate with elliptical, in-folded leaflets to 1″ long; FLOWERS pink and crowded in terminal, globose clusters.

ECOLOGY: Subalpine and alpine in moisture.

LOCATION: Mitchell Lake Trail, Brainerd Lake Rec. Area, Ward, CO 7/00 10,500′

LOOK FOR a pink flower head with 8–12 leguminous flowers on a short scape.

■ LIFE LIST   Where _____ NUMBER _____

RED CLOVER
Trifolium pratense
Pea family   *Fabaceae (Leguminosae)*

BIENNIAL or perennial to 2½′ tall, in clumps; STEMS hairy and leafy with terminal flower clusters; LEAVES trifoliate with ovate leaflets to 1″ long, often hairy, with white "V" patches; FLOWERS pink, in globose heads to 1″ wide, collared with leaf-like bracts.

ECOLOGY: Plains to subalpine in moisture.

LOCATION: Copper Mt. bike trail, CO 8/91 10,000′

LOOK FOR white "V" patches on the leaves.

■ LIFE LIST   Where _____ NUMBER _____

STORKBILL (FILAREE)

Erodium cicutarium
Geranium family   *Geraniaceae*

ANNUAL or biennial to 8″ high; SCAPES hairy,
reddish and supporting 1–4 blooms; LEAVES rosetted,
pinnate to 3″ long with pinnatifid leaflets to ½″ long;
FLOWERS pink to white, 5-petaled, to ½″ across;
PODS with elongated styles resembling stork bills.

ECOLOGY: Plains and foothills on open sites.

LOCATION: Boyd Lake S.P., Loveland, CO 5/02
5000′

LOOK FOR pink flowers, stork bills and a rosette of
carrot-like foliage.

■ **LIFE LIST** Where _____ NUMBER _____

PINEYWOODS GERANIUM

Geranium caespitosum
Geranium family   *Geraniaceae*

PERENNIAL to 12″, in bushy clumps; STEMS
sprawling, hairy and leafy; LEAVES palmately
dissected into 5-toothed lobes; FLOWERS to 1½″
across with pink petals and purple veins; PODS like
crane bills, to 1½″ long.

ECOLOGY: Foothills to subalpine.

LOCATION: Gem Lake Trail, RMNP, CO 6/00 8500′

LOOK FOR pink, saucer-shaped flowers, 5
overlapping petals and exserted styles.

■ **LIFE LIST** Where _____ NUMBER _____

STICKY GERANIUM

Geranium viscosissimum
Geranium family   *Geraniaceae*

PERENNIAL to 12″ tall in clumps; STEMS twisted,
erect and sticky; LEAVES sticky and deeply cut into
coarsely toothed segments; FLOWERS pink, to ¾″
wide with 5 separated, horizontal petals.

ECOLOGY: Foothills and montane.

LOCATION: Boulder Creek Trail, Boulder, CO 6/92
5500′

LOOK FOR a sticky plant with pink flowers and 3-
lobed leaves with sharp teeth.

■ **LIFE LIST** Where _____ NUMBER _____

WAX CURRANT
Ribes cereum
Gooseberry family   *Grossulariaceae*

THORNLESS SHRUB to 5´ tall; STEMS smooth, brown and reddish near the tips; LEAVES palmately veined with 3 indistinct, toothed lobes; FLOWERS pink, tubular and drooping, in groups of 1–4; BERRIES red, sticky and translucent.

ECOLOGY: Foothills and montane in canyons.

LOCATION: Young Gulch, Poudre Canyon, CO 5/03 7000´

LOOK FOR glossy leaves and pink tubular flowers.

■ **LIFE LIST**   Where _____ NUMBER _____

MOTHERWORT
Leonurus cardiaca
Mint family   *Lamiaceae (Labiatae)*

PERENNIAL to 3´ tall; STEMS square and grooved; LEAVES opposite, to 2˝ long, palmately cleft into 3 sharp lobes; FLOWERS pinkish white to ¼˝ long, clustered in axillary whorls; stamens purple and exserted.

ECOLOGY: Plains and foothills.

LOCATION: Chautauqua Park, Boulder, CO 6/99 6000´

LOOK FOR 3-pointed leaves and whorls of pinkish flowers.

■ **LIFE LIST**   Where _____ NUMBER _____

HORSEMINT (BEEBALM)
Monarda fistulosa
Mint family   *Lamiaceae (Labiatae)*

PERENNIAL to 2´ tall; STEMS erect and square; LEAVES opposite, ovate and finely toothed to 4˝ long with ¼˝ petioles; FLOWERS pink to 1˝ long, clustered on a domed disc subtended by leaf-like bracts.

ECOLOGY: Plains to montane in the open.

LOCATION: Shore Trail, Lory S.P., Ft. Collins, CO 7/04 5500´

LOOK FOR opposite leaves and a terminal cluster of pink flowers.

■ **LIFE LIST**   Where _____ NUMBER _____

SHORT STYLED ONION
Allium brevistylum
Lily family   *Liliaceae*

PERENNIAL to 16″ tall from a stout bulb; SCAPES upright supporting a solitary umbel; LEAVES grass-like to 10″ long; FLOWERS pink to 1″ high with pointed lobes, short styles and 1″ pedicles; umbels with 6–12 flowers.

ECOLOGY: Montane and subalpine.

LOCATION: Medicine Bow N.F., WY 7/00 10,500′

LOOK FOR an upright onion umbel with pink flowers and pointed lobes.

■ **LIFE LIST** Where _____ NUMBER _____

NODDING ONION
Allium cernuum
Lily family   *Liliaceae*

PERENNIAL to 18″ tall from elongated bulbs; SCAPES upright with terminal umbels; LEAVES basal, to 9″ long; FLOWERS pink or white, cup-shaped and nodding to ¼″ wide with exserted stamens and styles.

ECOLOGY: Foothills to subalpine on grassy slopes.

LOCATION: Coyote Ridge Rec. Area, Ft. Collins, CO 6/05 5500′

LOOK FOR nodding, pink flowers and exserted stamens.

■ **LIFE LIST** Where _____ NUMBER _____

WOOD LILY
Lilium philadelphicum
Lily family   *Liliaceae*

PERENNIAL to 2′ tall; STEMS erect, leafy and smooth, usually with a solitary flower; LEAVES linear to 4″ long, whorled above and alternate below; FLOWERS erect to 4″ across, open bell-shaped with 6 orange to reddish tepals with purple spots in the center.

ECOLOGY: Foothills and montane in moisture – a beautiful, rare and endangered species.

LOCATION: Cub Lake Trail, RMNP, CO 7/97 8500′

LOOK FOR a 4″ lily, there's only one.

■ **LIFE LIST** Where _____ NUMBER _____

COPPER MALLOW

Sphaeralcea coccinea
Mallow family   *Malvaceae*

BIENNIAL or perennial to 12″ tall; STEMS silvery
and hairy; LEAVES deeply palmately incised and
hairy; FLOWERS saucer-shaped to ¾″ across, with 5
overlapping orange petals.
ECOLOGY: Plains and foothills.
LOCATION: Bitterbrush Trail, Hall Ranch, Lyons, CO
5/01 6000′
LOOK FOR a 5-petaled orange flower and deeply
incised leaves.

◼ **LIFE LIST** Where _____ NUMBER _____

PINE DROPS

Pterospora andromedea
Pinesap family   *Montopaceae*

SAPROPHYTIC PERENNIAL to 1′ tall with no
chlorophyll; STEMS unbranched, stout, sticky and
reddish to purple; LEAVES scale-like to 1″ long;
FLOWERS look like orange beads hanging by short
red stalks, on 3″ racemes.
ECOLOGY: Foothills and montane – associated with
pine forests, in deep shade.
LOCATION: Cub Lake Trail, RMNP, CO 7/99 8500′
LOOK FOR a reddish asparagus-like stalk and
orange bead-like flowers on a raceme.

◼ **LIFE LIST** Where _____ NUMBER _____

ALPINE WILLOWHERB

Epilobium anagallidifolium (alpinum)
Evening Primrose family   *Onagraceae*

PERENNIAL to 6″ tall in communities; STEMS
slender, curved and leafy; LEAVES bright green and
ovate to ½″ long; FLOWERS pinkish to lavender, ¼″
wide with 4 notched petals; PODS red and wire-like
to 2″ long.
ECOLOGY: Subalpine and alpine in moisture.
LOCATION: Mitchell Lake Trail, Brainard Lake Rec.
Area, Ward, CO 7/00 11,000′
LOOK FOR a pink flower on a long red stem that
becomes a seed pod.

◼ **LIFE LIST** Where _____ NUMBER _____

FIREWEED
Epilobium (Chamerion) angustifolium
Evening Primrose family   *Onagraceae*

PERENNIAL to 5´ tall; STEMS erect and shiny;
LEAVES alternate to 6˝ long, narrow-lanceolate with
short petioles; FLOWERS rose, purple or white, to ¾˝
long in racemes to 12˝ long.
ECOLOGY: Foothills to subalpine.
LOCATION: Horseshoe Trail, Golden Gate S.P.,
Golden, CO 7/99 8500´
LOOK FOR pink flowers with exserted styles in
loosely flowered racemes.

■ LIFE LIST Where _____ NUMBER _____

ANNUAL WILLOWHERB
Epilobium brachycarpum (paniculatum)
Evening Primrose family   *Onagraceae*

ANNUAL or perennial to 2´ tall; STEMS leafy and
branching; LEAVES linear and alternate to 2˝ long;
FLOWERS pink to ⅜˝ wide with 4 petals cut almost
to the base; POD cylindrical to 2˝ long.
ECOLOGY: Montane in disturbed areas.
LOCATION: Dowdy Lake Rec. Area, Red Feathers, CO
8/01 8000´
LOOK FOR an open, bushy plant and solitary
terminal flowers with petals split almost to the base.

■ LIFE LIST Where _____ NUMBER _____

PURPLE LEAVED WILLOWHERB
Epilobium ciliatum (adenocaulon)
Evening Primrose family   *Onagraceae*

PERENNIAL to 5´ tall; STEMS upright, leafy, reddish
and branched; LEAVES elliptical to 2˝ long, sparingly
toothed and sessile; FLOWERS pink to 1˝ across,
saucer shaped with 4 overlapping, notched petals;
PODS 1¾˝ long releasing seed attached to fuzz.
ECOLOGY: Plains, in or near moving water.
LOCATION: Spring Creek Trail, Ft. Collins, CO 8/02
5000´
LOOK FOR pink solitary flowers or masses of
cottony fuzz at the top of the plant.

■ LIFE LIST Where _____ NUMBER _____

SCARLET GAURA
Gaura coccinea
Evening Primrose family *Onagraceae*

PERENNIAL to 1´ tall; STEMS slender, leafy and
erect or curved; LEAVES sessile, lanceolate to 1˝ long,
ascending and overlapping; FLOWERS white, pink or
red, ⅜˝ with drooping, protruding styles on racemes
to 4˝ long.
ECOLOGY: Plains to montane.
LOCATION: Eldorado Canyon S.P., Eldorado Springs,
CO 6/00 6500´
LOOK FOR red, pink and white flowers as they pass
from bud to flower to senescence.

■ **LIFE LIST** Where _____ NUMBER _____

COLORADO GAURA
Gaura longiflora
Evening Primrose family *Onagraceae*

PERENNIAL to 30˝ tall; STEMS leafy with many
leafy axillary branches; LEAVES alternate, elliptic,
sessile, wavy, to 2˝ long; FLOWERS red or white to 1˝
long with exserted white filaments and red anthers,
on 8˝ racemes.
ECOLOGY: Plains and foothills.
LOCATION: Eldorado Canyon S.P., Eldorado Springs,
CO 5/01 6500´
LOOK FOR the unusual bright red anthers.

■ **LIFE LIST** Where _____ NUMBER _____

VELVET WEED
Gaura parviflora
Evening Primrose family *Onagraceae*

ANNUAL to 6´ tall; STEMS leafy, branched, willowy
and reddish; LEAVES lanceolate to 4˝ long;
FLOWERS pink, tubular to ½˝ long and borne on
curved spikes to 12˝ long.
ECOLOGY: Plains and foothills.
LOCATION: Lower Narrows Campground, Poudre
Canyon, CO 6/04 7500´
LOOK FOR a tall slender plant with 1 or more, long,
curved, slender spikes.

■ **LIFE LIST** Where _____ NUMBER _____

FAIRY SLIPPER
Calypso bulbosa
Orchid family   *Orchidaceae*

PERENNIAL to 5″ tall arising from a bulb; STEMS
  succulent and bearing a single leaf and flower;
  LEAVES cordate, basal, singular, to 1″ long; FLOWER
  pink with 5 small petals above the "slipper".
ECOLOGY: Foothills to subalpine in deep, moist
  forests – a beautiful and endangered species.
LOCATION: Upper Hidden Valley, Trail Ridge Rd.,
  RMNP, CO 6/02 10,500′
LOOK FOR the unmistakable pink slipper.

LIFE LIST Where _____ NUMBER _____

CALIFORNIA POPPY
Eschscholtzia californica
Poppy family   *Papaveraceae*

ANNUAL or perennial to 12″ high; STEMS erect,
  smooth and wiry; LEAVES mostly basal, dissected
  into linear divisions; FLOWERS solitary, to 2″ wide,
  deep orange to pale yellow.
ECOLOGY: Plains and foothills, usually along
  roadsides – an escapee from cultivation.
LOCATION: Boyd Lake S.P., Loveland, CO 6/95
  5000′
LOOK FOR a garden-type orange or yellow poppy
  with carrot-like foliage.

LIFE LIST Where _____ NUMBER _____

TINY TRUMPET
Collomia linearis
Phlox family   *Polemoniaceae*

ANNUAL to 10″ high; STEMS reddish, unbranched
  and leafy; LEAVES alternate, narrow, pointed and
  sessile; FLOWERS pink to lavender, trumpet shaped
  to ½″ long, with 5 lobes.
ECOLOGY: Plains to montane.
LOCATION: Bitterbrush Trail, Hall Ranch, Lyons, CO
  6/99 6000′
LOOK FOR tiny, pink trumpet flowers protruding
  from a terminal cluster.

LIFE LIST Where _____ NUMBER _____

SCARLET GILA

Ipomopsis aggregata
Phlox family   *Polemoniaceae*

BIENNIAL or perennial to 2´ tall; STEMS slender and reddish; LEAVES alternate to 3˝ long, pinnately dissected into relatively few (3–9), widely spaced, string-like segments; FLOWERS red to 2˝ long, tubular with 5, reflexed, pointed lobes in a loose panicle to 12˝ long.
ECOLOGY: Foothills and montane.
LOCATION: Breckenridge Trail, Frisco, CO 7/98 10,000´
LOOK FOR bright red trumpet flowers.

☐ LIFE LIST Where _____ NUMBER _____

BISTORT

Polygonum bistortoides
Buckwheat family   *Polygonaceae*

PERENNIAL to 2´ tall; STEMS red and slender with reduced leaves upward; LEAVES mostly basal, lanceolate, to 8˝ long; FLOWERS tiny, red or white in a dense, 2˝ spike.
ECOLOGY: Subalpine and alpine in moisture.
LOCATION: Berthoud Pass, CO 7/01 11,500´
LOOK FOR a compact spike on a slender stalk.

☐ LIFE LIST Where _____ NUMBER _____

RED SMARTWEED

Polygonum coccineum
Buckwheat family   *Polygonaceae*

ANNUAL to 18˝ tall; STEMS erect, red and leafy with papery sheaths at the nodes; LEAVES lanceolate, to 6˝ long, petioled below and sessile upward; FLOWERS pink in spikes to 3˝ long.
ECOLOGY: Plains and foothills in moist, open areas.
LOCATION: Boyd Lake S.P., Loveland, CO 8/05 5000´
LOOK FOR red stems and rhizomes and pink spikes.

☐ LIFE LIST Where _____ NUMBER _____

PENNSYLVANIA SMARTWEED
Polygonum (Persicaria) pensylvanicum
Buckwheat family   *Polygonaceae*

ANNUAL to 3½´ tall; STEMS erect with swollen joints
surrounded by papery sheaths; LEAVES alternate,
lanceolate, to 8˝ long, pointed at both ends and short
petioled; FLOWERS bright rose in cylindrical spikes
to 1˝ long.
ECOLOGY: Plains in moisture, including cultivated
fields.
LOCATION: Avery Park, Ft. Collins, CO 9/00 5000´
LOOK FOR 1˝, rose colored, cylindrical spikes.

■ LIFE LIST   Where _____ NUMBER _____

LADY'S THUMB SMARTWEED
Polygonum persicaria (Persicaria maculata)
Buckwheat family   *Polygonaceae*

ANNUAL or perennial to 3´ tall; STEMS sprawling,
branching and rooting at the nodes; LEAVES
alternate, narrow-lanceolate to 8˝ long with a dark
spot (lady's thumb print) on the leaf; FLOWERS rose
to pink in 1˝ catkin-like racemes.
ECOLOGY: Plains and foothills in moisture.
LOCATION: Boyd Lake S.P., Loveland, CO 8/01
5000´
LOOK FOR the lady's thumb print.

■ LIFE LIST   Where _____ NUMBER _____

SHEEP SORREL
Rumex acetosella (Acetosella vulgaris)
Buckwheat family   *Polygonaceae*

PERENNIAL to 18˝ tall, spreading by suckers;
STEMS curved, slender and ribbed; LEAVES
lanceolate to 3˝ long and may have triangular lobes at
leaf bases; FLOWERS pinkish to red, ⅛˝ long, in
panicles to 10˝ long.
ECOLOGY: Plains to montane.
LOCATION: Eldorado Canyon S.P., Eldorado Springs,
CO 5/01 6500´
LOOK FOR a loose, branched, terminal inflorescence
with bud-like flowers.

■ LIFE LIST   Where _____ NUMBER _____

MARSH DOCK
Rumex densiflorus
Buckwheat family   *Polygonaceae*

PERENNIAL to 8″ tall; STEMS creeping and leafy; LEAVES lanceolate, wavy, to 5″ long; FLOWERS red, to ¼″ wide, in crowded panicles to 3″ long.
ECOLOGY: Plains and foothills.
LOCATION: Pawnee National Grasslands, Keota, CO 5/01 5000′
LOOK FOR a low growing plant with dark green glossy leaves and a red inflorescence.

■ LIFE LIST Where _____ NUMBER _____

BEGONIA DOCK
Rumex venosus
Buckwheat family   *Polygonaceae*

PERENNIAL to 6″ high; STEMS prostrate, leafy and inconspicuous; LEAVES wavy, irregular, petioled and fleshy, to 3″ long; FLOWERS with pink, winged sepals to 1″ wide.
ECOLOGY: Plains along roadsides and in disturbed areas with moisture.
LOCATION: Highland Canal Trail, Denver, CO 5/92 5000′
LOOK FOR a pink begonia-like flower on a prostrate plant.

■ LIFE LIST Where _____ NUMBER _____

PYGMY BITTERROOT
Lewisia (Oreobroma) pygmaea
Purslane family   *Portulacaceae*

PERENNIAL to 2″ high from a taproot; STEMS inconspicuous; LEAVES basal and linear to 2″ long; FLOWERS pink or white, to ¾″ across with 7–9 tepals (petals can't be distinguished from sepals).
ECOLOGY: Subalpine and alpine in moisture.
LOCATION: Mitchell Lake Trail, Brainard Lake Rec. Area, Ward, CO 8/99 11,000′
LOOK FOR a tiny rosette of narrow leaves and a saucer-shaped flower.

■ LIFE LIST Where _____ NUMBER _____

SHOOTING STAR
Dodecatheon pulchellum
Primrose family   *Primulaceae*

PERENNIAL to 15″ high; SCAPES slender and
reddish; LEAVES rosetted, glossy, spatulate, to 8″
long; FLOWERS to 1½″ long with pink reflexed
petals and 5, fused stamens, in terminal clusters of
1–5 flowers.

ECOLOGY: Foothills to subalpine in cool, shady, wet
places.

LOCATION: Sheep Creek Trail (44H Rd.), Larimer
Cty., CO 6/04 7500′

LOOK FOR a pink flower with swept back petals and
protruding stamens.

☐ **LIFE LIST**   Where _____ NUMBER _____

PARRY PRIMROSE
Primula parryi
Primrose family   *Primulaceae*

PERENNIAL to 15″ tall; SCAPES succulent and
bright green; LEAVES basal, rosetted and lanceolate
with winged petioles, to 10″ long; FLOWERS red to
1″ across with a yellow center, in loose panicles to 5″
long.

ECOLOGY: Subalpine and alpine in or near moving
water.

LOCATION: Mitchell Lake Trail, Brainard Lake Rec.
Area, Ward, CO 8/99 11,000′

LOOK FOR panicles of beautiful rose colored flowers
near, or in, running water.

☐ **LIFE LIST**   Where _____ NUMBER _____

PIPSISSEWA (PRINCE'S PINE)
Chimaphila umbellata
Wintergreen family   *Pyrolaceae*

DWARF evergreen shrub to 10″ tall; STEMS green
with basal leaves; LEAVES lanceolate, alternate,
glossy, thick and finely toothed to 3″ long; FLOWERS
¾″ wide, pink or white, 5-petaled in terminal
clusters.

ECOLOGY: Foothills and montane in moisture,
under conifers.

LOCATION: Ouzel Falls Trail, Wild Basin, RMNP, CO
7/99 9000′

LOOK FOR pink or white flowers, berry-like buds
and glossy, evergreen leaves.

☐ **LIFE LIST**   Where _____ NUMBER _____

BOG WINTERGREEN
Pyrola asarifolia (rotundifolia)
Wintergreen family   *Pyrolaceae*

PERENNIAL to 16″ high; SCAPES slender and smooth; LEAVES basal, glossy, thick, round, petioled, to 1½″ wide and bright green above, brownish beneath; FLOWERS nodding with 5 round, pinkish-white petals.

ECOLOGY: Montane and subalpine in moisture.

LOCATION: Ouzel Falls Trail, Wild Basin, RMNP, CO 7/99 9000′

LOOK FOR a rosette of glossy leaves, a red scape and a raceme of pink, nodding, globular flowers.

■ **LIFE LIST** Where _____ NUMBER _____

RED ANEMONE
Anemone multifida (globosa)
Buttercup family   *Ranunculaceae*

PERENNIAL to 12″ tall; STEMS slender and silky; LEAVES dissected into linear segments; FLOWERS to ¾″ across, having up to 9 red to pink petal-like sepals, petals absent.

ECOLOGY: Foothills to alpine in shade.

LOCATION: Flowers Rd. (FR150), Stove Prairie, CO 6/04 7500′

LOOK FOR a stem with a collar of sessile, dissected leaves and a solitary red flower a few inches above the collar.

■ **LIFE LIST** Where _____ NUMBER _____

RED COLUMBINE
Aquilegia elegantula
Buttercup family   *Ranunculaceae*

PERENNIAL to 16″ tall, in patches; STEMS slender, erect with 3 or 4 leafy nodes; some LEAVES are trifoliate with lobed leaflets, others are 3-lobed; FLOWERS usually solitary, nodding, to 2″ long, with red spurs trailing like a rocket in flight.

ECOLOGY: Montane and subalpine in shade.

LOCATION: Ten Mile Creek Trail, Frisco, CO 7/95 9500′

LOOK FOR a flower trailing 5 red spurs.

■ **LIFE LIST** Where _____ NUMBER _____

WILD ROSE
Rosa woodsii
Rose family   *Rosaceae*

SHRUB to 3′ tall; STEMS thorny and branching, twigs red; LEAVES pinnate with 5–9 toothed leaflets to ½″ wide; FLOWERS 2″ long with 5 pink to white petals surrounding a yellow center; FRUIT (hips) red, hard and round to ½″, over-wintering on the shrub.
ECOLOGY: Plains to subalpine in sun.
LOCATION: Ouzel Falls Trail, Wild Basin, RMNP, CO 7/99 9000′
LOOK FOR a rose with a single set of petals and a large yellow center.

■ LIFE LIST Where _____ NUMBER _____

JAMES SAXIFRAGE
Boykinia (Telesonix) jamesii
Saxifrage family   *Saxifragaceae*

PERENNIAL to 8″ tall; STEMS succulent, leafy and smooth; LEAVES petioled, round and scalloped to 1½″ wide; FLOWERS pinkish to 1″ across with 5, stalked petals, on racemes to 4″ long bearing up to 8 flowers.
ECOLOGY: Subalpine and alpine on rocky slopes.
LOCATION: Gem Lake Trail, RMNP, CO 6/00 8500′
LOOK FOR pink flowers with stemmed petals and round, scalloped leaves.

■ LIFE LIST Where _____ NUMBER _____

ORANGE PAINTBRUSH
Castilleja integra
Figwort family   *Scrophulariaceae*

PERENNIAL to 16″ tall; STEMS slender, erect and leafy; LEAVES alternate, narrow, to 2″ long; FLOWERS hidden by orange bracts and calyx lobes.
ECOLOGY: Plains to montane in open fields.
LOCATION: Mesa Trail, Eldorado Canyon S.P., Eldorado Springs, CO 6/00 6500′
LOOK FOR an orange paintbrush with linear leaves.

■ LIFE LIST Where _____ NUMBER _____

WYOMING PAINTBRUSH
Castilleja linariifolia
Figwort family   *Scrophulariaceae*

PERENNIAL to 2´ tall; STEMS erect, leafy and reddish upward; LEAVES grass-like, sessile, alternate, to 5″ long; FLOWERS enclosed in red, deeply cleft bracts.

ECOLOGY: Foothills to montane in forest openings – the state flower of Wyoming.

LOCATION: Cub Lake Trail, RMNP, CO 6/00 8500´

LOOK FOR a red paintbrush with a loose spike and narrow, twisted leaves.

█ **LIFE LIST** Where _____ NUMBER _____

SCARLET PAINTBRUSH
Castilleja miniata
Figwort family   *Scrophulariaceae*

PERENNIAL to 2´ high, quite variable in size, form and color; STEMS erect, leafy, reddish and unbranched; LEAVES alternate, lanceolate and sessile; FLOWERS are hidden by bracts that are red to rose, ascending and corrugated.

ECOLOGY: Montane and subalpine in moist, open areas.

LOCATION: 4th of July Trail, Eldora, CO 7/00 11,500´

LOOK FOR a dense raceme of red bracts.

█ **LIFE LIST** Where _____ NUMBER _____

ROSY PAINTBRUSH
Castilleja rhexiifolia
Figwort family   *Scrophulariaceae*

PERENNIAL to 12″ tall; STEMS erect, leafy and green; LEAVES sessile, ovate, to 2″ long; FLOWERS hidden by red or rosy bracts that are broad and blunt with a 3-lobed tip.

ECOLOGY: Subalpine and alpine.

LOCATION: Berthoud Pass, CO 7/01 11,500´

LOOK FOR a red paintbrush with broad leaves and bracts and a short raceme.

█ **LIFE LIST** Where _____ NUMBER _____

LITTLE PINK ELEPHANT
Pedicularis groenlandica
Figwort family   *Scrophulariaceae*

PERENNIAL to 1´ tall; STEMS erect, reddish, unbranched and leafy; LEAVES to 6″ long, alternate, pinnatifid with lobes similar to fern fronds; FLOWERS pink to purple, 2-lipped with upper lip curved like an elephant's trunk; lower lip 3-lobed; racemes densely flowered to 5″ long.
ECOLOGY: Montane to alpine in moisture.
LOCATION: Trail Ridge Rd., West Side, RMNP, CO 7/05 10,000´
LOOK FOR pink elephant heads.

■ **LIFE LIST** Where _____ NUMBER _____

FIRE CRACKER
Penstemon barbatus
Figwort family   *Scrophulariaceae*

PERENNIAL to 6´ tall; STEMS red, unbranched and erect with nodes several inches apart; LEAVES opposite and linear to 6″ long; FLOWERS scarlet, nodding, tubular, to 2″ long on racemes to 8″ long.
ECOLOGY: Plains and foothills on steep slopes and clearings.
LOCATION: Fossil Creek Trail, Ft. Collins, CO 5/98 5000´
LOOK FOR bright red, nodding, tubular flowers on a tall red stemmed plant.

■ **LIFE LIST** Where _____ NUMBER _____

ORCHID BEARDS TONGUE (ONE SIDED PENSTEMON)
Penstemon secundiflorus
Figwort family   *Scrophulariaceae*

PERENNIAL to 20″ tall; STEMS erect, green, smooth and unbranched; LEAVES opposite, ovate and clasping; FLOWERS 1″ long, pink to purple on a raceme that is often one-sided.
ECOLOGY: Plains to montane.
LOCATION: Horsetooth Falls Trail, Horsetooth Park, Ft. Collins, CO 6/05 5500´
LOOK FOR pink to purple flowers borne on short branches of a 1-sided raceme.

■ **LIFE LIST** Where _____ NUMBER _____

TALL PENSTEMON
Penstemon unilateralis
Figwort family   *Scrophulariaceae*

PERENNIAL to 3´ tall; STEMS smooth, green, leafy and erect; LEAVES narrow-lanceolate, opposite, clasping to 5″ long; FLOWERS 1″ long, pink, blue or purple; corolla with 2-lobed upper lip and 3-lobed lower lip on a raceme to 18″ long.
ECOLOGY: Foothills and montane.
LOCATION: S. Mesa Trail, Eldorado Canyon S.P., Eldorado Springs, CO 6/99 6500´
LOOK FOR pink flowers crowded on one side of a tall, spike-like raceme.

■ **LIFE LIST** Where _____ NUMBER _____

DUSKY BEARDS TONGUE
Penstemon whippleanus
Figwort family   *Scrophulariaceae*

PERENNIAL to 15″ tall; STEMS smooth, green, erect and leafy; stem LEAVES opposite, narrow and sessile to 3″ long, basal leaves petioled; FLOWERS to 1½″ long, maroon to white, in whorls around the upper 3 nodes.
ECOLOGY: Subalpine to alpine.
LOCATION: Trail Ridge Rd., RMNP, CO 6/02 10,500´
LOOK FOR corrugated corollas.

■ **LIFE LIST** Where _____ NUMBER _____

SALT CEDAR
Tamarix ramosissima
Tamarisk family   *Tamaricaceae*

SHRUB to 15´ tall; TWIGS reddish-brown and highly branched; LEAVES small and scale-like; FLOWERS pink to white and 5-petaled.
ECOLOGY: Plains and foothills near water. Regarded as an undesirable plant because of its heavy water consumption.
LOCATION: Boyd Lake S.P., Loveland, CO 6/01 5000´
LOOK FOR an inflorescence composed of many short spikes of tiny pink flowers.

■ **LIFE LIST** Where _____ NUMBER _____

SHOWY VERVAIN
Glandularia (Verbena) bipinnatifida
Vervain family   *Verbenaceae*

ANNUAL or perennial to 12″ high; STEMS leafy, erect
and succulent; LEAVES opposite, deeply pinnatifid
and fleshy; FLOWERS pink, to ½″ across with 5,
notched lobes.
ECOLOGY: Plains and foothills in open areas.
LOCATION: Rabbit Mt., Lyons, CO 5/01 6000′
LOOK FOR a terminal cluster composed of an outer
ring of pink flowers and a central cluster of pink
buds.

■ **LIFE LIST** Where _____ NUMBER _____

FOG FRUIT
Phyla cuneifolia
Vervain family   *Verbenaceae*

PERENNIAL trailing plant to 3″ high, rooting at
nodes; STEMS to 3′ long, branching, creeping and
producing whorls of leaves at 2″ intervals; LEAVES
linear, sessile with irregular pointed terminal lobes;
FLOWER heads to ¾″ wide with an outer ring of
pink flowers and purple centers.
ECOLOGY: Plains and foothills.
LOCATION: Coyote Ridge Rec. Area, Ft. Collins, CO
6/03 5500′
LOOK FOR little flower heads with purple centers on
a trailing vine.

■ **LIFE LIST** Where _____ NUMBER _____

AMBROSIA VERBENA
Verbena ambrosifolia
Vervain family   *Verbenaceae*

PERENNIAL to 3″ tall; STEMS inconspicuous;
LEAVES deeply lobed to 1½″ long with prominent
veins; FLOWERS pink, ½″ wide with 5, notched
lobes.
ECOLOGY: Plains and foothills on open ground.
LOCATION: Rabbit Mt., Lyons, CO 5/02 6000′
LOOK FOR clusters of pink flowers on a tiny rosetted
plant.

■ **LIFE LIST** Where _____ NUMBER _____

ROCKY MOUNTAIN FLORA

Blue
Flowers

COMMON CHICORY

Cichorium intybus
Aster family   *Asteraceae (Compositae)*

BIENNIAL or perennial to 4´ high; STEMS erect with milky sap, branching at upper nodes; basal LEAVES to 6″ long, pinnatifid and toothed with a large terminal lobe, stem leaves reduced to 1″ bracts; FLOWERS blue to 1″ wide and petals with blunt, toothed tips.
ECOLOGY: Plains in moist, deep soil.
LOCATION: Roadside, Ft. Collins, CO 8/01 5000´
LOOK FOR a skeleton plant with showy blue flowers having all blue parts.

■ **LIFE LIST**   Where _____ NUMBER _____

BUGLOSS

Anchusa azurea
Borage family   *Boraginaceae*

PERENNIAL to 3´ high; STEMS erect, hairy, leafy and branched; LEAVES lanceolate, sessile, to 1″ long, hairy and alternate; FLOWERS blue to ½″ wide with white centers and 5 round petals; flowering is continuous behind the apex.
ECOLOGY: Plains and foothills – an escapee.
LOCATION: Boulder Creek Trail, Boulder, CO 9/92 5500´
LOOK FOR saucer-shaped blue flowers with white centers.

■ **LIFE LIST**   Where _____ NUMBER _____

FALSE FORGET-ME-NOT

Hackelia floribunda
Borage family   *Boraginaceae*

BIENNIAL or perennial to 3´ high; STEMS stout and hairy; LEAVES to 6″ long, alternate, narrow, fleshy, grayish and hairy beneath; FLOWERS saucer shaped to ¼″ wide with 5 blue petals and yellow centers.
ECOLOGY: Foothills to subalpine.
LOCATION: Cow Creek Trail, McGraw Ranch, RMNP, CO 7/99 8000´
LOOK FOR axillary shoots emerging at 45 degrees and bearing clusters of tiny blue flowers.

■ **LIFE LIST**   Where _____ NUMBER _____

ALPINE MERTENSIA
Mertensia alpina
Borage family   *Boraginaceae*

PERENNIAL to 6″ high; STEMS curved, slightly
grooved and hairy; LEAVES lanceolate, sessile,
ascending, to 1½″ long; FLOWERS blue, to ½″ long,
tubular with non-flaring lobes and a calyx split to the
base, borne in axillary clusters.

ECOLOGY: Subalpine and alpine in moisture.

LOCATION: St. Alban's Chapel, Medicine Bow N.F.,
WY 8/99 10,500′

LOOK FOR a 6″ *Mertensia* at high elevations having
a calyx split to the base.

■ LIFE LIST   Where _____ NUMBER _____

TALL CHIMING BELLS
Mertensia ciliata
Borage family   *Boraginaceae*

PERENNIAL to 4′ tall; STEMS leafy, erect or curved;
LEAVES alternate, lanceolate, to 6″ long, sessile above
and petioled below; FLOWERS blue, bell-shaped with
calyxes split to the base, in nodding clusters borne on
axillary branches.

ECOLOGY: Montane to alpine in moisture.

LOCATION: Fish Creek, Estes Park, CO 6/92
8000′

LOOK FOR a tall *Mertensia* with nodding terminal
clusters on axillary branches.

■ LIFE LIST   Where _____ NUMBER _____

LANCELEAF CHIMING BELLS
Mertensia lanceolata
Borage family   *Boraginaceae*

PERENNIAL to 1′ tall; STEMS erect or ascending
and leafy; LEAVES alternate, to 3″ long, edges down-
rolled with veins obscured; FLOWERS blue, ¾″ long,
bell-shaped and 5 lobed with calyx not split to the
base.

ECOLOGY: Plains and foohills.

LOCATION: Rabbit Mt., Lyons, CO 6/99 6000′

LOOK FOR bell-shaped flowers, at lower elevations.

■ LIFE LIST   Where _____ NUMBER _____

GREEN MERTENSIA

Mertensia lanceolata (viridis) nivalis
Borage family   *Boraginaceae*

PERENNIAL to 14″ tall; STEMS leafy and ascending; LEAVES alternate, lanceolate, to 2″ long; sessile above and petioled below; FLOWERS blue, tubular with non-flaring lobes; clusters drooping with 10–20 flowers.
ECOLOGY: Montane to alpine in moisture.
LOCATION: Hidden Valley, RMNP, CO 6/02 9500′
LOOK FOR a *Mertensia* with a large number of flowers per cluster.

■ LIFE LIST Where _____ NUMBER _____

FORGET-ME-NOT

Myosotis scorpioides
Borage family   *Boraginaceae*

ANNUAL to 8″ tall; STEMS hairy, leafy and curved; LEAVES to ½″ long, sessile, lanceolate and hairy; FLOWERS blue to ⅛″ wide with exserted styles.
ECOLOGY: Foothills to subalpine in moisture.
LOCATION: Wild Basin, RMNP, CO 7/99 9000′
LOOK FOR a tiny plant with a single, blue flower in the axil of every leaf of the raceme.

■ LIFE LIST Where _____ NUMBER _____

COMMON HAREBELL

Campanula rotundifolia
Bellflower family   *Campanulaceae*

PERENNIAL to 18″ high, forming colonies; STEMS slender with terminal clusters of 2–5 bells; stem LEAVES linear and sessile, basal leaves lanceolate and petioled; FLOWERS blue bells to 1″ wide in nodding clusters.
ECOLOGY: Foothills to alpine.
LOCATION: 4th of July Trail, Eldora, CO 7/01 11,500′
LOOK FOR nodding, blue, bell-shaped flowers on slender plants.

■ LIFE LIST Where _____ NUMBER _____

WESTERN SPIDERWORT
Tradescantia occidentalis
Spiderwort family *Commelinaceae*

PERENNIAL to 18″ tall; STEMS smooth, erect and
leafy; LEAVES grass-like, in-folded to 10″ long;
FLOWERS to 1″ across with 3 blue, spreading petals.
ECOLOGY: Plains and foothills.
LOCATION: Coyote Ridge Rec. Area, Ft. Collins, CO
5/02 5500′
LOOK FOR a grass-like plant with blue, 3-petaled
flowers.

LIFE LIST Where _____ NUMBER _____

NUTTALL MORNING GLORY
Evolvulus nuttallianus
Morning Glory family *Convolvulaceae*

PERENNIAL to 4″ tall; STEMS semi-prostrate to 8″
long with overlapping leaves; LEAVES gray-green,
elliptical and hairy to ⅜″ long; FLOWERS pale blue
to ½″ wide, resembling miniature morning glories.
ECOLOGY: Plains and foothills.
LOCATION: Coyote Ridge Rec. Area, Ft. Collins, CO
6/05 5500′
LOOK FOR a small, gray-green plant with hairy
leaves and pale-blue flowers.

LIFE LIST Where _____ NUMBER _____

PLEATED GENTIAN
Gentiana (Pneumonanthe) affinis
Gentian family *Gentianaceae*

PERENNIAL to 9″ tall; STEMS leafy, erect or
ascending; LEAVES sessile, lanceolae, to 2″ long;
FLOWERS blue, tubular and pleated (corrugated) to
1″ long with 5, small lobes.
ECOLOGY: Foothills and montane.
LOCATION: Well Gulch, Lory S.P., Ft. Collins, CO
8/01 5500′
LOOK FOR a clump of whitish stems with opposite
leaves and tight, terminal clusters of pleated blue
flowers.

LIFE LIST Where _____ NUMBER _____

MOUNTAIN GENTIAN

Gentiana (Pneumonanthe) parryi
Gentian family   *Gentianaceae*

PERENNIAL to 1´ tall, in clumps; STEMS leafy and
  ascending; LEAVES opposite, sessile, ovate, to 1″ long;
  FLOWERS blue to ¾″ across, barrel-shaped with 5,
  pointed lobes, in terminal clusters of 1–3 flowers.
ECOLOGY: Montane to alpine in moisture.
LOCATION: S. Park Trail, Guanella Pass, CO 8/99
  11,500´
LOOK FOR a Gentian at high elevations with a 5-
  lobe blue flower and broad, opposite leaves.

■ **LIFE LIST** Where _____ NUMBER _____

MOSS GENTIAN

Gentiana (Chondrophylla) prostrata
Gentian family   *Gentianaceae*

ANNUAL or biennial to 3″ high; STEMS prostrate or
  erect and leafy; LEAVES smooth to ½″ long, opposite
  and ascending; FLOWERS blue to purple, tubular,
  solitary and terminal, to ⅜″ wide with 4 large and
  4 small pointed lobes.
ECOLOGY: Subalpine and alpine in moist places.
LOCATION: Copper Mt., CO 8/92 10,500´
LOOK FOR a small Gentian flower with short and
  long lobes and scale-like leaves.

■ **LIFE LIST** Where _____ NUMBER _____

WILD IRIS

Iris missouriensis
Iris family   *Iridaceae*

PERENNIAL to 15″; STEMS succulent and leafless;
  LEAVES linear, parallel veined, basal to 12″ long;
  FLOWERS blue with 3 drooping falls (sepals) and 3
  upright petals.
ECOLOGY: Foothills to subalpine in moisture.
LOCATION: Cow Creek Trail, McGraw Ranch, RMNP,
  CO 6/01 8000´
LOOK FOR 3 drooping petals and 3 upright petals,
  all blue.

■ **LIFE LIST** Where _____ NUMBER _____

BLUE EYED GRASS

Sisyrinchium montanum
Iris family   *Iridaceae*

PERENNIAL to 14″ tall; STEMS flattened, winged
and pale green; LEAVES grass-like, sessile, to ⅛″
wide; FLOWERS blue to violet with 3 petals and
3 similar sepals, to ¾″ across.
ECOLOGY: Foothills to subalpine.
LOCATION: Ten Mile Creek Trail, Frisco, CO 7/95
10,000′
LOOK FOR a grass-like plant with blue flowers
borne about 2″ below the tip of the plant.

■ **LIFE LIST** Where _____ NUMBER _____

BLUE FLAX

Linum (Adenolinum) lewisii
Flax family   *Linaceae*

PERENNIAL to 2′ tall; STEMS slender, willowy and
leafy; LEAVES alternate, ascending. linear. to 1″ long;
FLOWERS blue, 1″ wide and 5 petaled in a drooping
panicle with 1 to several flowers open.
ECOLOGY: Plains to montane.
LOCATION: Spring Creek Trail, Edora Park, Ft.
Collins, CO 5/03 5000′
LOOK FOR a blue, saucer-shaped flowers with 5 blue
petals on a slender plant.

■ **LIFE LIST** Where _____ NUMBER _____

WESTERN JACOBS LADDER

Polemonium occidentale
Phlox family   *Polemoniaceae*

PERENNIAL to 2′ high; STEMS pubescent, leafy,
succulent and branched; LEAVES pinnate to 4″ long
with up to 15 leaflets; FLOWERS pale blue to ½″
across with 5, pointed petals.
ECOLOGY: Montane and subalpine in bogs.
LOCATION: Horseshoe Trail, Golden Gate S.P.,
Golden, CO 7/00 8500′
LOOK FOR blue flowers with purple stripes and
pointed petals.

■ **LIFE LIST** Where _____ NUMBER _____

JACOBS LADDER
Polemonium pulcherrimum
Phlox family   *Polemoniaceae*

PERENNIAL to 4″ high; STEMS sparsely leafed and
bearing 1–5 terminal flowers; basal LEAVES pinnate
with up to 9 pairs of ½″ lanceolate leaflets;
FLOWERS mostly white with tinges of blue or purple,
bowl-shape, to 1½″ wide.
ECOLOGY: Subalpine and alpine in shade.
LOCATION: Berthoud Pass, CO 7/01 11,500′
LOOK FOR the ladder-like arrangement of the
leaflets on the midrib.

LIFE LIST Where _____ NUMBER _____

SKY PILOT
Polemonium viscosum
Phlox family   *Polemoniaceae*

PERENNIAL to 12″ high; STEMS erect, twisted,
sticky and hairy; LEAVES mostly basal, pinnate, to 6″
long; leaflets form whorls around the midrib at ½″
intervals; FLOWERS blue, trumpet shape to 1½″ long
in tight clusters.
ECOLOGY: Subalpine and alpine.
LOCATION: Mt. Evans, CO 6/05 11,000′
LOOK FOR clusters of 15–20 blue, tubular flowers on
a 10″ stalk.

LIFE LIST Where _____ NUMBER _____

MONKSHOOD
Aconitum columbianum
Buttercup family   *Ranunculaceae*

PERENNIAL to 2′ tall, usually in patches; STEMS
erect and leafy; LEAVES thin, to 4″ wide, deeply cleft
and toothed; FLOWERS blue, purple or white, sepals
assume role of petals with upper sepal becoming a
monk's hood.
ECOLOGY: Montane to alpine in moisture.
LOCATION: Hassell Lake Trail, URAD Mine Rd.,
Berthoud Pass, CO 7/01 11,000′
LOOK FOR a monk's hood flower that is about the
right size to wear on the little finger.

LIFE LIST Where _____ NUMBER _____

COLORADO COLUMBINE
Aquilegia coerulea
Buttercup family   *Ranunculaceae*

PERENNIAL to 2´ tall; STEMS upright and slender; LEAVES mostly basal with long slender petioles and deeply cut blades; FLOWERS to 3″ across with 5, spreading, blue or white sepals and 5, white, scoop-shaped petals with trailing spurs.
ECOLOGY: Foothills to alpine in moisture – Colorado's state flower.
LOCATION: Sheep Lake Trail, Medicine Bow N.F., WY 7/01 10,500´
LOOK FOR the classic Columbine flower.

LIFE LIST Where _____ NUMBER _____

BLUE CLEMATIS
Clematis occidentalis
Buttercup family   *Ranunculaceae*

PERENNIAL vine, climbing on rocks and trees; STEMS viney, slender and leafy; LEAVES trifoliate with broad lanceolate leaflets to 1½″ long; FLOWERS blue with 4, spreading, petal-like sepals to 2″ long, later forming a 2″ fuzz ball.
ECOLOGY: Foothills to subalpine.
LOCATION: Young Gulch, Poudre Canyon, CO 6/02 7000´
LOOK FOR a climbing vine with trifoliate leaves and broad, entire leaflets.

LIFE LIST Where _____ NUMBER _____

GEYER LARKSPUR
Delphinium geyeri
Buttercup family   *Ranunculaceae*

PERENNIAL to 1´ tall; STEMS erect, pubescent and slender; LEAVES mainly basal to 5″ long and cut into many narrow 1″ segments; FLOWERS blue, to ⅝″ wide with a single ⅝″ spur. Sepals predominate while petals are much reduced.
ECOLOGY: Plains to montane.
LOCATION: Timber Trail, Lory S.P., Ft. Collins, CO 6/05 5500´
LOOK FOR a raceme of blue flowers and string-like leaves.

LIFE LIST Where _____ NUMBER _____

EARLY LARKSPUR
Delphinium nuttallianum (nelsonii)
Buttercup family   *Ranunculaceae*

PERENNIAL to 12″ tall; STEMS slender and smooth; basal LEAVES long-petioled and digitally divided into narrow segments, stem leaves linear and sessile; FLOWERS well spaced with 5, blue, petal-like sepals, 1 having a spur.

ECOLOGY: Foothills to subalpine.

LOCATION: Arthur's Rock Trail, Lory S.P., Ft. Collins, CO 5/01 5500′

LOOK FOR tiny white petals in the center of the flower.

☐ **LIFE LIST** Where _____ NUMBER _____

BLUE-EYED MARY
Collinsia parviflora (tenella)
Figwort family   *Scrophulariaceae*

ANNUAL to 3″ tall; STEMS slender, reddish, succulent and leafy; LEAVES linear, opposite and fleshy to 1″ long; FLOWERS ¼″ long with a pink calyx, white corolla and blue lobes on the lower lip.

ECOLOGY: Plains to montane in shade.

LOCATION: Well Gulch, Lory S.P., Ft. Collins, CO 5/02 5500′

LOOK FOR a reddish plant with a little blue and white flower in the axils of upper leaves.

☐ **LIFE LIST** Where _____ NUMBER _____

NARROW-LEAVED PENSTEMON
Penstemon angustifolius
Figwort family   *Scrophulariaceae*

PERENNIAL to 1′ tall, in tufts; STEMS erect or ascending; LEAVES linear, sessile, in-folded to 4″ long; FLOWERS light blue or purple, to ¾″ long, tightly packed in racemes to 8″ long; corolla 2 lipped and lobed.

ECOLOGY: Plains and foothills.

LOCATION: Cherry Creek Trail, Denver, CO 5/93 5000′

LOOK FOR curved stems and racemes tightly packed with light-blue, tubular flowers.

☐ **LIFE LIST** Where _____ NUMBER _____

HALL'S BEARDTONGUE
Penstemon hallii
Figwort family   *Scrophulariaceae*

PERENNIAL to 8″ tall; STEMS curved, leafy and unbranched; LEAVES glossy, thick, narrow and opposite to 1½″ long; FLOWERS to 1″ long, tricolored with blue, purple and pink in varied proportions.
ECOLOGY: Subalpine and alpine.
LOCATION: Brown Lake Trail, Crown Pt. Rd. (FR139), Larimer Cty., CO 7/04 11,000′
LOOK FOR a tiny penstemon plant with multicolored flowers on a one-sided raceme.

■ **LIFE LIST** Where _____ NUMBER _____

SMALL FLOWERED PENSTEMON
Penstemon procerus
Figwort family   *Scrophulariaceae*

PERENNIAL to 16″ high, in clumps; STEMS smooth and upright; LEAVES opposite, lanceolate, leathery and glossy to 2″ long; FLOWERS blue-purple to ⅜″ long, densely packed in 1 or more whorled clusters.
ECOLOGY: Montane to alpine.
LOCATION: I-80 and Exit 323, WY 7/05 8500′
LOOK FOR a small penstemon with tiny, blue flowers in dense whorls.

■ **LIFE LIST** Where _____ NUMBER _____

TWO-LOBED SPEEDWELL
Veronica biloba
Figwort family   *Scrophulariaceae*

ANNUAL creeping ground cover to ½″ high; STEMS leafy to 4″ long; LEAVES opposite to ½″ long, toothed and sessile; FLOWERS saucer-shaped, blue and white to ¼″ wide.
ECOLOGY: Plains and foothills in small patches.
LOCATION: Avery Park, Ft. Collins, CO 8/05 5000′
LOOK FOR a small, dark green patch with tiny blue flowers.

■ **LIFE LIST** Where _____ NUMBER _____

ALPINE SPEEDWELL
Veronica wormskjoldii (nutans)
Figwort family   *Scrophulariaceae*

PERENNIAL to 10″ tall; STEMS erect and hairy; LEAVES opposite, ovate and sessile to 1″ long; FLOWERS blue in terminal clusters.
ECOLOGY: Subalpine and alpine in moisture.
LOCATION: Sheep Lake Trail, Medicine Bow N.F., WY 7/00 10,500′
LOOK FOR stems with opposite, uniformly sized leaves and a tight terminal flower cluster.

■ **LIFE LIST** Where _____ NUMBER _____

BLUE VERVAIN
Verbena hastata
Vervain family   *Verbenaceae*

ANNUAL or perennial to 4′ tall; STEMS erect, angular, hollow and leafy; LEAVES opposite and petioled to
6″ long, toothed and bristly beneath; FLOWERS ⅜″ across, pink to purplish, 5-lobed, in erect spikes of a candelabra-like panicle.
ECOLOGY: Plains and foothills near water.
LOCATION: Poudre River Trail, Ft. Collins, CO 7/02 5000′
LOOK FOR clusters of terminal spikes with whorls of blue flowers progressing upward.

■ **LIFE LIST** Where _____ NUMBER _____

MOUNTAIN BLUE VIOLET
Viola adunca

Violet family   *Violaceae*

PERENNIAL to 3″ high; SCAPES to 3″ long, supporting a single flower; LEAVES ovate, glossy, finely toothed and rolled inward, blade to 1½″ long and petiole to 2″ long; FLOWERS nodding, to ¾″ wide with 5, blue to purple petals, the lowest one being spurred.
ECOLOGY: Montane to alpine in meadows.
LOCATION: Mitchell Lake Trail, Brainard Lake Rec. Area, Ward, CO 7/00 11,000′
LOOK FOR a light blue violet with a spurred lower petal.

■ **LIFE LIST** Where _____ NUMBER _____

BLUE VIOLET
Viola nephrophylla

Violet family   *Violaceae*

ANNUAL or perennial to 6″ tall; STEMS mostly under ground, flowers borne on scapes; LEAVES heart-shaped (cordate) to 1½″ wide with 3″ petioles; FLOWERS blue to ¾″ wide.

ECOLOGY: Plains and foothills in moisture and shade.

LOCATION: Young Gulch, Poudre Canyon, CO 6/02 7500´

LOOK FOR a plant with a single blue violet and 3 or 4 leaves.

■ **LIFE LIST** Where _____ NUMBER _____

ROCKY MOUNTAIN FLORA

Purple
Flowers

BURDOCK
Arctium minus
Aster family   *Asteraceae (Compositae)*

BIENNIAL to 4´ tall; STEMS leafy and branched; basal LEAVES cordate, pubescent and large, with blades to 15″ and petioles to 10″ long; stem leaves reduced; FLOWERS purple to red, ½″ wide with tiered bracts bearing hooks that suggested the invention of "Velcro".

ECOLOGY: Plains and foothills – of European origin.

LOCATION: Mesa Trail, Eldorado Canyon S.P., Eldorado Springs, CO 6/00 6500´

LOOK FOR thistle flowers and rhubarb leaves.

■ **LIFE LIST** Where _____ NUMBER _____

WESTERN ASTER
Aster ascendens
Aster family   *Asteraceae (Compositae)*

PERENNIAL to 10″ tall; STEMS upright, leafy and branching only at the top; LEAVES ascending, acuminate, wavy, to 2″ long and little reduced upward; FLOWER head lavender to 1½″ wide with up to 60 rays.

ECOLOGY: Foothills to subalpine.

LOCATION: Young Gulch, Poudre Canyon, CO 7/03 7500´

LOOK FOR an aster with sharp-pointed, upright leaves, sized fairly uniformly.

■ **LIFE LIST** Where _____ NUMBER _____

SUNLOVING ASTER
Aster foliaceus
Aster family   *Asteraceae (Compositae)*

PERENNIAL to 12″ tall; STEMS erect and purplish at the base; lower LEAVES lanceolate and petioled to 4″ long, reduced and sessile upward; FLOWER head saucer-shaped to 2″ wide with pinkish to purple rays.

ECOLOGY: Subalpine and alpine.

LOCATION: Berthoud Pass, CO 7/01 11,500´

LOOK FOR an aster with a solitary, purple flower head and bright, alternating, wavy leaves.

■ **LIFE LIST** Where _____ NUMBER _____

VIOLET ASTER

Aster lanceolatus hesperius
Aster family   *Asteraceae*

PERENNIAL to 3´ tall; STEMS wiry and branching at the top; LEAVES narrow, sessile, smooth to 4˝ long; FLOWERS 1˝ across, in clusters, petals separated, pale-blue to lavender.
ECOLOGY: Plains to montane in moisture.
LOCATION: Well Gulch, Lory S.P., Ft. Collins, CO 8/01 5500´
LOOK FOR a sparsely leafed branching stem with up to 12 flowers heads.

■ **LIFE LIST** Where _____ NUMBER _____

SMOOTH ASTER

Aster laevis
Aster family   *Asteraceae (Compositae)*

PERENNIAL to 2´ tall; STEMS succulent, reddish, erect and leafy; LEAVES lanceolate, sessile and wavy; FLOWER heads lavender to pink, 1˝ wide with up 100 narrow rays.
ECOLOGY: Plains to montane.
LOCATION: Horse Trail, Wild Basin, RMNP, CO 7/00 9000´
LOOK FOR alternate, narrow, wavy leaves that are fairly uniformly sized upward, and 3–5 flower heads

■ **LIFE LIST** Where _____ NUMBER _____

WESTERN MOUNTAIN ASTER

Aster occidentalis
Aster family   *Asteraceae (Compositae)*

PERENNIAL to 7˝ tall; STEMS erect, arising from rhizomes, in groups of 1–4; LEAVES mostly basal, spatulate, to 3˝ long; FLOWERS reddish-purple to 1˝ across with 12–20 unruly rays.
ECOLOGY: Subalpine and alpine in meadows.
LOCATION: Boreas Pass, CO 8/99 11,500´
LOOK FOR a low growing aster at high elevations.

■ **LIFE LIST** Where _____ NUMBER _____

CANADIAN THISTLE
Cirsium arvense
Aster family   *Asteraceae (Compositae)*

PERENNIAL to 4´ high; STEMS leafy, erect and branching at the top; LEAVES wavy, lobed and pine-tipped, to 6″ long; FLOWERS purple or white, thistle-like, to 1″ wide.

ECOLOGY: Plains – an invasive and persistent, introduced weed.

LOCATION: Boyd Lake S.P., Loveland, CO 6/01 5000´

LOOK FOR a plant with spine tipped leaves and thistle flowers at low elevations.

■ **LIFE LIST** Where _____ NUMBER _____

TALL FLEABANE
Erigeron elatior
Aster family   *Asteraceae (Compositae)*

PERENNIAL to 2´ tall; STEMS erect, leafy, with some top branching; LEAVES mostly on stem to 4″ long, alternate, sessile, ascending and little reduced upward; FLOWER heads to 1½″ wide, light pink to rose with many rays.

ECOLOGY: Montane to alpine in moisture.

LOCATION: Young Gulch, Poudre Canyon, CO 9/04 7000´

LOOK FOR a relatively large domed disc.

■ **LIFE LIST** Where _____ NUMBER _____

SPRUCEFIR BEEBALM
Erigeron eximius
Aster family   *Asteraceae (Compositae)*

PERENNIAL to 20″ tall; STEMS erect, leafy and top branching; LEAVES lanceloate, alternate and clasping wih little reduction upward; FLOWER heads red-purple to 1½″ across with many rays.

ECOLOGY: Subalpine in meadows.

LOCATION: 4th of July Trail, Eldora, CO 7/00 11,500´

LOOK FOR red-purple flowers, and leaves that are little reduced upward.

■ **LIFE LIST** Where _____ NUMBER _____

BEAUTIFUL FLEABANE

Erigeron formosissimus
Aster family *Asteracea (Compositae)*

PERENNIAL to 12″ tall; STEMS succulent, hairy and
leafy; LEAVES mostly basal, spatulate to 4″ long, stem
leaves lanceolate, sessile and reduced; FLOWER heads
pale purple to 1″ wide with ⅜″ discs and over 100
rays.

ECOLOGY: Montane and subalpine.

LOCATION: Mill Creek Trail, RMNP, CO 8/99 9000′

LOOK FOR numerous light purple rays, a large
yellow disc and a succulent, hairy stem.

☐ LIFE LIST Where _____ NUMBER _____

ROCKSLIDE DAISY

Erigeron leiomerus
Aster family *Asteraceae (Compositae)*

PERENNIAL to 4″ tall; SCAPES reddish above with a
solitary flower head; LEAVES spatulate to 1″ long in a
rosette; FLOWER head 1⅛″ wide with lavender or
white rays.

ECOLOGY: Subalpine and alpine.

LOCATION: Sheep Lake Trail, Medicine Bow N.F.,
WY 6/02 10,500′

LOOK FOR a tiny daisy with lavender rays.

☐ LIFE LIST Where _____ NUMBER _____

PINNATE-LEAVED DAISY

Erigeron pinnatisectus
Aster family *Asteraceae (Compositae)*

PERENNIAL to 4″ tall, in clumps; SCAPES curved
and stout; LEAVES basal, pinnatafid with narrow
lobes; FLOWER heads solitary to 1″ wide with pink
to lavender rays.

ECOLOGY: Subalpine and alpine.

LOCATION: S. Park Trail, Guanella Pass, CO 8/99
11,500′

LOOK FOR a clump of dissected leaves and several
scapes, each with a single flower.

☐ LIFE LIST Where _____ NUMBER _____

ONE-HEADED DAISY
Erigeron simplex
Aster family   *Asteraceae (Compositae)*

PERENNIAL to 10″ tall; STEMS slender, curved and
leafy with a solitary flower head; lower LEAVES
petioled, to 3″ long; stem leaves alternate, sessile and
reduced; FLOWER heads to 1″ wide with pink to
purple rays.
ECOLOGY: Subalpine to alpine in moisture.
LOCATION: Sheep Lake Trail, Medicine Bow N.F.,
   WY 7/00 11,000′
LOOK FOR a clump of asters bearing a single flower
   on each leafy stem and rays that vary in form and
   count.

■ **LIFE LIST** Where _____ NUMBER _____

GAY FEATHER
Liatris punctata
Aster family   *Asteraceae (Compositae)*

PERENNIAL to 12″ tall; STEMS erect, leafy and
unbranched; LEAVES linear to 5″ long and reduced
upward; FLOWERS purple or white in a narrow spike,
opening first at the top then progressing downward;
corollas tubular with pointed, flaring lobes and erect
styles.
ECOLOGY: Plains and foothills.
LOCATION: Well Gulch Trail, Lory S.P., Ft. Collins, CO
   8/01 5500′
LOOK FOR a spike of feathery flowers that open
   from the top of the spike on down.

■ **LIFE LIST** Where _____ NUMBER _____

TALL TANSY ASTER
Machaeranthera bigelovii
Aster family   *Asteraceae (Compositae)*

BIENNIAL or perennial to 2′ tall; STEMS upright or
leaning and disorderly branching; LEAVES linear, in-
folded, thick, curved and sharply toothed, to 2″ long;
FLOWER heads purple or pink, to 1½″ wide with
tiered, sharp-pointed bracts.
ECOLOGY: Foothills and montane.
LOCATION: Lawn Lake Trail, RMNP, CO 8/05 8500′
LOOK FOR irregular wavy leaves, and flower heads
   with prominent bracts.

■ **LIFE LIST** Where _____ NUMBER _____

FIELD ASTER

Machaeranthera canescens
Aster family   *Asteraceae (Compositae)*

ANNUAL, biennial, or perennial to 15″ tall; STEMS
reddish, slender, sticky, leafy and much branched;
LEAVES narrow to 1½″ and sticky; FLOWER heads
pink to lavender, to 1¼″ wide, terminal on short
branches.
ECOLOGY: Montane and subalpine.
LOCATION: Parvin Lake Rec. Area, Red Feathers, CO
8/01 8000′
LOOK FOR red stems that are sparsely leafed and an
abundance of flowers.

☐ **LIFE LIST** Where _____ NUMBER _____

COLORADO TANSY ASTER

Machaeranthera coloradoensis
Aster family   *Asteraceae (Compositae)*

PERENNIAL to 8″ tall; STEMS erect to prostrate;
LEAVES linear, hairy, to 2″ long and toothed;
FLOWER heads to 1½″ across with lavender to
purple rays, and pointed bracts.
ECOLOGY: Montane to alpine in rocky areas.
LOCATION: 4th of July Trail, Eldora, CO 7/00
11,500′
LOOK FOR bowl-shaped flowers and narrow,
clasping, toothed leaves.

☐ **LIFE LIST** Where _____ NUMBER _____

DRUMMOND FALSE ARABIS

Arabis (Boechera) drummondii
Mustard family   *Brassicaceae (Cruciferae)*

BIENNIAL or perennial to 20″ high; STEMS singular,
erect and leafy; LEAVES linear, upright, to 1″ long;
FLOWERS white, yellow or purple, to ¼″ wide with
4 petals; PODS wire-like to 3″ long.
ECOLOGY: Montane to subalpine in meadows.
LOCATION: Cirque Meadow Trail, Pingree Park, CO
6/01 9500′
LOOK FOR a grass-like stem with 4-petaled flowers
at the top.

☐ **LIFE LIST** Where _____ NUMBER _____

BLUE MUSTARD
Chorispora tenella
Mustard family *Brassicaceae (Cruciferae)*

ANNUAL to 15″ high; STEMS stout and fleshy;
LEAVES ascending, fleshy, wavy and toothed to 1″
long; FLOWERS pinkish-purple, to ½″ wide with 4
spreading, petal like lobes; PODS tubular spikes, to
2″ long.

ECOLOGY: Plains, in open places.

LOCATION: Well Gulch, Lory S.P., Ft. Collins, CO
4/01 5500′

LOOK FOR flower lobes that are pinched inward at
the base – a diagnostic trait.

■ LIFE LIST Where _____ NUMBER _____

PURPLE BELLFLOWER
Campanula parryi
Bellflower family *Campanulaceae*

PERENNIAL to 4″ tall; STEMS slender and sparingly
leafed; rosette LEAVES spatulate to 2″ long; stem
leaves linear, up-right and reduced; FLOWERS violet-
blue, bell-shaped, 5-lobed, terminal and solitary to
1″ across.

ECOLOGY: Montane to subalpine in moisture.

LOCATION: Ski Trail, Brainard Lake Rec. Area, Ward,
CO 8/04 10,500′

LOOK FOR a solitary, terminal, 5-lobed, bell-shaped
flower on a slender stem.

■ LIFE LIST Where _____ NUMBER _____

BELLFLOWER (HAREBELL)
Campanula rapunculoides
Bellflower family *Campanulaceae*

PERENNIAL to 3′ high, spreading by rhizomes;
STEMS upright, leafy and flowering at nodes;
LEAVES prominently veined, petioled, serrated, to
4″ long; FLOWERS purple, bell-shaped, to 1″ wide
with 5-flaring lobes.

ECOLOGY: Plains, in moisture – an aggressive weed
in gardens.

LOCATION: Watson Lake, Bellvue, CO 8/05 5000′

LOOK FOR purple, bell-shaped flowers and long,
pointed leaves.

■ LIFE LIST Where _____ NUMBER _____

VENUS LOOKING GLASS
Triodanis perfoliata
Bellflower family   *Campanulaceae*

ANNUAL to 2´ tall; STEMS leafy and branching near the base; LEAVES ovate-cordate, clasping, to 1¼˝ long; FLOWERS purple to ½˝ wide in cups formed by clasping leaf bases; corolla split to the middle forming 5, flaring, pointed lobes.
ECOLOGY: Foothills in moisture.
LOCATION: Boulder Creek Trail, Boulder, CO 6/92 5500´
LOOK FOR a leafy, terminal cluster of little purple bellflowers.

■ LIFE LIST Where _____ NUMBER _____

TEASEL
Dipsacus fullonum (sylvestris)
Teasel family   *Dipsacaceae*

BIENNIAL to 6´ tall; STEMS corrugated with thorns along ridges; LEAVES lanceolate and prickly; CONES egg-shaped with sharp bracts; FLOWERS open in a purple center band which divides with one band migrating upward and the other downward.
ECOLOGY: Plains and foothills in moisture.
LOCATION: Poudre River Trail, Ft. Collins, CO 8/04 5000´
LOOK FOR a tall spiny plant with a spiny terminal cone bearing 1–2 bands of purple flowers.

■ LIFE LIST Where _____ NUMBER _____

LEADPLANT
Amorpha fruticosa (canescens)
Pea family   *Fabaceae (Leguminosae)*

PERENNIAL to 4´ tall; STEMS erect with alternate leaves; LEAVES pinnate with ½˝ leaflets that are lanceolate, pubescent and in-folded; FLOWERS dark purple, barrel-shaped, to ¼˝ with exserted yellow anthers, in spikes to 5˝ long; PODS to ⅜˝ long.
ECOLOGY: Plains and foothills.
LOCATION: Spring Creek Trail, Ft. Collins, CO 8/02 5000´
LOOK FOR tiny, deep purple flowers crowded on a spike.

■ LIFE LIST Where _____ NUMBER _____

TUFTED MILKVETCH
Astragalus sericoleucus
Pea family *Fabaceae (Leguminosae)*

PERENNIAL to 1″ high in tufted patches; STEMS hidden; LEAVES gray, trifoliate and pubescent; leaflets lanceolate, in-folded to ¼″ long; FLOWERS ¼″ wide with a purple banner having white vertical stripes, pointed wings and a tiny keel.
ECOLOGY: Prairie, in open, sandy ground.
LOCATION: Pawnee National Grasslands, Keota, CO 5/99 5000′
LOOK FOR a mat of miniature, soft leaflets and tiny purple leguminous flowers.

☐ LIFE LIST Where _____ NUMBER _____

EARLY PURPLE VETCH
Astragalus shortianus
Pea family *Fabaceae (Leguminosae)*

PERENNIAL to 6″ high; SCAPES leaning, stout and wiry; LEAVES pinnate, with up to 10 pairs of hairy, oval, in-folded leaflets to ½″ long; FLOWERS pink to lavender in rounded clusters; PODS hairy and leathery to 1¼″ long.
ECOLOGY: Plains and foothills.
LOCATION: Eldorado Canyon S.P., Eldorado Springs, CO 5/01 6500′
LOOK FOR a rosette of pinnate leaves and global clusters crowded with lavender, leguminous flowers.

☐ LIFE LIST Where _____ NUMBER _____

PURPLE PEAVINE
Lathyrus eucosmus
Pea family *Fabaceae (Leguminosae)*

PERENNIAL vine to 20″ long; STEMS angular and climbing or trailing; LEAVES pinnate with 4–8 elliptical leaflets and a tendril; FLOWERS white, pink or purple, to ¾″ across, in clusters of 2–4 on 2″ scapes.
ECOLOGY: Plains to montane.
LOCATION: Pine Ridge Nat. Area, Ft. Collins, CO 5/05 5000′
LOOK FOR a pea vine with tendrils and 2–4 flowers on short scapes.

☐ LIFE LIST Where _____ NUMBER _____

MANYSTEM PEA
Lathyrus polymorphus
Pea family   *Fabaceae (Leguminosae)*

PERENNIAL to 8″ high, in clumps; STEMS leafy,
hairy and leaning; LEAVES pinnate with linear
leaflets to ⅜″ long; FLOWERS purple and white to
¾″ long, in cluster of 2–5 flowers.

ECOLOGY: Plains to montane in open areas.

LOCATION: Pawnee National Grasslands, Keota, CO
4/00 5000′

LOOK FOR a tiny clump of leguminous plants with
miniature linear leaflets and purple flowers with
white keels.

■ LIFE LIST Where _____ NUMBER _____

SILVER LUPINE
Lupinus argenteus
Pea family   *Fabaceae (Leguminosae)*

PERENNIAL to 2′ tall; STEMS leafy and branched;
LEAVES palmately divided into 5–9 leaflets to 3″
long; FLOWERS blue, white or purple in racemes to
8″ long; PODS hairy, 6-seeded, to 1½″ long.

ECOLOGY: Foothills to subalpine.

LOCATION: Horse Trail, Wild Basin, RMNP, CO 7/00
9000′

LOOK FOR leaves with 5–9 finger-like leaflets and a
raceme of leguminous flowers.

■ LIFE LIST Where _____ NUMBER _____

ALFALFA
Medicago sativa
Pea family   *Fabaceae (Leguminosae)*

PERENNIAL to 3′ tall; STEMS slender, flexible and
leaning; LEAVES trifoliate with elliptical leaflets,
in-folded, to 1″ long; FLOWERS purple, blue, white
or pink, to ⅛″ long, in clusters of 8–25.

ECOLOGY: Plains to montane – an escapee from
cultivation.

LOCATION: Mountain Lion Trail, Golden Gate S.P.,
Golden, CO 7/00 8500′

LOOK FOR lush, green stems, trifoliate leaves and
axillary racemes of tiny flowers.

■ LIFE LIST Where _____ NUMBER _____

SLIM SCURFPEA
Psoralidium tenuiflorum
Pea family   *Fabaceae (Leguminosae)*

PERENNIAL to 2´ tall; STEMS branching to form a shrub-like plant; LEAVES trifoliate with linear leaflets to 1˝ long; FLOWERS purple, pea-like to ¼˝ wide on slender racemes.
ECOLOGY: Foothills among rocks in open areas.
LOCATION: Arthur's Rock Trail, Lory S.P., Ft. Collins, CO 6/03 5500´
LOOK FOR an alfalfa-like plant with fewer and smaller flowers.

■ LIFE LIST   Where _____ NUMBER _____

AMERICAN VETCH
Vicia americana
Pea family   *Fabaceae (Leguminosae)*

PERENNIAL vine to 2´ long, climbing via tendrils; LEAVES pinnate terminating in a tendril, leaflets linear, in-folded to 1˝ long; FLOWERS pink, purple or white to 1˝ long, in loose racemes of 2–5 flowers; PODS flat to 2˝ long.
ECOLOGY: Plains to montane.
LOCATION: Bitterbrush Trail, Hall Ranch, Lyons, CO 5/01 6000´
LOOK FOR tendrils, linear leaflets and leguminous flowers.

■ LIFE LIST   Where _____ NUMBER _____

NORTHERN GENTIAN
Gentianella amarella
Gentian family   *Gentianaceae*

ANNUAL or biennial to 8˝ tall; STEMS erect, reddish and often hidden by numerous flowers; LEAVES mostly on stems, opposite, lanceolate and sessile, to 1˝ long; FLOWERS upright, reddish-purple, to 1˝ long with 4–5 flaring, pointed lobes.
ECOLOGY: Subalpine and alpine in moisture.
LOCATION: Copper Mt. bike trail, CO 8/91 10,000´
LOOK FOR purple or pink barrel-shaped flowers with 5 lobes. Expect wide variation in this species.

■ LIFE LIST   Where _____ NUMBER _____

LITTLE GENTIAN
Gentianella amarella acuta
Gentian family   *Gentianaceae*

ANNUAL or biennial to 10″ tall; STEMS unbranched,
slender, green or red with 3–5 nodes; LEAVES mostly
stem, opposite, sessile and lanceolate to 1½″ long;
FLOWERS reddish-purple to ½″ long with 5 flaring
lobes, single or in small terminal and axillary
clusters.
ECOLOGY: Foothills to alpine in moisture.
LOCATION: Butler Gulch, Henderson Mine Rd.,
Berthoud Pass, CO 8/99 11,000′
LOOK FOR an upright, slender, delicate Gentian.

LIFE LIST Where _____ NUMBER _____

TWISTED GENTIAN
Gentianopsis barbellata
Gentian family   *Gentianaceae*

PERENNIAL to 4″ tall; STEMS with a terminal
flower; LEAVES to 2″ long narrow-spatulate, sessile
and in a rosette; FLOWERS solitary, purple to pink
and tubular with lobes that are quite variable.
ECOLOGY: Subalpine and alpine.
LOCATION: Boreas Pass, CO 8/99 11,500′
LOOK FOR tiny plant with narrow fleshy leaves and
a solitary terminal flower with 4 lavender lobes.

LIFE LIST Where _____ NUMBER _____

FRINGED GENTIAN
Gentianopsis detonsa (thermalis)
Gentian family   *Gentianaceae*

ANNUAL or biennial to 8″ tall; STEMS erect,
unbranched, slender and green or purple; LEAVES
opposite, sessile, lanceolate, to 1″ long; FLOWERS
purple, terminal, solitary, tubular, to 2″ long with
twisted and fringed lobes.
ECOLOGY: Montane and subalpine in bogs.
LOCATION: Roadside, Medicine Bow N.F., WY 7/00
10,500′
LOOK FOR a Gentian flower with round, twisted,
fringed, or toothed lobes.

LIFE LIST Where _____ NUMBER _____

STAR GENTIAN
Swertia perennis
Gentian family   *Gentianaceae*

PERENNIAL to 12″ high; STEMS reddish, slender, erect and unbranched with well-spaced nodes; LEAVES mainly basal, spatulate, to 3″ long; stem leaves few, sessile and opposite; FLOWERS star-shaped, reddish-purple, to ¾″ wide on ¾″ stalks arising from leaf axils.
ECOLOGY: Montane to alpine in moisture.
LOCATION: Copper Mt., CO 8/92 10,500′
LOOK FOR a rosette of glossy leaves, purple stems and 5-petaled, star-like flowers.

■ **LIFE LIST** Where _____ NUMBER _____

PURPLE FRINGE
Phacelia sericea
Waterleaf family   *Hydrophyllaceae*

BIENNIAL or perennial to 12″ tall; STEMS erect or curved, stout and leafy; LEAVES alternate, pinnatifid to 4″ long with rounded lobes; FLOWERS purple or pink, with exserted stamens, giving the clusters a pincushion appearance.
ECOLOGY: Montane to alpine.
LOCATION: Trail Ridge Rd., RMNP, CO 7/05 12,000′
LOOK FOR deeply lobed, pinnatafid leaves and purple or pink pincushion-like clusters.

■ **LIFE LIST** Where _____ NUMBER _____

WILD MINT
Mentha arvensis
Mint family   *Lamiaceae (Labiatae)*

PERENNIAL to 18″ tall, in patches; STEMS erect, square, with nodes at 2″ intervals, shortened upward; LEAVES paired, aromatic, elliptical, toothed and petioled to 3″ long; FLOWERS purple or pink, with 4 lobes, to ⅛″ across, in whorled clusters at leaf nodes.
ECOLOGY: Plains to montane in moisture.
LOCATION: Avery Park, Ft. Collins, CO 8/01 5000′
LOOK FOR whorls of tiny flowers in axils of opposite leaves.

■ **LIFE LIST** Where _____ NUMBER _____

SELF-HEAL
Prunella vulgaris
Mint family   *Lamiaceae (Labiatae)*

PERENNIAL to 15″ tall; STEMS leafy and ascending, to 16″ long; LEAVES opposite, lanceolate, to 2″ long; FLOWERS to ¼″ across, purple or pink, and clustered in terminal spikes to 2″ long.

ECOLOGY: Foothills and montane.

LOCATION: FR129 off 44H Rd., Buckhorn area, Larimer Cty., CO 6/04 8000′

LOOK FOR narrow, opposite leaves and a short, terminal spike, crowded with tiny flowers.

☐ **LIFE LIST** Where _____ NUMBER _____

SKULLCAP
Scutellaria brittonii
Mint family   *Lamiaceae (Labiatae)*

PERENNIAL to 10″ high; STEMS erect, hairy and leafy; LEAVES elliptical, sessile, pubescent, opposite and upright to 1¼″ long; FLOWERS purple with white centers, tubular, to 1¼″ long and borne in leaf axils.

ECOLOGY: Plains and foothills.

LOCATION: Young Gulch, Poudre Canyon, CO 6/02 7000′

LOOK FOR a beaked flower with a patch of white on the lower lip.

☐ **LIFE LIST** Where _____ NUMBER _____

SUGAR BOWL (VASE FLOWER)
Clematis hirsutissima
Buttercup family   *Ranunculaceae*

PERENNIAL to 2′ tall; STEMS leafy, purplish and slender with a nodding terminal flower; LEAVES opposite to 6″ long, divided into many linear segments; FLOWERS bell-shaped, hanging and purple to 2″ long.

ECOLOGY: Foothills to montane.

LOCATION: Horsetooth Trail, Lory S.P., Ft. Collins, CO 5/02 5500′

LOOK FOR a large, solitary, bell-shaped flower and opposite leaves dissected into string-like segments.

☐ **LIFE LIST** Where _____ NUMBER _____

SUBALPINE LARKSPUR
Delphinium barbeyi
Buttercup family   *Ranunculaceae*

PERENNIAL to 4´ tall; STEMS smooth, erect, hollow and leafy; LEAVES palmately cleft into 3–7 narrow, pointed, leafy segments; FLOWERS purple, tubular and spurred, to 1˝ long, in racemes.

ECOLOGY: Subalpine and alpine in moisture.

LOCATION: S. Park Trail, Guanella Pass, CO 8/99 11,500´

LOOK FOR a raceme of purple, spurred flowers on a plant that has sharply lobed leaves.

■ **LIFE LIST**   Where _____ NUMBER _____

PASQUE FLOWER
Pulsatilla patens
Buttercup family   *Ranunculaceae*

PERENNIAL to 10˝ tall; STEMS with a solitary flower and a single whorl of leaves; LEAVES consists of a single pair of stem leaves divided into many linear segments; FLOWER to 2˝ across with 6 light purple sepals (petals absent); SEED head is a fuzzy ball of silky filaments.

ECOLOGY: Plains to alpine.

LOCATION: Arthur's Rock Trail, Lory S.P., Ft. Collins, CO 5/01 5500´

LOOK FOR string-like leaves, a bowl-shaped terminal flower or a seed-bearing, fuzzy ball.

■ **LIFE LIST**   Where _____ NUMBER _____

ALPINE PENSTEMON
Penstemon glaber (alpinus)
Figwort family   *Scrophulariaceae*

PERENNIAL to 2´ tall; STEMS erect, smooth and leafy; LEAVES opposite, broad, shiny and sessile to 2˝ long, reduced upward; FLOWERS blue to red-purple to ¾˝ long, in whorls subtended by reduced leaves.

ECOLOGY: Montane and subalpine slopes.

LOCATION: Bierstadt Lake Trail, RMNP, CO 7/99 9500´

LOOK FOR whorls of flowers occurring at every other node and pairs of large leaves alternating with smaller ones.

■ **LIFE LIST**   Where _____ NUMBER _____

SLENDER PENSTEMON

Penstemon gracilis
Figwort family   *Scrophulariaceae*

PERENNIAL to 12″ tall; STEMS slender, erect, green and leafy; stem LEAVES finely toothed and glossy; basal leaves elliptic and petioled, stem leaves opposite, sessile and lanceolate to 1½″ long; FLOWERS ¾″ long, lavender to blue, with 5 lobes.
ECOLOGY: Foothills on grassy slopes.
LOCATION: Shore Trail, Lory S.P., Ft. Collins, CO 6/05 5500′
LOOK FOR opposite leaves and purple-blue flowers at the upper nodes.

■ **LIFE LIST**   Where _____ NUMBER _____

RYDBERG PENSTEMON

Penstemon rydbergii
Figwort family   *Scrophulariaceae*

PERENNIAL to 12″ tall, in clumps; STEMS numerous, curved, slender and leafy; stem LEAVES opposite, narrow and reduced, basal leaves petioled to 4″ long; FLOWERS blue to reddish purple, to ½″ wide, in whorls on the upper ½ of the stem.
ECOLOGY: Foothills to subalpine.
LOCATION: Cirque Meadow, Pingree Park, CO 6/01 9500′
LOOK FOR a penstemon with narrow, in-folded, bright green leaves and ascending stems..

■ **LIFE LIST**   Where _____ NUMBER _____

AMERICAN SPEEDWELL

Veronica americana
Figwort family   *Scrophulariaceae*

PERENNIAL to 14″ high; STEMS succulent and leafy bearing many axillary branches; LEAVES opposite, sessile, lanceolate to 3″ long; FLOWERS purple, dish-shaped, to ½″ wide in terminal clusters.
ECOLOGY: Plains and foothills near water.
LOCATION: Orchard Cove, Lory S.P., Ft. Collins, CO 6/03 5500′
LOOK FOR terminal clusters of tiny purple flowers on a short, upright, succulent plant.

■ **LIFE LIST**   Where _____ NUMBER _____

WATER SPEEDWELL

Veronica anagallis-aquatica
Figwort family   *Scrophularicaeae*

BIENNIAL or perennial to 5´ tall; STEMS succulent, reddish and leafy; LEAVES opposite, sessile lanceolate, minutely toothed, to 6″ long and mostly on the stem; FLOWERS saucer shaped, purplish, to ½″ across, on racemes.

ECOLOGY: Plains in or near running water.
LOCATION: Avery Park, Ft. Collins, CO 6/02 5000´
LOOK FOR a tall plant with opposite leaves and racemes with light purple flowers.

◼ LIFE LIST Where _____ NUMBER _____

PURPLE-FLOWERED GROUND CHERRY

Quincula (Physalis) lobata
Potato family   *Solancaeae*

PERENNIAL to 4″ tall, in patches; STEMS branching, creeping and leafy; LEAVES to 3″ long, lobed and velvety; FLOWERS pink, blue or violet to ¾″ across.

ECOLOGY: Plains and foothills on sandy soil.
LOCATION: Coyote Ridge Rec. Area, Ft. Collins, 5/04 5500´
LOOK FOR lobed leaves, and a purple corolla with a white center.

◼ LIFE LIST Where _____ NUMBER _____

PROSTRATE VERVAIN

Verbena bracteata
Vervain family   *Verbenaceae*

ANNUAL, biennial, or perennial to 3″ high, in mats; STEMS branching, leafy, hairy and creeping to 18″ long; LEAVES hairy with lower leaves lobed to 1″ long and upper leaves sessile and linear to ½″ long; FLOWERS in leafy spikes, pink to purple, 5-petaled, to ⅛″ across.

ECOLOGY: Plains and foothills.
LOCATION: Horsetooth Trail, Lory S.P., Ft. Collins, CO 5/04 5500´
LOOK FOR miniature flowers and linear leaves at the tip of creeping stems.

◼ LIFE LIST Where _____ NUMBER _____

ROCKY MOUNTAIN FLORA

Flowers
of Other
Colors

ROCKY MOUNTAIN MAPLE

Acer glabrum
Maple family   *Aceraceae*

TREE to 15´ tall; TWIGS reddish-brown; LEAVES 3-lobed, sharply toothed and borne on long, slender petioles that turn red in autumn; FLOWERS green, to 1˝ across with up to 10 separated petals and stamens; FRUIT winged and doubled to form a 1˝ wide "V".

ECOLOGY: Plains to montane in moisture.

LOCATION: Arthur's Rock Trail, Lory S.P., Ft. Collins, CO 5/01 5500´

LOOK FOR a sharply toothed maple leaf and a "V"-shaped fruit.

■ **LIFE LIST** Where _____ NUMBER _____

BOX ELDER

Acer negundo
Maple family   *Aceraceae*

TREE to 20´ tall, male and female trees; LEAVES trifoliate with toothed, lanceolate leaflets; male FLOWERS are whorls of 1˝ dangling stamens, females are on a raceme; FRUIT is a double-winged "V" to 1˝ long.

ECOLOGY: Plains and foothills in moisture.

LOCATION: Legacy Park, Ft. Collins, CO 5/02 5500´

LOOK FOR trifoliate leaves and "V"-shaped fruit.

■ **LIFE LIST** Where _____ NUMBER _____

SILVER MAPLE

Acer saccharinum
Maple family   *Aceraceae*

TREE to 70´ high; trunk short, dividing and sub-dividing to produce a broad-topped tree, easily damaged by storms; LEAVES with 3 major-toothed lobes to 4˝ wide with a red, 1¾˝ petiole; FLOWERS inconspicuous; FRUIT a 2-seeded, winged "V".

ECOLOGY: Plains in moisture – an escapee from cultivation.

LOCATION: Spring Creek Trail, Ft. Collins, CO 8/02 5000´

LOOK FOR a 3-lobed maple with coarse teeth.

■ **LIFE LIST** Where _____ NUMBER _____

PROSTRATE PIGWEED
Amaranthus albus (graecizans)
Amaranth family   *Amaranthaceae*

ANNUAL to 2″ high forming mats of several square
feet; STEMS yellowish, leafy, branched and spreading;
LEAVES alternate, bristle-tipped to ⅜″ long;
FLOWERS tiny and greenish.

ECOLOGY: Plains and foothills, often in cultivated
fields.

LOCATION: Eltuck Bay, Lory S.P., Ft. Collins, CO 8/01
5500′

LOOK FOR a yellow-stemmed mat with bristle-
tipped leaves.

■ **LIFE LIST**   Where _____ NUMBER _____

ROUGH PIGWEED
Amaranthus retroflexus
Amaranth family   *Amaranthaceae*

ANNUAL to 4′ high; STEMS succulent, leafy, branched,
upright and reddish; LEAVES alternate, lanceolate and
petioled, to 3″ long; FLOWERS are tiny, green and
clustered at terminals of stems and branches.

ECOLOGY: Plains, on disturbed land, especially
cultivated fields.

LOCATION: Boyd Lake S.P., Loveland, CO 8/01
5000′

LOOK FOR a tall, succulent plant with a bristly
inflorescence.

■ **LIFE LIST**   Where _____ NUMBER _____

STAGHORN SUMAC
Rhus hirta (typhina)
Sumac family   *Anacardiaceae*

SHRUB to 12′ tall; TWIGS pubescent and reddish;
LEAVES to 20″ long with lanceolate leaflets to 5″
long; FLOWERS in upright clusters to 5″ long; FRUIT
are in red, velvety spikes.

ECOLOGY: Plains; an escapee from cultivation.

LOCATION: Ft. Collins, CO 7/02 5000′

LOOK FOR large, pinnate leaves and red velvet
spikes.

■ **LIFE LIST**   Where _____ NUMBER _____

POISON IVY

Toxicodendron rydbergii (Rhus radicans)
Sumac family   *Anacardiaceae*

SHRUB to 2´ high, growing in patches; LEAVES alternate and trifoliate with shiny, ovate leaflets that can cause a skin rash on contact; BERRIES are yellowish-white and borne in clusters.
ECOLOGY: Plains and foothills in moisture.
LOCATION: Young Gulch, Poudre River Canyon, CO 6/01 7000´
LOOK FOR a shrub that has long-stemmed, glossy, trifoliate leaves and stay clear.

☐ **LIFE LIST** Where _____ NUMBER _____

SILVERLEAF POVERTYWEED

Ambrosia tomentosa (Franseria discolor)
Aster family   *Asteraceae (Compositae)*

PERENNIAL to 14˝ tall in patches; STEMS erect, alternate leafed, with racemes of globular flower heads; LEAVES pinnatifid, silvery beneath with irregular lobes; FLOWERS heads gray and nodding to ¼˝ wide.
ECOLOGY: Plains to montane – a persistent weed in cultivated fields.
LOCATION: Boyd Lake S.P., Loveland, CO 5/03 5000´
LOOK FOR cut, gray-green leaves.

☐ **LIFE LIST** Where _____ NUMBER _____

ARCTIC SAGE

Artemisia arctica
Aster family   *Asteraceae (Compositae)*

PERENNIAL to 16˝ tall; STEMS form a thick, branched tap root; LEAVES mainly basal with dense, silky pubescent, blades cut into linear segments; FLOWER heads nodding on an elongated, narrow raceme.
ECOLOGY: Subalpine and alpine.
LOCATION: Herman Gulch Trail, Bakerville, CO 8/00 11,000´
LOOK FOR a slender raceme with nodding, button-like, solitary flower heads on upright, axillary stems.

☐ **LIFE LIST** Where _____ NUMBER _____

WILD TARRAGON
Artemisia (Oligosporus) dracunculus
Aster family   *Asteraceae (Compositae)*

PERENNIAL to 2´ high; STEMS slender, erect, leafy, unbranched and reddish; LEAVES linear and drooping to 1″ long; FLOWERS inconspicuous, but soft, gray-green, globular leaf clusters occur late in the season.
ECOLOGY: Plains to montane in moisture.
LOCATION: Eltuck Bay, Lory S.P., Ft. Collins, CO 8/01 5500´
LOOK FOR stems that are red and unbranched, supporting little balls of gray leaves.

■ LIFE LIST Where _____ NUMBER _____

SILVER SAGEBRUSH
Artemisia ludoviciana
Aster family   *Asteraceae (Compositae)*

PERENNIAL to 3´ tall; STEMS leafy and yellowish at maturity; LEAVES silvery, pubescent, alternate, to 2″ long with pointed lobes at the apex; FLOWERS greenish and borne in terminal spikes.
ECOLOGY: Plains and foothills.
LOCATION: Coyote Ridge Rec. Area, Ft. Collins, CO 7/01 5500´
LOOK FOR a silvery plant, and leaves with sharp apex lobes.

■ LIFE LIST Where _____ NUMBER _____

MOUNTAIN SAGEBRUSH
Artemisia tridentata
Aster family   *Asteraceae (Compositae)*

SHRUB to 5´ tall; STEMS woody and branching; LEAVES silvery, pubescent, to 1½″ long with 3, rounded lobes at the tip; FLOWERS appear as tiny green balls.
ECOLOGY: Plains to montane.
LOCATION: Dowdy Lake Rec. Area, Red Feathers, CO 7/01 8000´
LOOK FOR triangular leaves with 3 apex lobes.

■ LIFE LIST Where _____ NUMBER _____

TALL MARSH ELDER
Iva xanthifolia
Aster family   *Asteraceae (Compositae)*

ANNUAL to 8´ tall; STEMS upright with opposite leaves; LEAVES toothed to 6˝ wide with 6˝ petioles; FLOWERS tiny, round balls, male and female, crowded on spikes.

ECOLOGY: Plains and foothills in moisture.

LOCATION: Boyd Lake S.P., Loveland, CO 8/01 5000´

LOOK FOR large, ovate leaves with irregular serration.

■ **LIFE LIST**   Where _____ NUMBER _____

COMMON COCKLEBUR
Xanthium strumarium
Aster family   *Asteraceae (Compositae)*

ANNUAL to 4´ tall; STEMS erect, branched, spotted and rough; LEAVES alternate, petioled, ovate and lobed; FLOWERS inconspicuous; FRUIT are oval burs to 1˝ long that readily adhere to fur and cloth.

ECOLOGY: Plains and foothills in moisture.

LOCATION: Boyd Lake S.P., Loveland, CO 8/01 5000´

LOOK FOR the big leaves and burs with hooks that stick like "Velcro."

■ **LIFE LIST**   Where _____ NUMBER _____

ROCKY MOUNTAIN ALDER
Alnus incana
Birch family   *Betulaceae*

TREE to 18´ tall with scaly gray to reddish bark; LEAVES oval, toothed and prominently veined to 3˝ long; male CATKINS to ⅜˝ and female CONES to ¾˝ long on separate trees.

ECOLOGY: Foothills to subalpine in moisture.

LOCATION: Young Gulch, Poudre Canyon, CO 6/01 7000´

LOOK FOR oval, toothed leaves with prominent herringbone venation.

■ **LIFE LIST**   Where _____ NUMBER _____

DWARF BIRCH
Betula nana (glandulosa)
Birch family *Betulaceae*

SHRUB to 4´ tall; STEMS reddish near the tips, turning to mahogany below with prominent lenticles; LEAVES toothed, nearly round, glossy and leathery to ¾″ wide; CATKINS ½″ long with sexes on different trees.
ECOLOGY: Montane to alpine in moisture.
LOCATION: Mitchell Lake Trail, Brainard Lake Rec. Area, Ward, CO 7/00 11,000´
LOOK FOR round, glossy, serrated leaves and red twigs.

☐ **LIFE LIST** Where _____ NUMBER _____

RIVER BIRCH
Betula occidentalis (fontinalis)
Birch family *Betulaceae*

TREE to 20´ tall; STEMS many, mahogany color with white lenticels; LEAVES ovate, toothed and glossy with blades 1¾″ and ¾″ petioles; male CATKINS 2″ long and females oval and 1″ long on separate trees.
ECOLOGY: Foothills to subalpine in moisture.
LOCATION: Lion Gulch, Roosevelt N.F., US 36, CO 6/00 7500´
LOOK FOR thin, oval, serrated leaves and slender branch terminals.

☐ **LIFE LIST** Where _____ NUMBER _____

DRUMMOND CAMPION
Silene (Lychnis) drummondii
Pink family *Caryophyllaceae*

PERENNIAL to 16″ tall; STEMS green, upright, slender and leafy; basal LEAVES petioled and stem leaves narrow, up-right, paired, sessile and reduced; FLOWERS erect, with flower parts retained within the calyx tube.
ECOLOGY: Subalpine and alpine.
LOCATION: Sheep Lake Trail, Medicine Bow N.F., WY 8/99 10,500´
LOOK FOR racemes bearing tubular calyxes that retain all flower parts inside.

☐ **LIFE LIST** Where _____ NUMBER _____

LAMB'S QUARTER (PIGWEED)
Chenopodium album
Goosefoot family   *Chenopodaceae*

ANNUAL to 4´ tall; STEMS erect, leafy and green; LEAVES lanceolate to 4″ long, often white beneath; FLOWERS bractless, in spikes.

ECOLOGY: Plains to montane, edible – a common weed in cultivated fields.

LOCATION: Lion Gulch, Roosevelt N.F., US 36, CO 7/01 7500´

LOOK FOR little, green, berry-like flowers on axillary spikes. Leaves may be opposite and alternate on the same plant.

■ LIFE LIST Where _____ NUMBER _____

JERUSALEM OAK
Chenopodium botrys
Goosefoot family   *Chenopodiaceae*

ANNUAL to 30″ tall; STEMS succulent, upright and leafy; LEAVES fleshy, lobed, to 2½″ long; FLOWERS green and ball-like, to ⅛″ in racemes to 12″ long.

ECOLOGY: Plains and foothills in drying mud.

LOCATION: Orchard Cove, Lory S.P., Ft. Collins, CO 8/02 5500´

LOOK FOR plants with bright green racemes in open, wet sites.

■ LIFE LIST Where _____ NUMBER _____

OAK-LEAVED GOOSEFOOT
Chenopodium glaucum
Goosefoot family   *Chenopodiaceae*

ANNUAL, sprawling plant to 20″ high; STEMS upright to horizontal, succulent, branched, leafy and green to red; LEAVES to 1″ long and lanceolate with blunt lobes; FLOWERS look like gray berries, in axillary spikes.

ECOLOGY: Plains and foothills in drying mud, late in the season.

LOCATION: Eltuck Bay, Lory S.P., Ft. Collins, CO 8/01 5500´

LOOK FOR a sprawling plant with flowers resembling clusters of tiny, gray berries.

■ LIFE LIST Where _____ NUMBER _____

NARROWLEAF GOOSEFOOT
Chenopodium leptophyllum
Goosefoot family *Chenopodiaceae*

ANNUAL to 3´ tall; STEMS light green to yellowish, branching and leafy; LEAVES dark green above, pale green beneath, narrow lanceolate to 1″long; FLOWERS round to ⅛″, gray-green and glaucous.
ECOLOGY: Foothills in dry areas.
LOCATION: Arthur's Rock Trail, Lory S.P., Ft. Collins, CO 7/04 5500´
LOOK FOR yellowish stems with ascending, narrow leaves and clusters of flowers resembling little, gray berries.

■ **LIFE LIST** Where _____ NUMBER _____

RED GOOSEFOOT
Chenopodium rubrum
Goosefoot family *Chenopodiaceae*

ANNUAL to 4´ high; STEMS upright, succulent, stout and leafy; LEAVES sessile, lanceolate and irregularly lobed; FLOWERS green berry-like balls on leafy axillary spikes.
ECOLOGY: Plains in wet areas, often associated with cattails.
LOCATION: Prospect Ponds, Ft. Collins, CO 8/02 5000´
LOOK FOR unique, sharp-lobed leaves and leafy, axillary, flowering spikes.

■ **LIFE LIST** Where _____ NUMBER _____

BURNING BUSH
Kochia scoparia
Goosefoot family *Chenopodaceae*

ANNUAL to 3´ tall; STEMS branching to produce a cone-shape, shrub-like plant; LEAVES sparse and narrow to 3″ long; FLOWERS resemble little green balls crowded in spikes.
ECOLOGY: Plains and foothills – adapted to wet or dry conditions – very common.
LOCATION: Rolland Moore Park, Ft. Collins, CO 8/02 5000´
LOOK FOR a bushy plant with light green foliage that turns red in fall. Seed distributed by tumbling across plains.

■ **LIFE LIST** Where _____ NUMBER _____

WINTER FAT
Krascheninnikovia (Ceratoides) lanata
Goosefoot family *Chenopodiaceae*

PERENNIAL to 2´ high; STEMS branched and
woolly; LEAVES linear and upward curved to 1″ long;
FLOWERS in axillary clusters on terminal spikes,
hidden by woolly fuzz.

ECOLOGY: Foothills on dry, open slopes.

LOCATION: Coyote Ridge Rec. Area, Ft. Collins, CO
9/04 5500´

LOOK FOR a small, dense, shrub-like plant with
woolly stems.

■ **LIFE LIST** Where _____ NUMBER _____

RUSSIAN THISTLE (TUMBLEWEED)
Salsola kali (iberica)
Goosefoot family *Chenopodiaceae*

ANNUAL to 3´ tall; STEMS usually red or purple
striped; early LEAVES alternate, soft and string-like,
late leaves scale-like and tipped with a stiff spine;
FLOWERS inconspicuous; SEED dispersed as the
wind rolls the plant across the prairie.

ECOLOGY: Plains and foothills on over-grazed or
disturbed land.

LOCATION: S. Platte River Trail, Denver, CO 1/01
5000´

LOOK FOR a round, free-rolling plant.

■ **LIFE LIST** Where _____ NUMBER _____

COMMON JUNIPER
Juniperus communis
Cypress family *Cupressaceae*

SHRUB to 5´ tall; LEAVES linear, to ½″ and sharply
pointed; FLOWERS on separate plants, males have
tiny brown cones with overlapping scales, females
produce powdery blue, ¼″ berries, used to flavor gin.
Over 18 varieties are recognized, some being trees.

ECOLOGY: Plains to montane in dry areas.

LOCATION: Arthur's Rock Trail, Lory S.P., Ft. Collins,
CO 5/05 5500´

LOOK FOR a cascading, woody, evergreen shrub
with sharp, awl-like leaves.

■ **LIFE LIST** Where _____ NUMBER _____

ROCKY MOUNTAIN JUNIPER
Juniperus scopulorum
Cypress family   *Cupressaceae*

TREE to 30´ tall; LEAVES scale-like, green and often
waxy; male FLOWERS on cones with brown, over-
lapping scales, females produce powdery-blue
BERRIES on separate trees.
ECOLOGY: Plains and foothills in dry open areas,
usually on southern slopes.
LOCATION: Shadow Canyon Trail, Eldorado Canyon
S.P., Eldorado Springs, CO 6/00 6500´
LOOK FOR a round, cone-shaped, evergreen tree.

■ **LIFE LIST** Where _____ NUMBER _____

CANADIAN BUFFALOBERRY
Shepherdia canadensis
Oleaster family   *Elaeagnaceae*

SHRUB to 7´ tall; TWIGS with dark brown, smooth
bark; LEAVES ovate, dark green, leathery to 2½˝ long
and rolled down at the margins; FLOWERS green and
inconspicuous; FRUIT a bright red egg-shaped berry
to ⅜˝ long.
ECOLOGY: Plains to subalpine in moisture.
LOCATION: Herman Gulch Trail, Bakerville, CO 8/00
11,000´
LOOK FOR rolled down leaf margins and red, egg-
shaped berries.

■ **LIFE LIST** Where _____ NUMBER _____

TOOTHED SPURGE
Euphorbia dentata
Spurge family   *Euphorbiaceae*

ANNUAL to 1´ tall; STEMS red, with milky sap,
sparingly branched and leafed; LEAVES narrow and
slightly toothed with most of them whorled beneath
terminal flower clusters; FLOWERS clustered at
terminals in Poinsettia fashion.
ECOLOGY: Plains in moist, open areas.
LOCATION: Boyd Lake S.P., Loveland, CO 8/01
5000´
LOOK FOR a red stemmed plant with milky sap,
resembling a Poinsettia.

■ **LIFE LIST** Where _____ NUMBER _____

GAMBLE OAK

Quercus gambelii
Beech family   *Fagaceae*

SHRUB to 15´ tall; LEAVES alternate, ovate, with rounded lobes extending halfway to the midrib, glossy above and pubescent beneath; NUT is half enclosed by the cap.

ECOLOGY: Plains to montane on dry slopes.

LOCATION: Roxborough S.P., Littleton, CO 9/99 6000´

LOOK FOR leaves with rounded lobes that extend halfway to the midrib and a nut that is half enclosed by its cap.

■ **LIFE LIST** Where _____ NUMBER _____

GREEN GENTIAN (MONUMENT PLANT)

Frasera speciosa
Gentian family   *Gentianaceae*

PERENNIAL to 5´ tall; STEMS stiff and unbranched; LEAVES sessile, narrow and downward curved, to 18" long, reduced upward; FLOWERS clustered at nodes, 4-petaled, greenish-white with brown spots.

ECOLOGY: Foothills to subalpine in moisture.

LOCATION: Mesa Trail, Eldorado Canyon S.P., Eldorado Springs, CO 6/99 6500´

LOOK FOR an erect plant with lily-like leaves and whorls of greenish-white flowers.

■ **LIFE LIST** Where _____ NUMBER _____

PRICKLY CURRANT

Ribes lacustre
Goooseberry family   *Grossulariaceae*

SHRUB to 2´ tall, sprawling, in patches; STEMS densely covered with prickly spines, especially near the growing tip; LEAVES lobed, glossy and petioled, to 1" wide; FLOWERS greenish or purple in drooping racemes with up to 20 blooms; FRUIT purple and bristly.

ECOLOGY: Montane to alpine.

LOCATION: Mirror Lake, Medicine Bow N.F., WY 8/00 10,500´

LOOK FOR reddish twigs crowded with thorns.

■ **LIFE LIST** Where _____ NUMBER _____

RED PRICKLY CURRANT
Ribes montigenum
Gooseberry family   *Grossulariaceae*

SHRUB to 2´ tall with spreading, spiny branches; LEAVES cleft into 3 or more toothed lobes with spines located at the base of leaves; FLOWERS ⅛″ across with white, reddish or green petals; BERRIES red and bristly to ⅜″.

ECOLOGY: Montane to alpine.

LOCATION: Sheep Lake Trail, Medicine Bow N.F., WY 7/00 10,500´

LOOK FOR reddish-brown stems with yellow tips and spines at the base of leaves.

■ **LIFE LIST** Where _____ NUMBER _____

COMMON DUCKWEED
Lemna minor
Duckweed family   *Lemnaceae*

PERENNIAL to ½″ wide, floating on surface of quiet water; LEAVES (fronds) to ⅛″ across, usually in threes; ROOTS to 2″ long, trailing in the water.

ECOLOGY: Free floating in quiet, stagnant water.

LOCATION: Swamp along Poudre River Trail, Ft. Collins, CO 7/03 5000´

LOOK FOR a green scum on quiet water and check to see if it's Duckweed.

■ **LIFE LIST** Where _____ NUMBER _____

WING-FRUITED SAND VERBENA
Tripterocalyx micranthus
Four o'clock family   *Nyctaginaceae*

ANNUAL to 2´ tall; STEMS branching and sprawling; LEAVES leathery, lanceolate to 3″ long; FLOWERS enfolded in a bract that opens into a papery disc to ¾″ across.

ECOLOGY: Plains, on open, dry areas.

LOCATION: Colfax and Kipling, Wheat Ridge, CO 7/02 5000´

LOOK FOR dark green leaves, many branches and papery bracts.

■ **LIFE LIST** Where _____ NUMBER _____

GREEN ASH
Fraxinus pennsylvanica
Olive family   *Oleraceae*

TREE to 60´ tall; bark gray and becoming rough with age; LEAVES to 12″ long with up to 9 elliptical leaflets to 1¼″ long; FLOWERS inconspicuous; SEED a single winged samara to 2″ long, borne on female trees.
ECOLOGY: Plains and foothills – native and widely used in landscapes.
LOCATION: Prospect Ponds, Ft. Collins, CO 8/02 5000´
LOOK FOR a tree with 5–9 leaflets and a single winged seed.

☐ **LIFE LIST** Where _____ NUMBER _____

SUBALPINE FIR
Abies lasiocarpa
Pine family   *Pinaceae*

TREE to 80´ tall; BRANCHLETS gray; needles 1½″ long, pale, bluish-green with white stripes and upward curved; female CONES to 4″ long, male cones, clustered and tiny; both on same tree, females high and males low.
ECOLOGY: Montane to subalpine on N slopes.
LOCATION: Brainard Lake Rec. Area, Ward, CO 6/02 10,500´
LOOK FOR curved needles with white stripes.

☐ **LIFE LIST** Where _____ NUMBER _____

KRUMMHOLZ (SUBALPINE FIR)
Abies lasiocarpa
Pine family   *Pinaceae*

SHRUB, when grown under alpine conditions, *A. lasiocarpa* becomes dwarfed, to 5´ or less. The NEEDLES are proportionally dwarfed and curved. In this form it is known as Krummholz, a name applied to all dwarfed alpine evergreens.
ECOLOGY: Alpine.
LOCATION: Crown Pt., Brown Lake Trail, Larimer Cty., CO 7/04 11,500´
LOOK FOR an evergreen shrub on tundra, with up-turned, striped needles to ½″ long.

☐ **LIFE LIST** Where _____ NUMBER _____

ENGELMANN SPRUCE

Picea engelmannii
Pine family *Pinaceae*

TREE to 100´ tall; NEEDLES bluish-green, 4-angled and slightly flattened, to 1˝ long; CONES 2½˝ long with papery scales.

ECOLOGY: Montane to subalpine on N slopes and as Krummholz (stunted shrubbery) at timberline.

LOCATION: Libby Flats, Medicine Bow N.F., WY 8/00 10,500´

LOOK FOR short, straight, slightly flattened needles and stately trees usually occurring in pure stands.

☐ LIFE LIST Where _____ NUMBER _____

COLORADO BLUE SPRUCE

Picea pungens
Pine family *Pinaceae*

TREE to 100´ tall; BRANCHLETS yellow-brown; NEEDLES 4-angled, to 1¼˝ long, radiating around the branchlet, stiff, sharp-pointed and usually bluish green; CONES to 4˝ long with papery scales.

ECOLOGY: Foothills and montane in moisture – generally solitary, never in pure stands.

LOCATION: Three Mile Creek Trail, Grant, CO 8/00 9500´

LOOK FOR needles sharp enough to penetrate skin and a tree that usually stands alone.

☐ LIFE LIST Where _____ NUMBER _____

BRISTLECONE PINE

Pinus aristata
Pine family *Pinaceae*

TREE to 40´ tall, but may be prostrate and shrubby; NEEDLES in bundles of 5, to 2˝ long, curved, with sticky, white resin spots; CONES to 3˝ long with woody scales that are upturned and pointed at the tips.

ECOLOGY: Montane and subalpine – specimens up to 2000 years old.

LOCATION: Three Mile Creek Trail, Grant, CO 8/99 9500´

LOOK FOR bottlebrush terminals and white resin spots on the needles.

☐ LIFE LIST Where _____ NUMBER _____

LODGEPOLE PINE
Pinus contorta
Pine family   *Pinaceae*

TREE to 100´ tall, but much shorter in the Rocky
  Mts.; NEEDLES in bundles of 2, stiff and twisted, to
  2½˝ long; CONES oval and woody to 2˝ long.
ECOLOGY: Foothills to subalpine in burned areas
  and dry slopes.
LOCATION: Lost Lake Trail, Eldora, CO 9/99 9000´
LOOK FOR twisted needles.

■ **LIFE LIST** Where _____ NUMBER _____

LIMBER PINE
Pinus flexilis
Pine family   *Pinaceae*

TREE to 25´ tall, usually with multiple trunks (not a
  good timber tree); NEEDLES in bundles (fascicles) of
  5, stiff, yellow-green to 3˝ long; CONES oval, 3–5˝
  long and glossy.
ECOLOGY: Foothills to subalpine on rocky slopes
  and windy ridges.
LOCATION: Mt. Evans, CO 6/05 13,000´
LOOK FOR 5 needles per bundle without white resin
  spots (as Bristlecone Pine has).

■ **LIFE LIST** Where _____ NUMBER _____

PONDEROSA PINE
Pinus ponderosa
Pine family   *Pinaceae*

TREE to 100´ but much shorter in the Rockies; BARK
  reddish; NEEDLES dark green, in bundles of 2 and 3
  and from 5–10˝ long; CONES oval and woody from
  3–8˝ long.
ECOLOGY: Foothills to montane on S slopes.
LOCATION: Bitterbrush Trail, Hall Ranch, Lyons, CO
  5/02 6000´
LOOK AT needle bundles, some will have 2 needles
  and others will have 3. Only Ponderosa pine has this
  combination.

■ **LIFE LIST** Where _____ NUMBER _____

DOUGLAS FIR
Pseudotsuga menziesii
Pine family   *Pinaceae*

TREE to 200´ but much shorter in the Rockies;
NEEDLES flat with a round tip, to 1˝ long; CONES to
4½˝ long, with reflexed bracts having 3 pointed
lobes. A major timber tree in Oregon.
ECOLOGY: Foothills to subalpine in moisture.
LOCATION: Young Gulch, Poudre Canyon, CO 5/02
7000´
LOOK FOR cones with 3-lobed bracts. These are
diagnostic.

■ LIFE LIST Where _____ NUMBER _____

COMMON PLANTAIN
Plantago major
Plantain family   *Plantaginaceae*

PERENNIAL to 14˝ tall; STEMS inconspicuous;
SCAPES curves with upper ⅓ to ½ a flower-bearing
spike; LEAVES broad-lanceolate to 10˝ long;
FLOWERS greenish, berry-like balls to ⅛˝, turning
brown at maturity.
ECOLOGY: Plains in damp places.
LOCATION: Eltuck Bay, Lory S.P., Ft. Collins, CO 8/01
5500´
LOOK FOR a broad-leafed rosette, and curved scapes
with 6˝ spikes.

■ LIFE LIST Where _____ NUMBER _____

TWEEDY PLANTAIN
Plantago tweedyi
Plantain family   *Plantaginaceae*

PERENNIAL to 10˝ tall; STEMS inconspicuous;
SCAPES upright, leafless, with 2˝ spikes; LEAVES
lanceolate to 5˝ long, parallel veined and basal;
FLOWERS inconspicuous; FRUIT brown and
seed-like.
ECOLOGY: Montane and subalpine.
LOCATIONS: Roadside, Medicine Bow N.F., WY
7/00 10,500´
LOOK FOR wiry scapes with brown racemes and
upright, narrow leaves.

■ LIFE LIST Where _____ NUMBER _____

ALPINE SORREL

Oxyria digyna
Buckwheat family   *Polygonaceae*

PERENNIAL to 10″ tall; LEAVES basal, palmately veined with long petioles; FLOWERS small, greenish and in racemes; FRUIT peripherally winged with reddish margins.

ECOLOGY: Subalpine and alpine in wet shady places.

LOCATION: Berthoud Pass, CO 7/01 11,500′

LOOK FOR kidney-shaped leaves with radial venation and scapes with racemes of green flowers.

■ **LIFE LIST** Where _____ NUMBER _____

WESTERN DOCK

Rumex aquaticus (occidentalis)
Buckwheat family   *Polygonaceae*

PERENNIAL to 18″ tall; STEMS erect with upper half given to a panicle; LEAVES lanceolate, to 10″ long, basal, erect and wavy; FLOWERS green to tan with papery, winged sepals, densely packed in tight panicles.

ECOLOGY: Montane and subalpine near moving water.

LOCATION: Medicine Bow N.F., WY 7/02 10,500′

LOOK FOR upright, narrow, wavy leaves and papery, winged fruit.

■ **LIFE LIST** Where _____ NUMBER _____

CURLY DOCK

Rumex crispus
Buckwheat family   *Polygonaceae*

PERENNIAL to 5′ tall; STEMS erect, leafy, smooth and branched; LEAVES lanceolate with wavy margins to 12″ long; FLOWERS small and crowded in long clusters; SEEDS are winged.

ECOLOGY: Plains and foothills in moisture.

LOCATION: Jefferson County Fairgrounds, CO 5/02 6500′

LOOK FOR wavy leaf margins and winged seed (fruit).

■ **LIFE LIST** Where _____ NUMBER _____

WILLOW DOCK
Rumex salicifolius
Buckwheat family   *Polygonaceae*

PERENNIAL to 2´ tall; STEMS ascending or erect, leafy, with well developed axillary shoots; LEAVES narrow-lanceolate, and sessile to 4˝ long; FLOWERS greenish to pink, with winged, papery sepals, densely packed onto a raceme to 5˝ long.
ECOLOGY: Foothills and montane.
LOCATION: Berthoud Pass, CO 7/01 11,500´
LOOK FOR narrow, willow-like leaves.

LIFE LIST Where _____ NUMBER _____

KNOTTY PONDWEED
Potamogeton nodosus
Pondweed family   *Potamogetonaceae*

PERENNIAL pond weed of shallow water; STEMS succulent, white and branching; submerged LEAVES lanceolate, aerial leaves spatulate, paired and shifting 90 degrees at each node; FLOWERS green and inconspicuous.
ECOLOGY: Plains in slow-moving water.
LOCATIONS: Spring Creek, Rolland Moore Park, Ft. Collins, CO 8/02 5000´
LOOK FOR alternating pairs of leaves on an anchored plant in shallow, moving water.

LIFE LIST Where _____ NUMBER _____

GREEN FLOWERED WINTERGREEN
Pyrola chlorantha
Wintergreen family   *Pyrolaceae*

PERENNIAL to 8˝ tall; SCAPES red, bearing greenish, ball-like flowers; LEAVES round, leathery, basal, to 1½˝ wide; FLOWERS green, round to ½˝, borne on reddish racemes.
ECOLOGY: Montane and subalpine in moist, shady places.
LOCATION: Bierstadt Lake Trail, RMNP, CO 7/99 9500´
LOOK FOR a rosette of round leaves and a red scape with several, round, greenish flowers.

LIFE LIST Where _____ NUMBER _____

FENDLER MEADOW RUE
Thalictrum fendleri
Buttercup family *Ranunculaceae*

PERENNIAL to 3´ tall; STEMS erect, slender and leafy; LEAVES trifoliate with circular leaflets having rounded lobes; FLOWERS apetalous with pointed sepals; sexes on separate plants.
ECOLOGY: Montane and subalpine in shade.
LOCATION: Lost Lake Trail, Eldora, CO 6/02 9000´
LOOK FOR a delicate, thin-leafed plant, the male will have yellow anthers and the female will have only small, green flowers.

■ LIFE LIST Where _____ NUMBER _____

FEW FLOWERED MEADOW RUE
Thalictrum sparsiflorum
Buttercup family *Ranunculaceae*

PERENNIAL to 30˝ high; STEMS slender, branched and re-branched; LEAVES trifoliate with irregular, round lobes; FLOWERS few, perfect, with green sepals and no petals.
ECOLOGY: Foothills and montane in shade.
LOCATION: Lion Gulch, Roosevelt N.F., US 36, CO 7/01 7500´
LOOK FOR slender stems, flat trifoliate leaves, and perfect (bi-sexual) flowers.

■ LIFE LIST Where _____ NUMBER _____

NARROWLEAF COTTONWOOD
Populus angustifolia
Willow family *Salicaceae*

TREE to 50´ tall; TWIGS light gray with orange at the nodes; LEAVES narrow, to 3˝ long with a ½˝ petiole and pale under; female CATKINS to 4˝ long, male catkins to ½˝ long, found on separate trees.
ECOLOGY: Plains to montane near water.
LOCATION: Prospect Ponds Rec. Area, Ft. Collins, CO 5/04 5000´
LOOK FOR an undivided trunk and a form similar to Aspen to avoid confusing it with Peachleaf Willow (see opposite page).

■ LIFE LIST Where _____ NUMBER _____

COTTONWOOD

Populus deltoides (sargentii)
Willow family   *Salicaceae*

TREE to 80´ tall, with male and female trees; LEAVES triangular with a straight-line base to 5″ wide; male CATKINS to 2″ long and female catkins to 8″ long composed of 10–30 pods that release seed on tiny, cottony clouds.

ECOLOGY: Plains and foothills in moisture.
LOCATION: Prospect Ponds Rec. Area, Ft. Collins, CO 5/04 5000´
LOOK FOR large, triangular leaves that are toothed on the sides but not on the bottom.

■ **LIFE LIST** Where _____ NUMBER _____

ASPEN

Populus tremuloides
Willow family   *Salicaceae*

TREE to 70´ tall with smooth, whitish bark, and famous for its display of golden foliage in the fall; LEAVES rounded to 1½″ wide, finely toothed, with flat, 1″ petioles; male and female CATKINS are on separate trees.

ECOLOGY: Montane to subalpine in moisture.
LOCATION: Mill Creek Trail, RMNP, CO 6/01 9000´
LOOK FOR a grove of columnar trees with leaves that twist and dance in the wind (due to the flat petiole) and turn golden in fall.

■ **LIFE LIST** Where _____ NUMBER _____

PEACHLEAF WILLOW

Salix amygdaloides
Willow family   *Salicaceae*

TREE to 40´ tall with separate male and female trees; TWIGS yellow, tan or reddish; LEAVES narrow-lanceolate, serrated and shiny to 6″ long.

ECOLOGY: Plains to montane in moisture.
LOCATION: Spring Creek Trail, Ft. Collins, CO 8/02 5000´
LOOK FOR narrow, peach-like leaves that are over 3″ long; shorter ones are likely to be from a Narrowleaf Cottonwood.

■ **LIFE LIST** Where _____ NUMBER _____

ARCTIC WILLOW

Salix arctica
Willow family   *Salicaceae*

SHRUB to 6″ high forming mats; STEMS reddish and creeping; LEAVES elliptical to 1″ long, dark green above and pale beneath; male CATKINS ½″ and females 1″ long, found on separate plants.
ECOLOGY: Subalpine and alpine in moisture.
LOCATION: Loveland Pass, CO 8/00 12,000′
LOOK FOR a low growing shrub with reddish twigs, little leaves and male or female catkins.

█ **LIFE LIST** Where _____ NUMBER _____

WEEPING WILLOW

Salix babylonica
Willow family   *Salicaceae*

TREE to 50′ high; TRUNKS usually multiple; BRANCHES extending horizontally; BRANCHLETS hanging to 10′ long with yellow tips; LEAVES narrow-lanceolate to 4½″ long and minutely toothed; female CATKINS to 2″ and males to 1″ long on separate trees.
ECOLOGY: Plains; an escapee from cultivation – of European origin.
LOCATION: Spring Creek Trail, Ft. Collins, CO 8/02 5000′
LOOK FOR long, hanging branchlets.

█ **LIFE LIST** Where _____ NUMBER _____

SHORT FRUITED WILLOW

Salix brachycarpa
Willow family   *Salicaceae*

SHRUB to 5′ high, forming thickets; LEAVES bright green turning bluish with age, to 1½″ long; female CATKINS to ¾″ and males to ½″ long; sexes on different plants.
ECOLOGY: Foothills to alpine in moisture.
LOCATION: Cirque Meadow, Pingree Park, CO 6/01 9500′
LOOK FOR crowded, pubescent leaves at the tips of branches.

█ **LIFE LIST** Where _____ NUMBER _____

BLUE WILLOW

Salix drummondiana
Willow family *Salicaceae*

SHRUB to 9´ tall; TWIGS chalky white near terminals going to smooth, brown bark downward; LEAVES narrow, tapered at both ends, pale beneath, to 2″ long; both male and female CATKINS are ½″ long and produced on separate shrubs.
ECOLOGY: Foothills to subalpine.
LOCATION: Mt. Margaret, Red Feathers, CO 6/02 8000´
LOOK FOR chalky, white branch tips.

☐ **LIFE LIST** Where _____ NUMBER _____

PETIOLE COLLARED WILLOW

Salix eriocephala
Willow family *Salicaceae*

SHRUB to 6´ tall; TWIGS slender, yellow-green and leafy; LEAVES narrow-lanceolate and acuminate to 6″ long, with a leafy collar around the petiole base.
ECOLOGY: Plains and foothills near water.
LOCATION: Orchard Cove, Lory S.P., Ft. Collins, CO 8/02 5500´
LOOK FOR a leafy collar at the base of petioles.

☐ **LIFE LIST** Where _____ NUMBER _____

SANDBAR WILLOW

Salix exigua
Willow family *Salicaceae*

SHRUB to 12´ tall growing in thickets along shores; STEMS whitish and pubescent at tips; LEAVES linear, pubescent on both sides, minutely toothed to 3″ long; CATKINS, both male and female, 1″ long.
ECOLOGY: Plains and foothills along shores of ponds and rivers.
LOCATION: Dowdy Lake, Red Feathers, CO 7/01 8000´
LOOK FOR thickets of 10´ shrubs, with very narrow leaves.

☐ **LIFE LIST** Where _____ NUMBER _____

CRACK WILLOW
Salix fragilis
Willow family *Salicaceae*

SHRUB to 15´ tall forming thickets; TWIGS greenish maturing to gray; LEAVES narrow-elliptical to 2″ long; CATKINS – female to 4″ long, males to 2″ long.
ECOLOGY: Plains and foothills.
LOCATION: Dixon Reservoir, Ft. Collins, CO 5/03 5000´
LOOK FOR a willow thicket near water and observe leaves and catkins.

LIFE LIST Where _____ NUMBER _____

GEYER WILLOW
Salix geyeriana
Willow family *Salicaceae*

SHRUB to 12´ tall; TWIGS dark, reddish-brown and slender; LEAVES narrow-lanceolate and acuminate to 2″ long; female CATKINS to ¾″ long and males to ½″, resembling a round pussy willow early in the season.
ECOLOGY: Foothills to subalpine near bogs.
LOCATION: Lower Narrows Campground, Poudre Canyon, CO 6/00 6500´
LOOK FOR a tall shrub with dark twigs, narrow leaves and short catkins.

LIFE LIST Where _____ NUMBER _____

GRAYLEAVED WILLOW
Salix glauca
Willow family *Salicaceae*

SHRUB to 5´ tall, in thickets; TWIGS grayish to reddish-brown; LEAVES alternate, narrow elliptic to 1″ long, gray-green above and whitish beneath; CATKINS yellowish to light brown to 1″ long.
ECOLOGY: Montane to alpine in bogs.
LOCATION: Mt. Evans, CO 6/05 10,000´
LOOK FOR a 3´ high willow thicket with gray-green, elliptical leaves.

LIFE LIST Where _____ NUMBER _____

BLUE STEM WILLOW
Salix irrorata
Willow family   *Salicaceae*

SHRUB to 12´ tall; TWIGS reddish-brown; LEAVES alternate, elliptic, pale beneath to 1½˝ long; female CATKINS to 2˝ long and males to 1½˝ long on separate shrubs.

ECOLOGY: Foothills to alpine near water.

LOCATION: Dowdy Lake Rec. Area, Red Feathers, CO 8/02 8000´

LOOK FOR a white bloom on lateral twigs and bright, reddish-brown bark on the central stem.

☐ **LIFE LIST**   Where _____ NUMBER _____

GREENLEAF WILLOW
Salix lucida (caudata)
Willow family   *Salicaceae*

SHRUB to 15´ high forming thickets; TWIGS light gray darkening on maturity; LEAVES narrow-lanceolate to 5˝ long at maturity; CATKINS – males to 1˝ x ½˝ and curved, females to 2˝ long.

ECOLOGY: Plains and foothills near water.

LOCATION: Spring Creek Trail, Ft. Collins, CO 5/03 5000´

LOOK FOR the short, curved male catkins and nearby female shrubs with 2˝ catkins.

☐ **LIFE LIST**   Where _____ NUMBER _____

YELLOW WILLOW
Salix lutea
Willow family   *Salicaceae*

SHRUB to 15´ high; TWIGS yellow and shiny, becoming reddish with age and sun exposure; LEAVES shiny, bright green, mostly elliptic, to 2˝ long; both male and female CATKINS to 1˝ long.

ECOLOGY: Foothills and montane in moisture.

LOCATION: Well Gulch, Lory S.P., Ft. Collins, CO 7/05 5500´

LOOK FOR yellow twigs and 1˝ catkins.

☐ **LIFE LIST**   Where _____ NUMBER _____

PLANE-LEAF WILLOW
Salix planifolia
Willow family   *Salicaceae*

SHRUB to 4´ tall; TWIGS dark brown and shiny; LEAVES elliptic, alternate, bright green above and pale beneath, to 1˝ long; male and female CATKINS both 1˝ long, on separate shrubs.

ECOLOGY: Montane and subalpine near water.

LOCATION: Sheep Lake Trail, Medicine Bow N.F., WY 7/01 10,500´

LOOK FOR small elliptical, shiny leaves on dark brown, shiny branches.

■ **LIFE LIST** Where _____ NUMBER _____

SNOW WILLOW
Salix reticulata (nivalis)
Willow family   *Salicaceae*

SHRUB to 3˝ high; STEMS inconspicuous; LEAVES oval, glossy above, reticulate beneath, to 1˝ long; CATKINS reddish to ½˝ long.

ECOLOGY: Subalpine to alpine in meadows and on tundra.

LOCATION: Silver Dollar Lake Trail, Guanella Pass, CO 8/99 11,000´

LOOK FOR glossy, oval, leathery leaves on a woody plant to 3˝ high.

■ **LIFE LIST** Where _____ NUMBER _____

SCOULER WILLOW
Salix scouleriana
Willow Family   *Salicaceae*

SHRUB to 18´ tall; BRANCHES dark brown and slender; LEAVES mostly narrow-elliptic to 2˝ long, shiny above and pale beneath; CATKINS to 1½˝ long, females with curled styles, on separate shrubs.

ECOLOGY: Foothills to subalpine, not necessarily near water like other Salix.

LOCATION: Young Gulch, Poudre Canyon, CO 6/01 7000´

LOOK FOR dark brown twigs and shiny leaves that are pale beneath.

■ **LIFE LIST** Where _____ NUMBER _____

DWARF ALUMROOT
Heuchera parvifolia nivalis
Saxifrage family   *Saxifragaceae*

PERENNIAL to 6″ tall; SCAPES green, smooth and
topped with a 1″ spike; LEAVES round and toothed to
1″ wide; FLOWERS green to ⅛″ with exserted
stamens.
ECOLOGY: Montane and subalpine on rocky ledges.
LOCATION: Gem Lake Trail, RMNP, CO 6/00 8500′
LOOK FOR a basal rosette of sharply toothed leaves
and a nodding, grass-like flower spike.

■ **LIFE LIST** Where _____ NUMBER _____

FIVE STAMENED MITREWORT
Mitella pentandra
Saxifrage family   *Saxifragaceae*

PERENNIAL to 7″ tall; SCAPES with up to 12
nodding flowers near the top; LEAVES to 1½″ wide,
rounded, crinkled and toothed; FLOWERS greenish,
spaced and button-like to ¼″ wide.
ECOLOGY: Montane to alpine.
LOCATION: Cirque Meadow Trail, Pingree Park, CO
6/01 9500′
LOOK FOR a plant that resembles the common
"Cheeseweed" (*Malva neglecta*; see page 52). Now
note the scape that is absent in "Cheeseweed."

■ **LIFE LIST** Where _____ NUMBER _____

HACKBERRY
Celtis laevigata (reticulata, occidentalis)
Elm family   *Ulmaceae*

TREE to 50′ high; BARK resembles tread of
snowtires; LEAVES alternate, broad-lanceolate, not
quite bisymmetrical, to 3″ long and often infected
with "Nipple Gall"; FRUIT is a drupe to ⅜″ wide, that
was eaten by Native Americans.
ECOLOGY: Plains and foothills in moisture.
LOCATION: Poudre River Trail, Ft. Collins, CO 7/02
5000′
LOOK FOR unique bark, lop-sided leaves and
"Nipple Gall."

■ **LIFE LIST** Where _____ NUMBER _____

AMERICAN ELM
Ulmus americana
Elm family   *Ulmaceae*

TREE to 100´ tall with a vase-like shape; LEAVES elliptical, toothed and prominently veined to 5˝ long; FRUIT are oval, papery discs to ½˝ wide with a small seed in the center.

ECOLOGY: Plains in rich, moist soil. Native to eastern U.S., but an escapee from cultivation in this area.

LOCATION: Poudre River Trail, Ft. Collins, CO 7/02 5000´

LOOK FOR large, elliptical, serrated leaves.

■ **LIFE LIST** Where _____ NUMBER _____

SIBERIAN ELM
Ulmus pumila
Elm family   *Ulmaceae*

TREE to 40´ tall; BARK rough, furrowed and gray; LEAVES elliptical, toothed and prominently veined to 2½˝ long; FRUIT is a papery disc to ½˝ wide with a seed in the center.

ECOLOGY: Plains – an introduced species.

LOCATION: Spring Creek Trail, Ft. Collins, CO 8/02 5000´

LOOK FOR an elm tree that lacks the vase-shape form, and has smaller leaves than the American Elm.

■ **LIFE LIST** Where _____ NUMBER _____

AMERICAN STINGING NETTLE
Urtica dioica
Nettle family   *Urticaceae*

PERENNIAL to 4´ tall, in clumps; STEMS erect, leafy and unbranched; LEAVES narrow-lanceolate to 4˝ long, toothed, with prominent veins; FLOWERS in 1˝ catkin-like racemes borne in leaf axils.

ECOLOGY: Foothills to montane in moisture.

LOCATION: Dowdy Lake Rec. Area, Red Feathers, CO 7/01 8000´

LOOK FOR a thicket of green stems, crowded with narrow, toothed leaves – and be sure not to touch it.

■ **LIFE LIST** Where _____ NUMBER _____

ROCKY MOUNTAIN FLORA

Grasses

CRESTED WHEATGRASS
Agropyron cristatum
Grass family   *Poaceae (Gramineae)*

PERENNIAL bunch grass; CULMS erect to 18″ tall with 4–5 alternate leaves; LEAVES ascending and straight to 6″ long; SPIKE tapered to 2″ long with 2 ranks of spikelets bearing ¼″ awns.

ECOLOGY: Plains and foothills – an Asian species much used for stabilizing soil.

LOCATION: Prospect Ponds, Ft. Collins, CO 8/02 5000′

LOOK FOR an upright, tapered seed head with 2 ranks of spikelets.

■ **LIFE LIST** Where _____ NUMBER _____

RED TOP
Agrostis stolonifera (alba, gigantea)
Grass family   *Poaceae (Gramineae)*

PERENNIAL forming clumps; CULMS erect to 2′ tall with upper half being a panicle; LEAVES mostly basal to 8″x ⅛″; PANICLE loose, reddish, to 12″ long with slender, horizontal branches.

ECOLOGY: Foothills to subalpine in meadows.

LOCATION: Dowdy Lake Rec. Area, Red Feathers, CO 8/02 8000′

LOOK FOR a clump of short, fine grass with red panicles to half the length of the culms.

■ **LIFE LIST** Where _____ NUMBER _____

RED THREE-AWN
Aristida purpurea (longiseta)
Grass family   *Poaceae (Gramineae)*

PERENNIAL tufted grass; CULMS to 12″ tall and nearly leafless; LEAVES mostly basal, in-folded and curled, to 6″ long; PANICLE erect, narrow, with branches ascending, FLOWERS few, 3-awned, to 2″ long.

ECOLOGY: Plains and foothills.

LOCATION: Coyote Ridge Rec. Area, Ft. Collins, CO 7/02 5500′

LOOK FOR three 2″ awns extending from each flower.

■ **LIFE LIST** Where _____ NUMBER _____

WILD OATS

Avena fatua
Grass family   *Poaceae (Gramineae)*

ANNUAL; CULMS to 30″ high, stout and leafy; LEAVES numerous with flat blades to ⅜″ wide; PANICLES to 6″ long, open during pollination and closed before and after; SPIKELETS usually 2 flowered with 1″ awns.

ECOLOGY: Plains on disturbed land including cultivated fields.

LOCATION: Donath Lake, Loveland, CO 8/04 5000′

LOOK FOR elongated spikelets with straight awns.

LIFE LIST   Where _____ NUMBER _____

SIDE-OATS GRAMA

Bouteloua curtipendula
Grass family   *Poaceae (Gramineae)*

PERENNIAL; CULMS to 30″ tall, erect with 3–6 leaves; LEAVES mostly basal, curved, narrow, to 10″ long; SPIKES 2-sided to 10″ long with 30–50, ¾″ long, hanging, alternate spikelets.

ECOLOGY: Plains and foothills.

LOCATION: Spring Creek Trail, Ft. Collins, CO 8/02 5000′

LOOK FOR a spike with hanging spikelets.

LIFE LIST   Where _____ NUMBER _____

HAIRY GRAMA

Bouteloua hirsuta
Grass family   *Poaceae (Gramineae)*

PERENNIAL, densely tufted; CULMS to 2′ tall, erect with few leaves; LEAVES mostly basal, narrow, to 10″ long; INFLORESCENCE composed of 1 or 2 rachi, bearing hanging spiklets. Tips of rachi and culms are extended by ¼″ spurs.

ECOLOGY: Plains to montane.

LOCATION: Three Mile Creek Trail, Grant, CO 8/99 9500′

LOOK FOR a stem with flag-like branches and hanging flowers on the lower side.

LIFE LIST   Where _____ NUMBER _____

FRINGED BROME

Bromus (Bromopsis) ciliatus
Grass family   *Poaceae (Gramineae)*

PERENNIAL; CULMS to 4´ tall, leafy, and curved near the top; culm LEAVES broad to 10˝ long, basal leaves narrow and curved; PANICLE to 10˝ long, slender and nodding with drooping branches and hanging spikelets.

ECOLOGY: Foothills to subalpine.

LOCATION: Herman Gulch Trail, Bakerville, CO 8/00 11,000´

LOOK FOR flowers dangling on hair-like branches from a nodding panicle.

■ LIFE LIST Where _____ NUMBER _____

SMOOTH BROME

Bromus (Bromopsis) inermis
Grass family   *Poaceae (Gramineae)*

PERENNIAL spreading by rhizomes; CULMS to 30˝ tall, erect and leafy; LEAVES smooth and wide to 7˝ long; PANICLE to 8˝ long, erect, with whorled branches, spreading at pollination and contracting at maturity.

ECOLOGY: Plains to subalpine – used for hay and pasture.

LOCATION: Horseshoe Trail, Golden Gate S.P., Golden, CO 7/99 8500´

LOOK FOR a smooth flower head that slides easily through the hand.

■ LIFE LIST Where _____ NUMBER _____

JAPANESE CHESS

Bromus (Bromopsis) japonicus
Grass family   *Poaceae (Gramineae)*

ANNUAL bunch grass; CULMS to 18˝ tall, erect and leafy; LEAVES reddish and flat to 6˝ long; PANICLES to 6˝ long with 1–5 branches per node, SPIKELETS ⅜˝ long, abruptly tapered to ⅜˝ awns.

ECOLOGY: Plains and foothills.

LOCATION: Boyd Lake S.P., Loveland, CO 7/02 5000´

LOOK FOR a reddish clump of grass with upright stems and awned spikelets.

■ LIFE LIST Where _____ NUMBER _____

PUMPELLY'S BROME

Bromus (Bromopsis) pumpellianus
Grass family *Poaceae (Gramineae)*

PERENNIAL to 5′ tall and spreading by rhizomes; CULMS tall, erect and leafy; LEAVES smooth and wide to 8″ long; PANICLE to 10″ long, erect, with whorled branches and fruit bearing ¼″ awns.

ECOLOGY: Plains to montane, often in association with Smooth Brome.

LOCATION: Arthur's Rock Trail, Lory S.P., Ft. Collins, CO 6/03 5500′

LOOK FOR a patch of grass among Smooth Brome that is a little taller and bears ¼″ awns.

LIFE LIST Where _____ NUMBER _____

DOWNY CHESS (CHEAT)

Bromus (Bromopsis) tectorum
Grass family *Poaceae (Gramineae)*

ANNUAL, undesirable import; CULMS to 20″ tall, leafy and curved; LEAVES mostly on stems to 6″ x ⅜″; PANICLE drooping, dense and soft with narrow spikelets and 1″ awns.

ECOLOGY: Plains and foothills – awns make it unpalatable and early demise make it a natural fire hazard.

LOCATION: Jefferson County Fairground, Golden, CO 5/02 6500′

LOOK FOR a drooping panicle with dangling spikelets and 1″ awns.

LIFE LIST Where _____ NUMBER _____

BUFFALO GRASS

Buchloe dactyloides
Grass family *Poaceae (Gramineae)*

PERENNIAL sod former; CULMS to 10″ tall, erect with 2–3 narrow leaves; LEAVES mostly basal to 7″ x ⅛″; PANICLE to ½″ long with 1–2 side branches, to ½″ long, bearing spikelets on the upper and lower surfaces.

ECOLOGY: Plains, forming a turf that is gaining favor in xerophytic landscapes.

LOCATION: Rolland Moore Park, Ft. Collins, CO 7/02 5000′

LOOK FOR a patch of soft turf and flag-like seed heads.

LIFE LIST Where _____ NUMBER _____

PURPLE REEDGRASS
Calamagrostis purpurascens
Grass family   *Poaceae (Gramineae)*

PERENNIAL forming tufts; CULMS to 2′ tall bearing
2–3 leaves; LEAVES mostly basal to 7″ x ⅜″;
PANICLE dense, spike-like to 5″ long with yellow-
green to purplish spikelets.

ECOLOGY: Foothills to subalpine among rocks.

LOCATION: Timber Trail, Lory S.P., Ft. Collins, CO
6/05 5000′

LOOK FOR a columnar panicle with soft, yellow or
purple spikelets.

█ **LIFE LIST**   Where _____ NUMBER _____

NORTHERN REEDGRASS
Calamagrostis scopulorum
Grass family   *Poaceae (Gramineae)*

PERENNIAL forming tufts; CULMS to 2′ tall with
2–3 leaves; LEAVES mostly basal to 7″ x ¼″;
PANICLE loose, spike-like to 5″ long with pale green
to purplish spikelets.

ECOLOGY: Foothills to subalpine.

LOCATION: Nighthawk Trail, Hall Ranch, Lyons, CO
5/01 6000′

LOOK FOR a loose columnar panicle having about
half as many branches as the denser panicle of
"Purple Reedgrass."

█ **LIFE LIST**   Where _____ NUMBER _____

WINDMILL GRASS
Chloris verticillata
Grass family   *Poaceae (Gramineae)*

PERENNIAL; CULMS to 12″ tall, upward curved,
with 2–3 leaves; stem LEAVES to 2″ long and basal
leaves to 5″; PANICLE consists of 2–3 whorls of 2–8
evenly spaced, horizontal branches to 3½″ long.

ECOLOGY: Plains in moisture.

LOCATION: Spring Creek Trail, Ft. Collins, CO 9/02
5000′

LOOK FOR a 3-whorled panicle with evenly spaced,
horizontal branches, typically with 8–4–2 branches
on nodes 1–3.

█ **LIFE LIST**   Where _____ NUMBER _____

BERMUDA GRASS

Cynodon dactylon
Grass family   *Poaceae (Gramineae)*

PERENNIAL creeping grass, rooting at nodes; CULMS to 10″ high; STEMS (stolons) prostrate to 1½′ long; LEAVES light green to 1½″ long occurring in tufts at nodes; one culm is produced per node, bearing 2 or 3 branches.

ECOLOGY: Plains, becoming more frequent further south where it is a major lawn grass.

LOCATION: Ft. Collins, CO 7/05 5000′

LOOK FOR creeping stolons with tufts of leaves at 2″ intervals.

■ **LIFE LIST** Where _____ NUMBER _____

ORCHARD GRASS

Dactylis glomerata
Grass family   *Poaceae (Gramineae)*

PERENNIAL in large tussocks; CULMS leafy, to 4′ tall; LEAVES coarse, mostly basal to 10″ x ⅜″; PANICLE 2 dimensional to 8″ long with alternating branches, opening during pollination and contracting at maturity.

ECOLOGY: Plains and foothills – used for pasture and hay.

LOCATION: Eldorado Canyon S.P., Eldorado Springs, CO 5/01 6500′

LOOK FOR a panicle branches with oval, terminal heads.

■ **LIFE LIST** Where _____ NUMBER _____

TUFTED HAIRGRASS

Deschampsia caespitosa
Grasss family   *Poaceae (Gramineae)*

PERENNIAL tufted grass; CULMS to 5′ tall with 1–2 leaves; LEAVES mostly basal, narrow, to 10″ long; PANICLES loose to 10″ long with 8–12 branches to 4″ long, sparsely flowered with reddish spikelets.

ECOLOGY: Foothills to subalpine in moist areas – a desirable forage grass.

LOCATION: Spring Creek Trail, Ft. Collins, CO 8/02 5000′

LOOK FOR a loose panicle sparsely flowered with reddish spikelets.

■ **LIFE LIST** Where _____ NUMBER _____

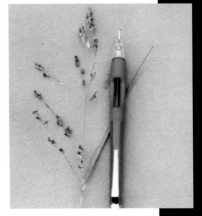

LANCE LEAF WITCHGRASS
Dichanthelium scabriusculum
(Panicum lanuginosum)
Grass family   *Poaceae (Gramineae)*

PERENNIAL in clumps; CULMS to 12″ high bearing several ascending leaves; LEAVES mainly on stems, lanceolate, to 3″ long; PANICLES to 3″ long, loose, with slender branches to 1″ long bearing sessile flowers.
ECOLOGY: Plains and foothills among rocks.
LOCATION: Bitterbrush Trail, Hall Ranch, Lyons, CO 6/00 6000′
LOOK FOR a loose panicle subtended by an upright, lanceolate leaf.

■ LIFE LIST Where _____ NUMBER _____

CRABGRASS
Digitaria sanguinalis
Grass family   *Poaceae (Gramineae)*

ANNUAL, prostrate grass forming mats to 2′ across; CULMS leafy, decumbent with heads ascending to 10″ high; LEAVES on stems only, to 7″ long; PANICLE with 4–6 spreading branches to 5″ long arising from approximately a common point.
ECOLOGY: Plains, as a common lawn weed.
LOCATION: Ft. Collins, CO 8/01 5000′
LOOK AT lawns for a sprawling mat of grass with pinwheel seed heads.

■ LIFE LIST Where _____ NUMBER _____

DESERT SALTGRASS
Distichlis spicata (stricta)
Grass family   *Poaceae (Gramineae)*

PERENNIAL forming dense colonies; CULMS to 10″ tall, yellowish with 2–5 alternating leaves; LEAVES to 4″ long; PANICLES 1″ long with 8–12 spikelets that turn yellow and contrast sharply with the green leaves.
ECOLOGY: Plains and foothills in swales.
LOCATION: Boyd Lake S.P., Loveland, CO 5/03 5000′
LOOK FOR a patch of light green turf in depressions that may be crusted with salt.

■ LIFE LIST Where _____ NUMBER _____

BARNYARD GRASS
Echinochloa crus-galli
Grass family   *Poaceae (Gramineae)*

ANNUAL, prostrate to erect; CULMS to 5′ tall and leafy; LEAVES to 12″ long, all on stems; PANICLES to 8″ long with spikelets crowded on branches to 4″ long that open for pollination and remain open; awns vary in length.

ECOLOGY: Plains, especially in cultivated fields – noted for its variability.

LOCATION: Boyd Lake S.P., Loveland, CO 8/01 5000′

LOOK FOR a panicle with round spikelets uniformly packed over the branches.

■ LIFE LIST Where _____ NUMBER _____

CANADIAN WILD RYE
Elymus canadensis
Grass family   *Poaceae (Gramineae)*

PERENNIAL forming tufts; CULMS to 5′ tall and leafy; LEAVES to 12″ x ¾″; SPIKES nodding, bristly and thick to 10″ long with awns to ¾″ long.

ECOLOGY: Plains and foothills in moisture.

LOCATION: Well Gulch, Lory S.P., Ft. Collins, CO 7/04 5500′

LOOK FOR a drooping spike with awns extending in bottlebrush fashion.

■ LIFE LIST Where _____ NUMBER _____

SLENDER WHEATGRASS
Elymus trachycaulus (Agropyron trachycaulum)
Grass family   *Poaceae (Gramineae)*

PERENNIAL bunchgrass; CULMS to 18″ tall, numerous, erect and leafy; LEAVES blue-green to 7″ long; SPIKES to 8″ long with awnless, pointed, alternating, appressed spikelets.

ECOLOGY: Plains to alpine.

LOCATION: Coyote Ridge Rec. Area, Ft. Collins, CO 7/01 5500′

LOOK FOR a blue-green bunchgrass that is not over 2′ tall with appressed spikelets.

■ LIFE LIST Where _____ NUMBER _____

TALL WHEATGRASS
Elytrigia (Agropyron) elongatum
Grass family   *Poaceae (Gramineae)*

PERENNIAL bunchgrass; CULMS to 6′ tall, straight and leafy; LEAVES blue-green to 5″ x ⅜″; SPIKES to 14″ long with 2 rows of alternating, appressed, awnless spikelets.

ECOLOGY: Plains and foothills – an Asian species.

LOCATION: Boyd Lake S.P., Loveland, CO 6/01 5000′

LOOK FOR a blue-green bunchgrass that is 4′ tall with appressed spikelets.

■ **LIFE LIST** Where _____ NUMBER ____

QUACKGRASS
Elytrigia (Agropyron) repens
Grass family   *Poaceae (Gramineae)*

PERENNIAL spreading by rhizomes; CULMS to 40″ tall with 3–5 leaves; LEAVES mainly on stems, in-folded to 8″ x ¼″; SPIKES 2-sided to 8″ long with alternating ½″ spikelets.

ECOLOGY: Plains to montane – a troublesome weed in lawns and fields.

LOCATION: Boyd Lake S.P., Loveland, CO 6/01 5000′

LOOK FOR patches of coarse grass with white rhizomes, in-folded leaves and stout culms with awnless spikelets.

■ **LIFE LIST** Where _____ NUMBER ____

PRAIRIE CUPGRASS
Eriochloa contracta
Grass family   *Poaceae (Gramineae)*

ANNUAL; CULMS to 30″ tall, slender with 2–3 small leaves; LEAVES mostly basal to 6″ x ⅛″; PANICLE to 3″ long with 6–12 branches to 1″ long, bearing tiny spikelets.

ECOLOGY: Plains and foothills.

LOCATION: Nighthawk Trail, Hall Ranch, Lyons, CO 5/01 6000′

LOOK FOR a slender culm with a short, compact head and a tuft of basal leaves.

■ **LIFE LIST** Where _____ NUMBER ____

SHEEP FESCUE
Festuca ovina (saximontana)
Grass family   *Poaceae (Gramineae)*

PERENNIAL forming tufts; CULMS to 16″ tall,
bearing 1–2 leaves; LEAVES mostly basal, slender, in-
folded to 10″ x ⅛″; PANICLE to 3″ long, branches
alternate to 1″ long with spikelets to ⅜″ long.
ECOLOGY: Plains and foothills.
LOCATION: Boyd Lake S.P., Loveland, CO 5/05
5000′
LOOK FOR a tussock with fine, narrow leaves and
small, smooth flower heads on slender culms.

☐ LIFE LIST Where _____ NUMBER _____

FOWL MANNAGRASS
Glyceria striata
Grass family   *Poaceae (Gramineae)*

PERENNIAL forming large tussocks; CULMS to 30″
tall with 2–3 ascending leaves; LEAVES mostly basal
to 10″ x ⅜″; PANICLE open, slender and nodding to
8″ long with 2–5 branches to 6″ long at each node;
SPIKELETS egg-shaped resembling beads on a string.
ECOLOGY: Plains to montane in moisture.
LOCATION: Boyd Lake S.P., Loveland, CO 5/05
5000′
LOOK FOR a drooping panicle with evenly spaced
seed on slender branches.

☐ LIFE LIST Where _____ NUMBER _____

FOXTAIL BARLEY
Hordeum (Cristesion) jubatum
Grass family   *Poaceae (Gramineae)*

PERENNIAL forming tussocks; CULMS to 2′ tall
bearing 2–3 leaves; LEAVES mostly basal to 10″ x
⅜″; SPIKES nodding, soft, pale, to 4″ long;
SPIKELETS imbricated upward with awns to 3″ long,
giving a paint brush appearance.
ECOLOGY: Plains to montane – awns injurious to
livestock.
LOCATION: Coyote Ridge Rec. Area, Ft. Collins, CO
7/01 5500′
LOOK FOR a soft, white-topped clump of grass with
curved, "foxtail" spikes.

☐ LIFE LIST Where _____ NUMBER _____

ITALIAN RYEGRASS
Lolium perenne (multiflorum)
Grass family   *Poaceae (Gramineae)*

ANNUAL, biennial, or perennial; CULMS to 2´ tall
   bearing 2–3 leaves; LEAVES mostly basal, to 6˝ long;
   SPIKES 2-sided to 8˝ long with 8–10 spikelets.

ECOLOGY: Plains and foothills in moist areas. Has
   been used for hay and turf.

LOCATION: Avery Park, Ft. Collins, CO 9/00 5000´
   Detail photo: Spring Creek Trail, Ft. Collins, CO
   6/05 5000´

LOOK FOR alternating, well-spaced spikelets on a
   long straight rachis. Wheatgrass spikelets tend to
   overlap.

■ LIFE LIST Where _____ NUMBER _____

INDIAN RICEGRASS
Oryzopsis (Achnatherum) hymenoides
Grass family   *Poaceae (Gramineae)*

PERENNIAL tufted grass; CULMS to 30˝ tall, slender
   with 2–3 leaves; LEAVES mostly basal, slender, in-
   folded, to 10˝ long; PANICLE loose, 6˝ x 7˝ with
   single seeded flowers suspended on thread-like
   branches.

ECOLOGY: Plains and foothills.

LOCATION: Coyote Ridge Rec. Area, Ft. Collins, CO
   5/04 5500´

LOOK FOR a clump of grass with flowers that are
   suspended by filamentous branches.

■ LIFE LIST Where _____ NUMBER _____

WITCHGRASS
Panicum capillare
Grass family   *Poaceae (Gramineae)*

ANNUAL; CULMS semi-prostrate and leafy to 15˝
   high; LEAVES hairy, sheathed at the stem to 6˝ x ½˝;
   PANICLES open to 8˝ x 6˝ with flowers suspended
   on thread-like branches.

ECOLOGY: Plains and foothills.

LOCATION: Eltuck Bay, Lory S.P., Ft. Collins, CO 8/01
   5500´

LOOK FOR a spreading panicle subtended by a wide
   blade of grass and flowers suspended by filamentous
   branches.

■ LIFE LIST Where _____ NUMBER _____

SWITCHGRASS
Panicum virgatum
Grass family   *Poaceae (Gramineae)*

PERENNIAL forming large tussocks and numerous
rhizomes; CULMS to 9′ tall bearing 3–7 leaves;
LEAVES mostly on stems to 2′ x ⅝″, reduced
upward; PANICLE loose to 1′ long with branches to
5″ long, bearing well spaced ⅛″ flowers.
ECOLOGY: Prairies and foothills, near water.
LOCATION: Avery Park, Ft. Collins, CO 9/01 5000′
LOOK FOR tussocks with tall stalks and loose
panicles on marshy ground.

■ LIFE LIST   Where _____ NUMBER _____

REED CANARYGRASS
Phalaris arundinacea
Grass family   *Poaceae (Gramineae)*

PERENNIAL with creeping rhizomes; CULMS to 6′
tall; LEAVES on the lower half of culms, ascending,
alternate, 1″ apart, to 8″ x ⅝″; PANICLE to 5″ long
with alternating branches to 1½″ long, reduced
upward, spreading during pollination and then
contracting.
ECOLOGY: Plains, near water.
LOCATION: Prospect Ponds, Ft. Collins, CO 5/04
5000′
LOOK FOR a clump of tall grass with leaves half-way
up the stalk and a yellow panicle, at maturity.

■ LIFE LIST   Where _____ NUMBER _____

ALPINE TIMOTHY
Phleum alpinum (commutatum)
Grass family   *Poaceae (Gramineae)*

PERENNIAL forming clumps; CULMS to 15″ bearing
2–3 leaves; LEAVES mostly basal to 4″ x ¼″; SPIKE
dense to 1″ x ⅜″, green to purple.
ECOLOGY: Subalpine to alpine.
LOCATION: Berthoud Pass, CO 7/02 11,500′
LOOK FOR a dwarf Timothy plant that is often
mistaken for a sedge.

■ LIFE LIST   Where _____ NUMBER _____

TIMOTHY
Phleum pratense
Grass family   *Poaceae (Gramineae)*

PERENNIAL forming large clumps; CULMS to 3′ from a swollen bulb-like base; LEAVES mostly basal to 8″ x ¼″; SPIKES to 6″ long, crowded with spikelets.

ECOLOGY: Plains and foothills – commonly cultivated as a forage crop.

LOCATION: Roadside, Lory S.P., Ft. Collins, CO 6/03 5500′

LOOK FOR the typical cylindrical spike that is diagnostic.

■ LIFE LIST   Where _____ NUMBER _____

ANNUAL BLUEGRASS
Poa annua
Grass family   *Poaceae (Gramineae)*

ANNUAL or biennial forming bright green mats by rooting at lower nodes; CULMS ascending to 6″ tall; LEAVES mostly on stems to 1″ x ⅛″; PANICLE open to 1″ long with 4–8 branches to ½″ long.

ECOLOGY: Plains, in wet, compact soil – a major weed of golf greens.

LOCATION: Avery Park, Ft. Collins, CO 6/02 5000′

LOOK FOR bright, light green patches in a lawn.

■ LIFE LIST   Where _____ NUMBER _____

BIGELOW BLUEGRASS
Poa bigelovii
Grass family   *Poaceae (Gramineae)*

ANNUAL bluegrass; CULMS erect to 12″ high bearing 2 or 3 appressed leaves; LEAVES mostly basal to 6″ x ⅛″; PANICLES narrow and interrupted to 6″ long.

ECOLOGY: Plains to montane.

LOCATION: Jefferson County Fairground, CO 5/02 6500′

LOOK FOR a tuft of bright green grass with short culms bearing tight heads.

■ LIFE LIST   Where _____ NUMBER _____

BOG BLUEGRASS
Poa leptocoma
Grass family   *Poaceae (Gramineae)*

PERENNIAL producing small tufts; CULMS to 18″
  with 1 to a few per tuft; LEAVES mostly basal to 10″ x
  ¼″; PANICLES very loose, nodding, with drooping
  branches and few flowers.
ECOLOGY: Montane and subalpine.
LOCATION: Sheep Lake Trail, Medicine Bow N.F.,
  WY 7/00 10,500′
LOOK FOR a delicate, open, nodding panicle with
  few flowers.

■ **LIFE LIST** Where _____ NUMBER _____

KENTUCKY BLUEGRASS
Poa pratensis
Grass family   *Poaceae (Gramineae)*

PERENNIAL spreading by rhizomes and forming
  patches; CULMS to 2′ with 2–3 leaves; LEAVES
  mostly basal to 8″ x ⅜″; PANICLES, to 4″ long, loose,
  with 1–5 uneven branches per node, spreading at
  pollination.
ECOLOGY: Plains to montane – used extensively for
  forage and lawns.
LOCATION: Avery Park, Ft. Collins, CO 6/02 5000′
LOOK FOR a delicate panicle with whorls of
  branches of uneven lengths.

■ **LIFE LIST** Where _____ NUMBER _____

FABER FOXTAIL
Setaria faberi
Grass family   *Poaceae (Gramineae)*

ANNUAL forming patches; CULMS slender and leafy
  to 4′ tall; LEAVES bright green, mostly on stems to
  10″ x ½″; SPIKES to 6″ long, curved, dense, yellow
  and bristly.
ECOLOGY: Plains, probably introduced form China
  in millet seed.
LOCATION: Boyd Lake S.P., Loveland, CO 8/01 5000′
LOOK FOR a patch of vigorous grass to 4′ high with
  yellow, curved, bristly spikes to 6″ long.

■ **LIFE LIST** Where _____ NUMBER _____

GREEN BRISTLEGRASS (GREEN FOXTAIL)
Setaria viridis
Grass family   *Poaceae (Gramineae)*

ANNUAL in small tufts; CULMS leafy to 16″ high; LEAVES mostly on stems to 6″ x ⅜″; SPIKES dense, bristly, green or purple, to 4″ long.

ECOLOGY: Plains and foothills – a common weed in cultivated fields.

LOCATION: Poudre River Trail, Ft. Collins, CO 8/04 5000′

LOOK FOR a bristly, green to purple spike.

◾ LIFE LIST   Where _____ NUMBER _____

NEEDLE AND THREAD
Stipa comata
Grass family   *Poaceae (Gramineae)*

PERENNIAL forming tufts; CULMS to 2′ bearing 2–3 leaves; LEAVES mostly basal to 8″ x ¼″; PANICLE to 8″ bearing spikelets with awns to 1″ long.

ECOLOGY: Plains and foothills.

LOCATION: Towhee Trail, Eldorado Canyon S.P., Eldorado Springs, CO 6/02 6500′

LOOK FOR white, thread-like awns that give the plant its common name.

◾ LIFE LIST   Where _____ NUMBER _____

LETTERMAN NEEDLEGRASS
Stipa lettermanii
Grass family   *Poaceae (Gramineae)*

PERENNIAL forming large tufts; CULMS to 20″ tall; LEAVES mostly basal, slender to 12″ x ⅛″; PANICLES to 6″ long bearing spikelets with curled, hair-like awns to ¾″ long.

ECOLOGY: Plains to montane.

LOCATION: Three Mile Creek, Grant, CO 8/00 9500′

LOOK FOR a clump of bunchgrass with very narrow leaves, numerous stems and tight, shiny panicles with hair-like awns.

◾ LIFE LIST   Where _____ NUMBER _____

PORCUPINE GRASS

Stipa spartea
Grass family *Poaceae (Gramineae)*

PERENNIAL forming tufts; CULMS to 3´ tall, leafy at the base and sparse upward; LEAVES mostly on lower stem, narrow, curled to 7˝ x ¼˝; PANICLES to 12˝ long, seed to ⅝˝ and awns to 8˝ long.
ECOLOGY: Plains and foothills.
LOCATION: Devil's Backbone Rec. Area, Loveland, CO 6/03 5500´
LOOK FOR curled, 8˝ awns that exceed the length of all other grasses.

■ LIFE LIST Where _____ NUMBER _____

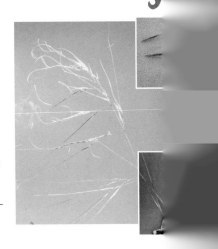

SPIKE TRISETUM

Trisetum spicatum
Grass family *Poaceae (Gramineae)*

PERENNIAL bunchgrass; CULMS to 18˝ with 1 to several leaves; basal and stem LEAVES a uniform 4˝ long; PANICLE spike-like, often interrupted at base, green and silvery to 3˝ long.
ECOLOGY: Subalpine and alpine.
LOCATION: Berthoud Pass, CO 7/02 11,500´
LOOK FOR a clump of grass with silvery heads, especially striking in the sunshine.

■ LIFE LIST Where _____ NUMBER _____

ROCKY MOUNTAIN FLORA

Sedges and Rushes

AQUA SEDGE
Carex aquatilis
Sedge family   *Cyperaceae*

PERENNIAL forming clumps; CULMS to 12″ tall; LEAVES mainly basal to 8″ x ¼″, reduced upward; SPIKES to 1½″ long in axils of reduced leaves; top SPIKE male, lower ones female bearing white stigmas.

ECOLOGY: Foothills to montane in bogs.

LOCATION: Horsetooth Trail, Lory S.P., Ft. Collins, CO 5/02 5500′

LOOK FOR multiple terminal spikes, the top spike being male.

█ **LIFE LIST**   Where _____ NUMBER _____

GOLDEN SEDGE
Carex aurea
Sedge family   *Cyperaceae*

PERENNIAL: CULMS to 7″ high with lateral flowering spikes; LEAVES 2–3 per culm, stiff and ascending at 45 degrees; SPIKELETS orange with yellow, silky hairs at the tips.

ECOLOGY: Plains to montane in moisture.

LOCATION: Boyd Lake S.P., Loveland, CO 7/01 5000′

LOOK FOR bright orange and yellow spikelets. Possibly the most colorful of all sedges.

█ **LIFE LIST**   Where _____ NUMBER _____

BREVIOR SEDGE
Carex brevior
Sedge family   *Cyperaceae*

PERENNIAL: CULMS to 20″ high and leafless; LEAVES basal and grass-like; SPIKES terminal in clusters of 2–5, to ½″ long; sexes on separate plants.

ECOLOGY: Foothills in meadows.

LOCATION: Boyd Lake S.P., Loveland, CO 6/02 5000′

LOOK FOR both narrow (male) and broad (female) spikes on separate plants.

█ **LIFE LIST**   Where _____ NUMBER _____

BLACK SEDGE

Carex ebenea
Sedge family   *Cyperaceae*

PERENNIAL forming tufts; CULMS to 2´ tall,
triangular in cross section; LEAVES basal, grass-like,
clasping, to 10″ long; FLOWER heads terminal, dark
brown and composed of 3–5 spikelets.
ECOLOGY: Subalpine to alpine in moisture.
LOCATION: Loveland Basin, CO 8/01 11,000´
LOOK FOR bright green stems and dark brown
terminal heads.

■ **LIFE LIST**   Where _____ NUMBER _____

FISH SCALE SEDGE

Carex heteroneura (albonigra)
Sedge family   *Cyperaceae*

PERENNIAL forming grassy clumps; CULMS to 12″
and not exceeding the height of leaves; LEAVES
mostly basal, grass-like with a pale green midrib to
12″ long; SPIKES 3–4, to ½″ long, whitish with black
tipped bracts.
ECOLOGY: Subalpine and alpine in bogs.
LOCATION: Sheep Lake Trail, Medicine Bow N.F.,
WY 7/01 10,500´
LOOK FOR a grass-like clump and white spikes with
black tipped bracts.

■ **LIFE LIST**   Where _____ NUMBER _____

YELLOW SEDGE

Carex hystricina
Sedge family   *Cyperaceae*

PERENNIAL: CULMS to 12″ high, 3-angled with 3 or
more leaves; LEAVES in-folded, linear, narrow and
stiff to 10″ long; SPIKES 3–5 to 1″ long, with top
spike male and lower ones female.
ECOLOGY: Foothills and montane in moisture.
LOCATION: Sheep Lake Trail, Medicine Bow N.F.,
WY 7/02 10,500´
LOOK FOR brown (male) and yellow (female) spikes
with long, sharp, subtending bracts (leaves).

■ **LIFE LIST**   Where _____ NUMBER _____

SUN LOVING SEDGE

Carex inops (heliophila)
Sedge family   *Cyperaceae*

PERENNIAL in prostrate patches; CULMS to 3″ long with 1–2 leaves; LEAVES grass-like to ¾″ x ⅛″; SPIKES purplish to ½″ x ⅛″.

ECOLOGY: Foothills and montane in moisture.

LOCATION: Eltuck Bay, Lory S.P., Ft. Collins, CO 8/01 5500′

LOOK FOR a grass-like patch that appears to be a miniature form of Alpine Timothy (*Phleum alpinum*; see p. 237).

■ LIFE LIST Where _____ NUMBER _____

ROCKY MOUNTAIN SEDGE

Carex scopulorum
Sedge family   *Cyperaceae*

PERENNIAL forming clumps; CULMS to 2′ high, slender and willowy; LEAVES in-folded, narrow to 10″ long; FLOWER heads nodding, composed of 1–4 spikes.

ECOLOGY: Subalpine and alpine in moisture.

LOCATION: Berthoud Pass, CO 7/02 11,500′

LOOK FOR a bright green clump with nodding, brown heads.

■ LIFE LIST Where _____ NUMBER _____

YELLOW NUTSEDGE

Cyperus esculentus
Sedge family   *Cyperaceae*

PERENNIAL to 12″ tall forming tufts; CULMS reclining, to 12″ long terminating in an umbel subtended by 3 or 4 bracts to 5″ long; LEAVES grass-like and basal to 8″ long; FLOWERS yellow or tan in ½″ flower heads borne on umbels.

ECOLOGY: Plains in moist places.

LOCATION: Boyd Lake S.P., Loveland, CO 8/05 5000′

LOOK FOR a many-headed umbel subtended by 5″ bracts.

■ LIFE LIST Where _____ NUMBER _____

NEEDLE SPIKE RUSH

Eleocharis acicularis
Sedge family   *Cyperaceae*

PERENNIAL to 2″ tall, forming sod; CULMS reclining, hair-like and leafless to 3″ long; LEAVES also hair-like to 2″ long; SPIKES to ¼″ long, purplish, turning white and falling.

ECOLOGY: Plains and foothills in drying mud of receding water.

LOCATION: Dixon Reservoir, Ft. Collins, CO 9/01 5000′

LOOK FOR a patch of fine, green turf with tiny, terminal spikes.

■ LIFE LIST Where _____ NUMBER _____

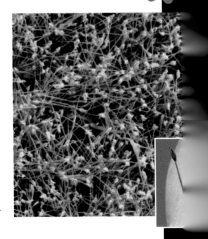

SPIKE RUSH

Eleocharis palustris (macrostachya)
Sedge family   *Cyperaceae*

PERENNIAL in patches in or near water; CULMS leafless to 10″ tall; LEAVES none, function is performed by spikeless culms; SPIKES terminal, solitary, to ½″ long, with male flowers upper and female flowers lower.

ECOLOGY: Plains to subalpine.

LOCATION: Boyd Lake S.P., Loveland, CO 5/02 5000′

LOOK FOR short, wire-like, green stems with or without short, terminal spikes.

■ LIFE LIST Where _____ NUMBER _____

SIBERIAN KOBRESIA

Kobresia sibirica
Sedge family   *Cyperaceae*

PERENNIAL forming dense clumps; CULMS to 6″ tall, erect and wiry, supporting a solitary spike; LEAVES basal, narrow and grass-like to 5″ long; SPIKES reddish to ½″ x ⅜″ having 3–4 spikelets with both male and female flowers.

ECOLOGY: Montane to alpine near water.

LOCATION: Cow Creek Trail, McGraw Ranch, RMNP, CO 7/99 8000′

LOOK FOR grassy clumps with tiny, reddish spikes.

■ LIFE LIST Where _____ NUMBER _____

THREE SQUARE
Scirpus americanus
Sedge family   *Cyperaceae*

PERENNIAL: CULMS 3-sided to 3′ tall; LEAVES grass-like, mostly basal to 12″ long; FLOWER clusters consist of 3 spikes to ⅝″ long, a large male and 2 smaller females.

ECOLOGY: Plains in wet places.

LOCATION: Coyote Ridge Rec. Area, Ft. Collins, CO 5/02 5500′

LOOK FOR a tall sedge with a flower cluster that appears to be 5″ below the tip of the culm; however, the 5″ extension is a bract.

■ **LIFE LIST** Where _____ NUMBER _____

SMALL FRUITED BULRUSH
Scirpus microcarpus
Sedge family   *Cyperaceae*

PERENNIAL: CULMS 3-sided to 4′ tall; LEAVES to 14″ long; PANICLE to 4″ tall with branches supporting terminal clusters of 1–5 round spikes to ¼″.

ECOLOGY: Plains in wet places.

LOCATION: Avery Park, Ft. Collins, CO 6/02 5000′

LOOK FOR a green panicle with terminal clusters of ¼″ balls.

■ **LIFE LIST** Where _____ NUMBER _____

PALE BULRUSH
Scirpus pallidus
Sedge family   *Cyperaceae*

PERENNIAL: CULMS stiff to 5′ tall; LEAVES pale green, grass-like to 12″ x ⅝″; male SPIKES suspended by slender stalks to 2″ long, female spikes clustered together on separate plants, both clusters are terminal and subtended by 3 bracts.

ECOLOGY: Plains and foothills in wet places.

LOCATION: Avery Lake, Ft. Collins, CO 7/02 5000′

LOOK FOR tripod of bracts subtending clusters of bur-like spikes.

■ **LIFE LIST** Where _____ NUMBER _____

SOFT STEM BULRUSH

Scirpus tabernaemontani (validus)
(Schoenoplectus lacustris creber)
Sedge family *Cyperaceae*

PERENNIAL: CULMS soft and round to 10´ tall;
LEAVES round to 16″ long; PANICLE of drooping
branches supporting ½″ brown spikes with male
flowers above and female flowers below.

ECOLOGY: Plains in wet places.

LOCATION: Avery Park, Ft. Collins, CO 9/00 5000´

LOOK FOR a tall, smooth stem with a nodding
panicle of brown spikes.

█ LIFE LIST Where _____ NUMBER _____

ARCTIC RUSH

Juncus arcticus (balticus)
Rush family *Juncaceae*

PERENNIAL: STEMS leafless to 15″ high; LEAVES
reduced to scales; FLOWER clusters appear laterally,
below the tip; actually they are terminal and the "tip"
is a subtending bract; clusters consist of several
spikes on stalks of various lengths.

ECOLOGY: Foothills to subalpine in bogs.

LOCATION: Mill Creek Trail, RMNP, CO 6/01 9000´

LOOK FOR a loose, single cluster 1½″ down from
the tip.

█ LIFE LIST Where _____ NUMBER _____

TOAD RUSH

Juncus bufonius
Rush family *Juncaceae*

ANNUAL to 12″ high in tufts; STEMS wiry and leafy;
LEAVES narrow, semi-round to 6″ long;
INFLORESCENCE making up more than half the
height of the plant and composed of upright clusters
with stalked, round, ⅛″ flowers.

ECOLOGY: Plains to montane in wet areas.

LOCATION: Boyd Lake S.P., Loveland, CO 6/02
5000´

LOOK FOR a forking panicle.

█ LIFE LIST Where _____ NUMBER _____

CHESTNUT RUSH

Juncus castaneus
Rush family   *Juncaceae*

PERENNIAL to 30″ tall; STEMS erect and wiry with
3 leaves; LEAVES upright, slender, to 6″ long;
FLOWER clusters terminal, brown and composed
of multiple heads with subtending bracts.
ECOLOGY: Montane to alpine in bogs.
LOCATION: Dowdy Lake Rec. Area, Red Feathers, CO
7/01 8000′
LOOK FOR a brown terminal cluster composed of
multiple heads and tan bracts.

■ **LIFE LIST** Where _____ NUMBER _____

DRUMMOND RUSH

Juncus drummondii
Rush family   *Juncaceae*

PERENNIAL to 12″ tall in tufts; STEMS terminate in
a flower cluster that is subtended by a bract that
extends about ½″ above the cluster; LEAVES reduced
to sheaths at the base of the stems; FLOWER clusters
consist of capsules to ¼″ long, with 1–3 per cluster.
ECOLOGY: Subalpine to alpine.
LOCATION: Sheep Lake Trail, Medicine Bow N.F.,
WY 7/00 10,500′
LOOK FOR oval capsules slightly below the "tip of
the stem."

■ **LIFE LIST** Where _____ NUMBER _____

INLAND RUSH

Juncus interior
Rush family   *Juncaceae*

PERENNIAL to 2′ tall; STEMS erect and slender
with 1–3 narrow leaves and a terminal bract that dies
back and droops; LEAVES mostly stem, narrow, in-
folded to 12″; FLOWERS on upright stalks subtended
by bracts of various lengths.
ECOLOGY: Plains to montane in wet areas.
LOCATION: Shore Trail, Lory S.P., Ft. Collins, CO
6/03 5500′
LOOK FOR die-back of the longest bract which
occurs during the season.

■ **LIFE LIST** Where _____ NUMBER _____

SUBALPINE RUSH

Juncus mertensianus
Rush family   *Juncaceae*

PERENNIAL to 16″ tall forming tussocks; STEMS round and erect with terminal, hemispheric heads subtended by a curved bract to 2″ long; LEAVES clasping to 6″ long; FLOWERS dark purple with exserted styles.

ECOLOGY: Montane and subalpine in meadows.

LOCATION: Loveland Basin, CO 8/01 11,000′

LOOK FOR a community of bright green stems with dark, hemispheric heads.

☐ LIFE LIST   Where _____ NUMBER _____

ROCKY MOUNTAIN RUSH

Juncus saximontanus
Rush family   *Juncaceae*

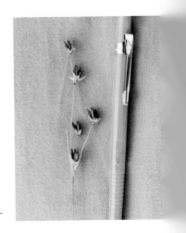

PERENNIAL to 2′ tall; STEMS erect, slender with usually 2 leaves; LEAVES slender to 7″ long; FLOWERS upright in cup-like receptacles to ¼″ high, with several heads per stem.

ECOLOGY: Montane and subalpine in bogs.

LOCATION: Dowdy Lake Rec. Area, Red Feathers, CO 7/01 8000′

LOOK FOR flower heads that are held at various levels by stiff, upright flower stems of unequal lengths.

☐ LIFE LIST   Where _____ NUMBER _____

TORREY RUSH

Juncus torreyi
Rush family   *Juncaceae*

PERENNIAL to 20″ tall; STEMS canted and straight with 3–4 leaves; LEAVES round and stiff to 9″ long; FLOWER heads reddish-tan and round, to ½″, in terminal clusters of 3–7.

ECOLOGY: Plains and foothills in wet places.

LOCATION: Boyd Lake S.P., Loveland, CO 7/01 5000′

LOOK FOR a terminal cluster composed of round, bur-like heads.

☐ LIFE LIST   Where _____ NUMBER _____

SMALL FLOWER WOODRUSH
Luzula parviflora
Rush family *Juncaceae*

PERENNIAL to 12″ tall; STEMS short and leafy; LEAVES grass-like to 6″ x ½″; FLOWERS brown or purple capsules to ⅛″ long in nodding panicles to 2″ long.

ECOLOGY: Montane and subalpine forests.

LOCATION: Cirque Meadow Trail, Pingree Park, CO 6/01 9500′

LOOK FOR a loose, unruly panicle with brown, bud-like capsules and wide, linear leaves.

■ LIFE LIST Where _____ NUMBER _____

NARROWLEAF CATTAIL
Typha angustifolia
Cattail family *Typhaceae*

PERENNIAL to 6′ high; STEMS erect and leafy with a terminal cattail; LEAVES to 30″ x ⅜″, stiff and projected upward at 45 degrees; male FLOWER head 7″ x $^5/_{16}$″, gap 1½″ x ⅛″, female flower head 5″ x ½″ cylinders.

ECOLOGY: Plains in standing water.

LOCATION: Poudre River Trail, Ft. Collins, CO 7/02 5000′

LOOK FOR the 1½″ gap between the male and female heads.

■ LIFE LIST Where _____ NUMBER _____

BROADLEAF CATTAIL
Typha latifolia
Cattail family *Typhaceae*

PERENNIAL to 6′ tall; STEMS round and smooth; LEAVES reed-like to 2′ long; FLOWERS tightly compacted in 2, 5″ x ⅝″ sausage-like clusters, male on top and female below, with no gap between; disintegration of the male after pollination leaves a sharp spindle.

ECOLOGY: Plains in standing water.

LOCATION: Avery Park, Ft. Collins, CO 6/02 5000′

LOOK FOR a cattail that has no gap between the male and female clusters.

■ LIFE LIST Where _____ NUMBER _____

ROCKY MOUNTAIN FLORA

Mushrooms

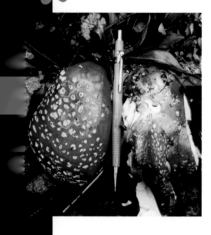

Amanita muscaria flavivolvata
FLY AGARIC
Family: *Amanitaceae*

CAP: 2–4″ wide, bright red, fading to dull pinkish red; GILLS white to cream.
EDIBILITY: Poisonous
ECOLOGY: Foothills to subalpine in conifer duff.
LOCATION: 4th of July Trail, Eldora, CO 7/01 11,500′
LOOK FOR a red ½ sphere with irregular white spots.

■ **LIFE LIST** Where _____ NUMBER _____

Suillus brevipes (Boletus luteus)
SLIPPERY JACK
Family: *Boletaceae*

CAP: 3–7″ wide, in various shades of brown; TUBES sulfur yellow.
EDIBILITY: Edible
ECOLOGY: Subalpine and always with conifers.
LOCATION: Berthoud Pass, CO 7/01 11,500′
LOOK FOR a convex to flat, reddish-brown cap and yellow tubes.

■ **LIFE LIST** Where _____ NUMBER _____

Suillus lakei
Family: *Boletaceae*

CAP: 1–3″ across, convex, margin in-rolled, covered with reddish brown fibrils; TUBES yellowish.
EDIBILITY: Edible
ECOLOGY: Foothills and montane under Douglas Fir.
LOCATION: Young Gulch, Poudre Canyon, CO 6/02 7500′
LOOK FOR a convex cap, to 3″ wide, covered with reddish fibrils.

■ **LIFE LIST** Where _____ NUMBER _____

Clavaria (Ramaria) botrytis
Family: *Clavariaceae*

CAP: to 12″ across, grayish-white, resembling an over-mature cauliflower head.
EDIBILITY: not recommended
ECOLOGY: Subalpine in coniferous forests.
LOCATION: Loveland Basin, CO 8/01 11,000′
LOOK FOR a large, spongy, off-white mass.

■ **LIFE LIST** Where _____ NUMBER _____

Coprinus comatus
SHAGGY MANE
Family: *Coprinaceae*

CAP: to 1 ½″ wide, egg-shaped, off-white with tan blotches; EPIDERMIS peeling in flaky scales; GILLS white going to grayish-pink to black.
EDIBILITY: Edible
ECOLOGY: Plains to montane.
LOCATION: Copper Mt. bike trail, CO 8/91 10,500′
LOOK FOR egg-shaped, white mushrooms with tan patches.

■ **LIFE LIST** Where _____ NUMBER _____

Bovista plumbea
TUMBLING PUFFBALL
Family: *Lycoperdaceae*

CAP: a nearly spherical spore case to 1½″ across.
EDIBILITY: Edible
ECOLOGY: Foothills to subalpine, widely distributed in leaf litter.
LOCATION: St. Alban's Chapel, Medicine Bow N.F., WY 8/99 10,500′
LOOK FOR a white golf ball.

■ **LIFE LIST** Where _____ NUMBER _____

Phallus impudicus
STINKHORN
Family: *Phallaceae*

CAP: to 2″ high, convoluted, olive-green and slimy; STEM white to 5″ tall.
EDIBILITY: Inedible
ECOLOGY: Plains and foothills.
LOCATION: Bitterbrush Trail, Hall Ranch, Lyons, CO 5/02 6000′
LOOK FOR a large, white stalk with a convoluted, olive-green cap and a torn covering.

■ **LIFE LIST** Where _____ NUMBER _____

Pluteus cervinus
Family: *Plutaceae*

CAP: 2–5″ across, white to tan and broadly convex to ¾″ deep; GILLS white.
ECOLOGY: Plains to subalpine, July–September, single or grouped.
EDIBILITY: Edible
LOCATION: Young Gulch, Poudre Canyon, CO 7/03 7000′
LOOK FOR and off-white, slightly domed, white gilled mushroom, about 3″ wide.

■ **LIFE LIST** Where _____ NUMBER _____

Fomitopsis pinicola
RED BELTED POLYPORE
Family: *Polyporaceae*

SHELF mushroom found on dead or dying conifer trees; BODY to 12″ across, pinkish-tan above and cream-yellow beneath; TUBES cream colored.
EDIBILITY: Inedible
ECOLOGY: Montane and subalpine on conifers.
LOCATION: Horse Trail, Wild Basin, RMNP, CO 7/00 9000′
LOOK FOR a pinkish-tan shelf mushroom attached to a conifer tree or log.

■ **LIFE LIST** Where _____ NUMBER _____

Neolentinus ponderosus
Family: *Polyporaceae*

CAP: to 12″ across, yellow-tan, cuticle breaking into concentric scales; GILLS white, going to yellow-orange.

EDIBILITY: Edible when young

ECOLOGY: Subalpine near dead conifer wood.

LOCATION: Cub Lake Trail, RMNP, CO 7/99 8500′

LOOK FOR a tan mushroom with white under tissue showing through growth cracks.

■ LIFE LIST Where _____ NUMBER _____

Phyllotopsis nidulans
Family: *Polyporaceae*

SHELF: to 3″ across, yellow and fan shaped; GILLS brilliant orange, fanning out from point of attachment.

EDIBILITY: Inedible

ECOLOGY: Montane and subalpine, saprophytic on dead logs.

LOCATION: Three Mile Creek, Grant, CO 8/99 9500′

LOOK FOR a little, yellow shelf mushroom growing on the side of a log.

■ LIFE LIST Where _____ NUMBER _____

Lactarus olympianus
Family: *Russulaceae*

CAP: 2½–6″ across, various shades of orange, becoming funnel shaped with age; GILLS light buff.

EDIBILITY: Poisonous

ECOLOGY: Subalpine in conifer forests.

LOCATION: Hassell Lake Trail, Urad Rd., Berthoud Pass, CO 8/99 11,000′

LOOK FOR an orange mushroom that has the appearance of a birdbath.

■ LIFE LIST Where _____ NUMBER _____

Russula brevipes
Family: *Russulaceae*

CAP: 2–6″ across, depressed in center and dingy white; GILLS white.
EDIBILITY: Non-poisonous but disagreeable
ECOLOGY: Montane to subalpine in coniferous forests.
LOCATION: Three Mile Creek, Grant, CO 8/99 9500′
LOOK FOR groups of white mushrooms, with concave upper surfaces, growing through conifer duff.

■ **LIFE LIST** Where _____ NUMBER _____

Russula emetica
Family: *Russulaceae*

CAP: 1–3″ wide, bright scarlet to red-orange; GILLS white to creamy.
EDIBILITY: Poisonous
ECOLOGY: Subalpine and alpine in single or small groups, in moist areas of conifer forests.
LOCATION: Copper Mt., CO 8/92 10,500′
LOOK FOR reddish, shiny mushroom at high elevations.

■ **LIFE LIST** Where _____ NUMBER _____

Russula paludosa
Family: *Russulaceae*

CAP: 2–5″ across, red, fading to uneven shades of orange; GILLS cream to pale yellow going to orange with time.
EDIBILITY: Not recommended
ECOLOGY: Montane and subalpine in boggy, conifer forests.
LOCATION: FR 139, Bennett Creek Rd., Larimer Cty., CO 6/04 8500′
LOOK FOR a pinkish, slightly domed mushroom.

■ **LIFE LIST** Where _____ NUMBER _____

Pholiota squarrosa
Family: *Strophariaceae*

CAP: 1–4″ wide, covered with brown scales on a brownish-yellow background; GILLS pale yellow going to dull brown.
EDIBILITY: Poisonous
ECOLOGY: Subalpine, at the base of dead or living trees.
LOCATION: Hassell Lake Trail, Urad Rd., Berthoud Pass, CO 8/99 11,000′
LOOK FOR a group of yellow-cream mushrooms with brown, concentric surface scales.

■ LIFE LIST Where _____ NUMBER _____

Citocybe dilatata
Family: *Trichlomataceae*

CAP: 1–5″ wide, convex and chalky white; GILLS white.
EDIBILITY: Poisonous
ECOLOGY: found in groups of 12 or more, usually at high elevations.
LOCATION: Hassell Lake Trail, Urad Rd., Berthoud Pass, CO 8/99 11,000′
LOOK FOR groups of snow white, domed mushrooms.

■ LIFE LIST Where _____ NUMBER _____

Tricholoma zelleri
Family: *Trichlomataceae*

CAP: 1½″–5″ across, COLORS streaked and varying from bright orange-brown to yellow-orange with olive tones; GILLS whitish, going to rust with time.
EDIBILITY: Not recommended
ECOLOGY: Montane and subalpine, associated with Lodgepole pine or Aspen.
LOCATION: Three Mile Creek, Grant, CO 8/99 9500′
LOOK FOR a mushroom with an irregular circumference and blended colors of orange, brown and white.

■ LIFE LIST Where _____ NUMBER _____

Tricholomapsis rutilans
PLUMS AND CUSTARD
Family: *Tricholomataceae*

CAP: to 5″ across, convex, margins in-rolled, yellow with purple dots; GILLS pale yellow; stalks short.

EDIBILITY: Edible

ECOLOGY: Montane and subalpine in coniferous forests.

LOCATION: Herman Gulch Trail, Bakerville, CO 8/99 11,000′

LOOK FOR a large, yellow mushroom with red dots.

■ **LIFE LIST** Where _____ NUMBER _____

ROCKY MOUNTAIN FLORA

Ferns &
Fern-like
Plants

MALE FERN
Dryopteris filix-mas
Fern family *Dryopteridaceae*

PERENNIAL to 2´ tall; STEMS green, woody, erect and slender; FRONDS (leaves) opposite and bipinnate to 10˝ long.
ECOLOGY: Foothills in moist areas with dense shade.
LOCATION: Big Bluestem Trail, Eldorado Canyon S.P., Eldorado Springs, CO 6/00 6500´
LOOK FOR a fern with a wiry stem and well spaced, opposite fronds.

◼ LIFE LIST Where _____ NUMBER _____

OREGON WOODSIA
Woodsia oregana
Fern family *Dryopteridaceae*

PERENNIAL forming tufts; FRONDS basal to 10˝ high, bright green with opposite leaflets to 1˝ long.
ECOLOGY: Foothills to subalpine in rocky areas.
LOCATION: Arthur's Rock Trail, Lory S.P., Ft. Collins, CO 6/99 5500´
LOOK FOR a small tuft of bright green fronds, with lobed leaflets.

◼ LIFE LIST Where _____ NUMBER _____

MOUNTAIN CLIFF FERN
(ROCKY MOUNTAIN WOODSIA)
Woodsia scopulina
Fern family *Dryopteridaceae*

PERENNIAL fern to 10˝ tall; FRONDS twice pinnate to 10˝ long; LEAFLETS pinnate to 1½˝ long.
ECOLOGY: Montane and subalpine in rock crevices.
LOCATION: Isabelle Glacier Trail, Brainard Lake Rec. Area, Ward, CO 7/00 11,000´
LOOK FOR a bright, light green fern, nestled among rocks.

◼ LIFE LIST Where _____ NUMBER _____

COMMON HORSETAIL
Equisetum arvense
Horsetail family *Equisetaceae*

PERENNIAL to 20″ tall; 2 forms: fertile to 6″ tall, brown and has only a brief existence early in the spring, and a non-fertile form that has wire-like leaves borne in whorls.
ECOLOGY: Plains to subalpine in wet areas.
LOCATION: McGraw Ranch, RMNP, CO 5/02 8000′
LOOK FOR a green plant with whorls of string-like leaves that are easily segmented by pulling.

 LIFE LIST Where _____ NUMBER _____

SCOURING RUSH
Equisetum laevigatum
(Hippochaete laevigata)
Horsetail family *Equisetaceae*

PERENNIAL to 3′ tall; STEMS hollow, jointed and may branch at top node; fruiting body develops as a brown terminal dome and elongates to form a white head with brown spots that enlarge and produce spores.
ECOLOGY: Plains to montane in wet areas.
LOCATION: Lion Gulch, Roosevelt N.F., US 36, CO 6/00 7500′
LOOK FOR a thin, single brown ring at each node and a constriction under the head.

LIFE LIST Where _____ NUMBER _____

ROCKY MOUNTAIN FLORA

Lichens

Alectoria sarmentosa
COMMON WITCH HAIR
Wood lichen

BODY: an aerial, green, hair-like growth on forest trees, especially dead conifer branches.
ECOLOGY: Foothills to subalpine.
LOCATION: Young Gulch, Poudre Canyon, CO 7/02 7500′
LOOK FOR an aerial, light green, hair-like growth, generally hanging from dead conifer branches.

■ LIFE LIST Where _____ NUMBER _____

Aspicilia desertorum
Rock lichen

BODY: light, gray-green with a sandy surface to 3″ across; SPORE cups have black centers and vary in size, shape and density.
ECOLOGY: Foothills on exposed surfaces.
LOCATION: Devil's Backbone Rec. Area, Loveland, CO 5/02 5500′
LOOK FOR a light gray-green, sandy surface with black spore cups.

■ LIFE LIST Where _____ NUMBER _____

Collema furfuraceum
Rock lichen

BODY: composed of black, overlapping leaves to ½″ wide, forming a rough surface and irregular outline.
ECOLOGY: Foothills on open hilltops.
LOCATION: Coyote Ridge Rec. Area, Ft. Collins, CO 5/02 5500′
LOOK FOR a lichen composed of black, overlapping leaves.

■ LIFE LIST Where _____ NUMBER _____

Flavopunctelia soredica
Rock lichen

BODY: a smooth single, shiny, light gray leaf with an
irregular outline, to 1″ long.
ECOLOGY: Foothills on exposed rocks.
LOCATION: Arthur's Rock Trail, Lory S.P., Ft. Collins,
CO 8/05 5500′
LOOK FOR a single, smooth, light gray leaf.

■ **LIFE LIST** Where _____ NUMBER _____

Haematomma subpuniceum
Rock lichen

BODY: light gray, sandy appearance to 2″ long with a
fairly smooth outline.
ECOLOGY: Foothills on exposed rock.
LOCATION: Devil's Backbone Rec. Area, Loveland,
CO 5/02 5500′
LOOK FOR light gray, sandy texture with a smooth
outline.

■ **LIFE LIST** Where _____ NUMBER _____

Lecidea atrobrunnea
Rock lichen

BODY: uniform, dark brown with a raised, grainy
texture, to 1″ long, with an irregular shape, but a
smooth outline.
ECOLOGY: Subalpine on marble rock.
LOCATION: North Gap Trail, Medicine Bow N.F., WY
8/00 10,500′
LOOK FOR a dark brown lichen with a grainy
surface.

■ **LIFE LIST** Where _____ NUMBER _____

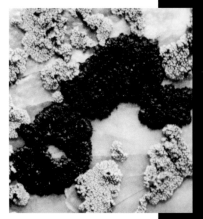

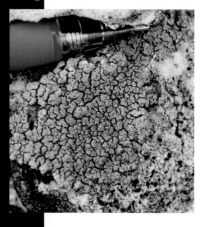

Lecidella euphorea
Rock lichen

BODY: blue-gray to 2″ across and fractured, like drying mud, with a semi-rough surface and a choppy outline.

ECOLOGY: Foothills on exposed rock.

LOCATION: Coyote Ridge Rec. Area, Ft. Collins, CO 5/02 5500′

LOOK FOR a blue-green lichen with an extensively cracked surface and a jagged outline.

■ **LIFE LIST** Where ＿＿＿＿＿ NUMBER ＿＿

Pleopsidium flavum
Rock lichens

BODY: greenish-yellow, fractured, to 2″ across, with a smooth outline and no black border.

ECOLOGY: Foothills on exposed rock.

LOCATION: Coyote Ridge Rec. Area, Ft. Collins, CO 5/02 5500′

LOOK FOR a greenish-yellow patch without a black border.

■ **LIFE LIST** Where ＿＿＿＿＿ NUMBER ＿＿

Ramalina intermedia
Rock lichen

BODY: light, gray-green, leafy surface, with rolled-down edges, to 2″ wide, with a jagged outline.

ECOLOGY: Foothills on exposed rock.

LOCATION: Horsetooth Trail, Lory S.P., Ft. Collins, CO 9/04 5500′

LOOK FOR gray-green, downward-rolled leaves.

■ **LIFE LIST** Where ＿＿＿＿＿ NUMBER ＿＿

Rhizocarpon disporum
Rock lichen

BODY: a dark, blue-gray, fractured patch to 2″ across, with large black spots of varying size, some coalescing.

ECOLOGY: Foothills on exposed rock.

LOCATION: Coyote Ridge Rec. Area, Ft. Collins, CO 5/02 5500′

LOOK FOR black spots of varying density and size on a dark, blue-green patch.

■ **LIFE LIST** Where _____ NUMBER _____

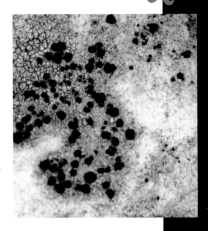

Rhizocarpon geographicum
Rock lichen

BODY: a bright yellow, fractured patch to 1″ across, underlaid and bordered by black, making a smooth outline.

ECOLOGY: Subalpine and alpine on marble rock.

LOCATION: North Gap Lake Trail, Medicine Bow N.F., WY 8/00 10,500′

LOOK FOR a yellow patch with fracture lines, underlaid with a black material.

■ **LIFE LIST** Where _____ NUMBER _____

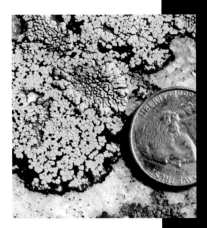

Sporastatia testudinea
Rock lichen

BODY: a uniformly light brown, fairly round patch with smooth edges, to 2″ wide.

ECOLOGY: Subalpine to alpine on marble rock.

LOCATION: North Gap Lake Trail, Medicine Bow N.F., WY 8/00 11,500′

LOOK FOR a light brown, circular lichen of sandy, uniform texture.

■ **LIFE LIST** Where _____ NUMBER _____

Xanthoparmelia cumberlandia
Rock lichen

BODY: light, gray-green, leafy at the edges and rough at the center with clusters of irregular cups. Small islands seem to coalesce to form large, irregular islands.

ECOLOGY: Plains and foothills on exposed rock.

LOCATION: Devil's Backbone Rec. Area, Loveland, CO 5/02 5500´

LOOK FOR colonies of light, gray-green islands of varying size.

■ **LIFE LIST** Where _____ NUMBER _____

Xanthoria elegans
ELEGANT ORANGE
Rock lichen

BODY: an orange patch to 2″ wide made up of large islands in the center surrounded by smaller islands near the edges, forming a smooth outline.

ECOLOGY: Subalpine and alpine on exposed rock.

LOCATION: Libby Flats, Medicine Bow N.F., WY 8/00 10,500´

LOOK FOR an orange patch with large and small islands.

■ **LIFE LIST** Where _____ NUMBER _____

ROCKY MOUNTAIN FLORA

Mosses

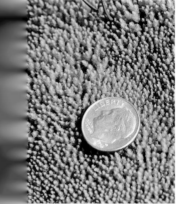

STRAW MOSS
Callier stramineum
Aquatic moss

PERENNIAL forming very shiny, yellow-green carpets; STEMS to 4″ tall, unbranched and either male or female; LEAVES tiny, crowded and overlapping.

ECOLOGY: Subalpine and alpine in bogs.

LOCATION: North Gap Lake Trail, Medicine Bow N.F., WY, in slowly moving water above tree line 8/00 10,500′

LOOK FOR a yellow-green, shiny carpet of moss in slowly moving water.

■ LIFE LIST Where _____ NUMBER _____

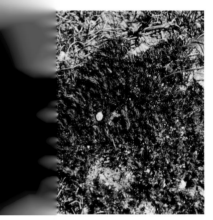

COPPER WIRE MOSS
Pohlia nutans
Terrestrial moss

PERENNIAL forming yellow-green or green carpets; STEMS reddish, slender, to 1½″ long and either male or female; LEAVES lanceolate, narrowing to a sharp point and ½″ long.

ECOLOGY: Foothills to alpine on open sites.

LOCATION: Twin Buttes Trail, Pawnee National Grasslands, Keota, CO 5/99, 5000′

LOOK FOR the tiny copper wires.

■ LIFE LIST Where _____ NUMBER _____

ROCKY MOUNTAIN FLORA

Edible
Native Plants

I would be remiss if I failed to express my concern for our Edible Native Plants. We should all be aware that plants are becoming extinct at an alarming rate. While I have no knowledge of the extinction of any plants described in this book, it would not surprise me if one or more are extinct. I say this because I have taken pictures of plants 15 years ago and have not seen them since, which is somewhat annoying because I was in need of better pictures.

By including this section it should not be construed that I approve harvesting native plants for consumption. On the contrary, I recommend that you bring water and food, leave nothing, and take only memories and pictures with you.

It's one thing to pick a leaf or a flower for closer examination when there are an abundance of leaves and flowers, and quite another to harvest a plant roots and all, especially if it's the only one of its kind in the vicinity.

This book is about education and appreciation of the plants that we are privileged to have in our midst. Knowing which ones are edible is part of that education.

While this list is complete for the species described in this book, it falls far short of being comprehensive. For an expanded listing, H.D. Harrington's *Edible Native Plants of the Rocky Mountains* is recommended.

Acer negundo, BOX ELDER. Sap used for making sugar using the technique employed for making maple sugar.

Allium cernuum, NODDING ONION. Leaves and bulbs used to flavor soup, stew or meat. Juice may be boiled to form a thick cough syrup.

Amaranthus albus, PROSTRATE PIGWEED and *A. retroflexus*, ROUGH PIGWEED. Young plants and tender shoots can be boiled as a potherb, and the seed may be boiled to make gruel, or ground to make flour for baking.

Amelanchier alnifolia, COMMON SHADBUSH. The fleshy fruit can be used just like any other fruit: fresh, dried as raisins, or cooked to make pies, jellies and jams.

Arctium minus, BURDOCK. Young leaves and shoots may be used in salads or boiled as potherbs. The roots of rosettes may be peeled and boiled if gathered before flowering.

Arctostaphylos uva-ursi, KINNIKINNIK. Berries may be eaten fresh, but are more palatable if cooked, and even more so when used with sugar to make jelly.

Argentina anserina, SILVERWEED. The roots have a nutty flavor and may be eaten raw or cooked.

Asclepias speciosa, SHOWY MILKWEED. Young shoots are harvested when up to 8″ high and boiled like asparagus. The water should be changed one or more times to remove the bitter taste.

Asparagus officinalis, ASPARAGUS. This is an escapee from cultivation and should be harvested and prepared just as it is under cultivation.

Avena fatua, WILD OATS. The gathered heads must first be abraded or singed to eliminate the sharp awns before grinding into flour.

Calochortus gunnisonii, MARIPOSA LILY. The whole plant can be used as a potherb, but there is little bulk in such a small plant. However, the bulb that is 6–8″ deep and often overlooked, has a potato flavor and is a good source of nutrition.

Caltha leptosepala, MARSH MARIGOLD. The leaves may be used as potherbs until the flowers emerge, and the roots may be boiled for a longer period to produce a food resembling sauerkraut.

Campanula rapunculoides, BELLFLOWER. Tender leaves shoots and roots may be boiled and eaten. Larger roots should have the rind removed before boiling or frying. Old, large roots will be too fibrous to eat.

Capsella bursa-pastoris, SHEPHERD'S PURSE. Young leaves are used as potherbs. The pods can be used fresh or dried as a flavoring for soups.

Ceanothus spp., BUCKBRUSH, MT. BALM, AND STICKY LAUREL, (NEW JERSEY TEA). All members of the genus may be used to make tea, by drying leaves and flowers and boiling or steeping them.

Chenopodium capitatum, STRAWBERRY BLITE. Tender leaves and shoots are used as potherbs, and the fleshy fruit clusters are used raw or cooked.

Cichorium intybus, COMMON CHICORY. Young leaves and shoots and used as potherbs, and roots have been ground and roasted as a substitute or additive to coffee. Its use for this purpose greatly increases during coffee shortages as it did during WWII.

Cirsium spp., THISTLE. Apparently all species of thistles in the region are edible. Certainly, the leaves and shoots should be harvested for potherbs before the spines develop. The pith of young stems and roots, when boiled, provide pleasant dishes.

Claytonia lanceolata, SPRING BEAUTY. The tuberous corms have a flavor similar to potatoes, and like potatoes, are more palatable after cooking.

Descurainia sophia, TANSY MUSTARD. Pods are harvested, dried and crushed to liberate the seed for grinding into flour. Tender leaves and shoots should be boiled with 2 or more changes of water before eating to rid them of bitterness.

Echinochloa crusgalli, BARNYARD GRASS. Seed are harvested, dried and ground into flour.

Elytrigia repens, QUACK GRASS. Rhizomes can be harvested and dried, then ground into flour for baking.

Epilobium angustifolium, FIREWEED. Young shoots may be used as asparagus, and tender leaves may be used for salad or potherbs.

Equisetum arvense, COMMON HORSETAIL. The reproductive shoots can be boiled and eaten before the cone scales loosen. However, this is regarded as a poisonous plant and as such, best avoided.

Erodium cicutarium, STORKBILL. When young it can be used for salad or potherbs. It is valued because it is available early in the season when there are few other edible plants.

Erythronium grandiflorum, AVALANCHE LILY. Leaves can be used as salad or potherbs and corms can be eaten raw or boiled as potatoes.

Fragaria vesca, WOODLAND STRAWBERRY and *F. virginiana*, WILD STRAWBERRY. Both produce fruit renown for their authentic flavor.

Helianthus annuus, COMMON SUNFLOWER. Sunflower seeds have been a dietary stable for countless years.

Juniperus scopulorum, ROCKY MT. JUNIPER. The fruit have been harvested and dried for off-season use by Indians. They are too astringent to enjoy, but are edible as a survival food. Boiling with several changes of water might improve their palatability.

Lactuca serriola, PRICKLY LETTUCE. Not surprisingly, when young and tender it may be used in salads, although it is quite bitter. It becomes less bitter when used as a potherb, especially if the water is changed 1 or more times.

Mahonia repens, HOLLYGRAPE. The berries can be eaten raw or processed into jelly or jam.

Malva neglecta, CHEESEWEED. Tender leaves and shoots may be used in salads or as potherbs. Fruit (cheese wheels) may be eaten raw or cooked with soups. Dried, older leaves can be used to make tea.

Nuphar polysepalum, YELLOW POND LILY. Roots are extracted from mud at the bottom of the pond. The roots, which may be 2′ long, are boiled, then peeled, cut and dried. The dried centers are then ground into flour that is used to thicken soups.

Oenothera villosa strigosa, HAIRY EVENING PRIMROSE. Young shoots and leaves may be used in salads or as potherbs, changing the water at least once to get rid of the bitter flavor. Tender roots may also be boiled like parsnips, peeled and eaten.

Opuntia macrorhiza, PRICKLY PEAR CACTUS. Before attempting to eat the fruit, the spines must be removed by either singeing the fruit over an open flame or boiling it for 15 minutes. Mechanically scraping them off does not disarm the spines, and any that remain can cause problems. Having done this, the fruit is split open and the edible pulp is removed. While this information is specific to this species, cacti are non-poisonous and most have pulp that is palatable.

Oryzopsis hymenoides, INDIAN RICEGRASS. The seed is rather large and easily gathered; however, they have objectionable hairs, which should be removed by singeing, prior to grinding the seed into flour. The Indians shook a mixture of seed and live coals to accomplish this; however shaking the seed on wire screen over an open flame, like popcorn, might be more efficient.

Oxyria digyna, ALPINE SORREL. Young leaves may be used in salads or eaten raw and older leaves are useful as potherbs.

Physalis spp., GROUND CHERRY. The berries of any of the yellow-flowered species may be eaten raw, or cooked and made into jams, jellies or pies.

Plantago major, COMMON PLANTAIN. Young leaves may be eaten raw or used in salad, while older leaves are better used as potherbs. Dried leaves have been used to make an herbal tea and fresh leaves are said to serve as bandages over cuts and bruises.

Polygonum bistortoides, BISTORT and *P. viviparum*, SERPENT GRASS. Young leaves of these two species may be used as potherbs, and their roots may be eaten raw or boiled, with boiling preferred for the larger roots.

Portulaca oleracea, PURSLANE. Tender shoots and leaves may be used in salads alone or in combination with other greens. Its high water content and astringent flavor make it useful for quenching thirst. It may also be used as a potherb.

although it does become mucilaginous when cooked. This attribute makes is useful for thickening soups, and suggests that it should be used with other potherbs rather than alone.

Potomogeton spp., PONDWEED. Thickened rootstocks and tubers of this genus are edible, although difficult to access when under water; however, they may be dug when the water recedes late in the season. The plants are easily recognized and the location is unique, so it is unlikely that they might be confused with a plant of a poisonous nature.

Prunus americana, WILD PLUM. The fruit of this shrub may be used for any purpose that the cultivated plum is used.

Prunus virginiana, WESTERN CHOKECHERRY. Like the wild plum, this fruit can be used like the cultivated cherry, making allowances for its astringency. It has found particular popularity when used to make chokecherry wine.

Quercus gambelii, GAMBLE OAK. Oaks are valued wherever they grow for the acorns they produce. These acorns are often the main food source of certain animals and this has been true of some Indian tribes. To be palatable, the meat must be removed from the shell, coarse ground, and leached to remove the tannins that give it a bitter flavor. After drying, it may be further ground and used as flour in producing cakes and breads.

Rhus glabra, SMOOTH SUMAC. The ripe red berries may be crushed in a small amount and strained through a cloth to remove the hairs, etc., then add water and sugar. One cluster per glass should produce a beverage that some compare to lemonade. It should be made fresh as it is reported to develop a rancid flavor after an hour.

Rhus triloba, THREE LEAF SUMAC. A handful of ripe berries, placed in a cloth bag and boiled, can be made up to a quart of orange liquid that has the flavor of lemonade. The berries can be eaten raw, or dried for future use. The consensus is that they are not very palatable, and are best used to make a beverage.

Ribes spp., GOLDEN CURRANT, WAX CURRANT, PRICKLY CURRANT, AND RED PRICKLY CURRANT. All Ribes may be eaten fresh, canned, frozen or used to make pies, jellies and jams. However, some species are preferred over others, with the Wax Currant being the least preferred.

Rorippa nasturtium-aquaticum, WATERCRESS. Tender leaves are used in salads to give the peppery flavor or bite that some people like. Older leaves can be used as potherbs or as a flavoring in soups. Watercress is grown and sold commercially and enjoys a small but steady market.

Rosa woodsii, WILD ROSE. This plant, as well as all roses, produces fruit called hips that are edible fresh, dried or cooked. The most common use for hips is the making of jelly. The recipe for this is included in many cookbooks as well as in the directions supplied with pectin.

Rubus idaeus, RED RASPBERRY. Eaten fresh, the flavor is wonderful, but the seeds are hard and large. Because of this, it is commonly used to make jelly, which of course, has no seeds.

Rumex acetosella, SHEEP SORREL. All species of this genus contain varying amounts of oxalates that are harmful if eaten in excess. However, the sour taste of these oxalates is what appeals to the users, and also what limits its use. It is generally thought of as a condiment for flavoring for salads and meats rather than an entree.

Rumex crispus, CURLY DOCK. This species apparently contains less oxalates that others and young leaves can be used as salads. Older leaves make good potherbs, becoming surprisingly tender after cooking.

Sagittaria latifolia, ARROWHEAD. Tubers are produced under water in mud. The usual procedure is to wade into the water and rake the bottom with a potato rake to bring up the tubers that float to the surface. These tubers are then boiled, peeled, and eaten like potatoes.

Salsola kali, RUSSIAN THISTLE. Young, rapidly growing shoots, up to 5″ long, make a very fine potherb. It is quite bland and accepts flavors from items such as bacon strips and boiled egg slices.

Sambucus canadensis., ELDERBERRY. Known as a black-fruited elderbery, its fruit can be eaten raw or used for pies, wine, jelly or jam. The red-fruited elderberry, as represented by *S. racemosa*, has an unpleasant taste that is not mitigated by cooking. In addition, it has been reported to have caused severe intestinal upsets and is generally regarded as inedible.

Sedum integrifolium, KING'S CROWN,
S. lanceolatum, YELLOW STONECROP and
S. rhodanthum, QUEEN'S CROWN. Young leaves and shoots of the above may be eaten fresh or boiled as potherbs.

Sisymbrium altissimum, TUMBLE MUSTARD. Tender shoots and leaves may be eaten fresh or used as potherbs. Seed may be harvested and ground into flour. It has been reported to have poisoned cattle, so caution is advised.

Maianthemum racemosum, FALSE SOLOMON'S SEAL and
M. stellatum, STAR SOLOMON'S SEAL. The berries may be eaten fresh or cooked, and young tender leaves and shoots may be used as potherbs. The berries have been reported to be laxative when eaten in quantities.

Solanum nigrum, BLACK NIGHTSHADE. When ripe (black) the fruit may be eaten fresh or used for a variety of things such as jellies, jams, pies and puddings. All green parts of this plant should be avoided.

Sonchus arvensis, SPINY SOWTHISTLE. This plant has milky juice that is generally associated with bitterness. Young leaves and shoots may be used in salads if their bitterness is not objectionable. When used as potherbs, the water may be changed to rid it of some of its bitterness.

Stellaria media, CHICKWEED. Young, tender shoots and leaves are bland and may be used alone for salad. They also can be substituted for spinach as a potherb.

Taraxacum officinale, COMMON DANDELION. Young, tender leaves may be used for salad, or used with older leaves as a potherb. The water should be changed 1 or more times during cooking to reduce the bitterness to tolerable levels. These greens are used world-wide for food and are available in the produce section of many stores.

Thelesperma megapotamicum, FIELD COREOPSIS. Tea can be made from this plant from the dried shoots, by boiling or steeping. The resulting tea is said to be delicious.

Thlaspi arvense, PENNYCRESS. Young, tender shoots and leaves may be used in salads or as potherbs. Being a Brassicaceae, it has the characteristic bitter taste that many people do not like. Several changes of water while cooking are the only practical answer to this bitterness.

Typha latifolia, BROADLEAF CATTAIL. This is probably the most important edible native plant that we have. No one should starve when a supply of these cattails are available. Shoots up to 2′ long may be cut and stripped of their leaves and eaten raw or as potherbs. Developing flower heads may be harvested, husked and eaten like corn-on the-cob. Surpluses can be dried and stored for future use.

Urtica dioica, AMERICAN STINGING NETTLE. This plant presents a problem in harvesting because it has spines that easily penetrate the skin, producing a sting similar to an ant sting. In both cases, formic acid is suspected. At any rate, shoots 4–8″ long are pulled as they emerge from the ground, and the rhizome to which they are attached is tender and may also be used. During boiling, the spines degenerate and loose their ability to sting and the resulting dish is reported to be quite tasty.

Valeriana edulis, WESTERN VALERIAN. The root is used after boiling as a vegetable root such as carrot or parsnip. While the Indians have used it, it has been reported to be all but inedible by any means of cooking, and without cooking, it is said to be poisonous.

Veronica americana, AMERICAN SPEEDWELL. Young, rapidly growing shoots can be used in salads to give a bitter taste that some people like. Using is alone gives more bitterness than most people want. This bitterness can be abated by changing the cooking water as often as necessary to attain a satisfactory potherb.

Viburnum edule, HIGH BUSH CRANBERRY. The berries may be eaten fresh, but the most common usage is to make jelly from the pulp. This is done by harvesting the ripe fruit after it has softened, and running it through a food processor to eliminate the tough skins and hard seeds.

Viola ssp., VIOLET. The young leaves and buds of all species of violets found in the Rocky Mountains may be used in salads, or boiled for potherbs. They are bland and benefit from being mixed with more flavorful greens.

Vitis spp., WILD GRAPE. Any of the wild grapes may be eaten fresh or used to make juice, jelly or wine.

Yucca glauca, SPANISH BAYONET. The immature fruit may be boiled and eaten with seeds and all; however, bitterness was reduced when the fruit was peeled before boiling. The flowers may be used in salads or boiled as a potherb.

ROCKY MOUNTAIN FLORA

Poisonous Native Plants

The plants cited below have been reported to be poisonous, contain poisonous substances such as alkaloids, or are generally regarded as poisonous. While these plants should be avoided, I would prefer that you regard any plant that you do not know is edible, to be poisonous. This particularly applies to mushrooms, which seem to have a sometimes-fatal attraction to those seeking new experiences in eating. My unsolicited advice in this matter is to bring your lunch with you so you don't have to forage.

Aconitum columbianum, MONKSHOOD. All parts of this plant are poisonous at all times.

Actaea rubra, RED BANEBERRY. The berries and rootstocks are poisonous.

Apocynum cannabinum, INDIAN HEMP. This is regarded as a poisonous plant although it has been reported that the seeds have been ground and used to make fried cakes.

Conium maculatum, POISON HEMLOCK. All parts of this plant are poisonous, and unfortunately, it resembles several edible plants, Queen Ann's Lace being one.

Delphinium geyeri, GEYER LARKSPUR. This is the worst cattle-poisoning plant in the United States. There is no record as to its effect on people, but it is assumed to be poisonous.

Iris missouriensis, WILD IRIS. The fleshy rhizomes are poisonous, and they are the plant part that is most tempting. The rest of the plant is assumed to be poisonous though less appealing.

Lupinus argenteus, SILVER LUPINE. This species is quite variable and botanists are not sure if more than this specie is involved; at any rate, all parts of this plant are poisonous. Sheep seem to be attracted to it more that other animals and suffer the highest mortality.

MUSHROOMS. Poisonous mushrooms are grouped together here because they are fungi. Of the 19 mushrooms described in the Mushroom section, 6 are designated edible, 5 are poisonous and 8 are listed as disagreeable, inedible, not recommended, or edible only at certain stages. The poisonous mushrooms are as follows:

Amanita muscaria   *Citocybe dilatata*
Lactarus olympianus   *Pholiota squarrosa*
Russula emetica

Oxypolis and *Oxytropis spp.*, COWBANE, COLORADO LOCO, FEW FLOWERED LOCO, WHITE LOCO, AND SHOWY LOCOWEED. All parts of these species are poisonous. They appeal to horses that become *loco* (crazy) before they die from the effects of the poison.

Ranunculus sceleratus, BLISTER BUTTERCUP. This plant contains an acrid juice that causes skin blisters on some people and is regarded as poisonous. It contains a narcotic (anemonal) that is especially lethal to cattle.

Toxicodendron rydbergii, POISON IVY. All parts of this plant contain a non-volatile oil that causes blisters when it comes in contact with the skin of most people. Birds and livestock do not seem to be bothered by it; however, it is not a preferred forage.

Zygadenus ssp., MT. DEATH CAMAS and MEADOW DEATH CAMAS. All parts of all species of the Zygadenus genus are poisonous. The bulbs are most dangerous because they are similar to wild onions and Mariposa Lily and have been mistakenly eaten with disastrous results.

REFERENCES
Books, Herbarium, and Websites

BOOKS

Beidleman, L. H., R. G. Beidleman, and B. E. Willard. 1994. *Plants of the Rocky Mountain National Park.* Rocky Mountain Nature Association and Falcon Publishing, Inc., Helena, Montana.

Carter J. L. 1988. *Trees and Shrubs of Colorado.* Johnson Books, Boulder, Colorado.

Evenson, V. S. 1997. *Mushrooms of Colorado.* Denver Museum of Natural History and Westcliffe Publishers, Inc., Englewood, Colorado.

Fernald, M.L. 1950. *Gray's Manual of Botany,* 8th ed., American Book Co., New York, New York.

Guennel, G. K. 1995. *Colorado Wildflowers.* Vol. 1. Plains and Foothills. Westcliffe Publishers, Inc., Englewood, Colorado.

Guennel, G. K. 1995. *Colorado Wildflowers.* Vol. 2. Mountains. Westcliffe Publishers, Inc., Englewood, Colorado.

Harrington, H. D., and Y. Matsumura. 1967. *Edible Native Plants of the Rocky Mountains.* University of New Mexico Press, Albuquerque, New Mexico.

Harris, J. G., and M. W. Harris. 1995. *Plant Identification Terminology.* 2nd ed., Spring Lake Publishing, Payson, Utah.

Hitchcock, A. S. 1971. *Manual of the Grasses of the United States.* Vol. 1 & 2. 2nd ed., Dover Publications, Inc., New York, New York.

Irwin, P. D., and D. H. Irwin. 1998. *Colorado's Best Wildflower Hikes.* Front Range. Westcliffe Publishers, Inc., Englewood, Colorado.

Kershaw, L., A. MacKinnon, and J. Pojar. 1998. *Plants of the Rocky Mountains.* Lone Pine Publishing, Edmonton, Alberta, Canada

Nelson, R. A., and R. L. Williams. 1992. *A Guide to Rocky Mountain Plants.* 5th ed., Roberts Rinehart Publishers, Lanham, Maryland.

St. Clair, L. L. 1999. *A Color Guidebook to Common Rocky Mountain Lichens.* Brigham Young University, Provo, Utah and San Juan-Rio Grande National Forest, Durango, Colorado.

Thornton, B. J., H. D. Harrington, and R. L. Zimdahl. 1974. *Weeds of Colorado.* Experiment Station, Colorado State University, Fort Collins, Colorado.

Weber, W. A. 1976. *Rocky Mountain Flora.* Colorado Associated University Press, Boulder, Colorado.

Whitson, T. D., *et al.* 1992. *Weeds of the West.* The Western Society of Weed Science, Newark, California.

HERBARIUM

Department of Biology, Colorado State University, Fort Collins, Colorado.

WEBSITES

http://www.mip.berkeley.edu/query_forms/browse_checklist.html
This website was initially used to verify the official Latin names of plants. It was called the 'Biota of North America Program' and was sponsored by the North Carolina Botanical Garden and the 'Museum Informatics Project', University of California at Berkeley. At one point, it became impossible to access this website and this forced a search for another authoritative website.

www.plants.usda.gov
This website was suggested as an alternative by the C.S.U. Herbarium, which had originally suggested the Berkeley site. They also found they could not assess the Berkeley website and were using this one. This website also gives common names for plants, which was not the case with the Berkeley site.

Glossary and Abbreviations

Achene: a small, dry, single-seeded fruit. Example: the 'seed' on the surface of a strawberry.

Acuminate: drawn to a point, as in stretching a plastic substance to its breaking point.

Alpine: as used in this book, refers to altitudes of above 11,500 ft.

Alternate: a leaf arrangement of left-then-right positioning of leaves ascending a stem.

Annual: a plant that lives for only one season.

Anther: a sac that contains pollen and is associated with a flower.

Apetalous: describes a flower without petals.

Apex: the highest or most remote point.

Appressed: refers to leaves or other structures being vertically pressed against the stem.

Aquatic: a plant that lives in or close to water.

Ascending: refers to a stem that grows laterally at first, usually to find sunlight, then curves upward.

Axil, axillary: the crotch formed by the leaf and the stem. Axillary buds form in these crotches.

Awl-like: refers to a leaf that resembles a point of an awl, a tool that is used to penetrate.

Awn: the bristle that extends from a grass flower.

Banner: the uppermost petal of a leguminous flower such as a pea. Its coloration is often a distinguishing feature.

Beaked: resembling the beak of a bird, most often used in reference to a flower with a downward hooked corolla.

Berry: a succulent fruit containing many seeds, such as tomatoes and blueberries.

Biennial: a plant that lives for 2 years.

Bipinnate: refers to a compound leaf with a row of leaflets on both side of the midrib (rachis), that in turn have similar leaflets.

Bipinnatifid: refers to a leaf that has a series of lobes arranged on both sides of the midrib. These lobes, in turn, have lobes that are similarly arranged. This usually is in reference to certain fern leaves (fronds).

Blade: refers to the flat part of the leaf, excluding the petiole.

Bloom: can refer to an open flower; but it also refers to a waxy powder that appears on certain leaves, twigs, and fruit. When present, it can be rubbed off, resulting an a glossy surface such as a polished apple.

Boreal: Northern

Bract: refers to leaf-like structure that usually subtend flowers or leaves. Some are quite colorful as the bracts on Poinsettias and Indian Paintbrushes.

Branchlet: a small branch most often used to describe the sub-branches of a grass inflorescence that produce the grass flowers.

Bristle: a stiff hair, but not pointed as a spine or thorn.

Bulblet or bulbil: a miniature bulb that may be produced in place of flowers as is the case with garlic. They represent an asexual method of cloning a plant.

Bur: a seed capsule that is characterized by thorns, for defense, or hooks, for seed distribution. Chestnuts and burdock are examples.

Calyx: a whorl of bracts (sepals) about the base of a flower. It may also be a tube, as with carnations.

Catkin: a spike, either stiff or dangling that holds the flower parts. They are generally associated with trees and use wind to disseminate both pollen and seed.

Caudex: is a woody stem of a perennial plant, mostly underground, that gives rise to the aerial part of the plant.

Clasping: refers to a leaf type that has a base which wraps around the stem. This trait is used to characterize certain plants.

Cleft: means split or lay open; an identifying characteristic.

Clump: a plant that has multiplied forming a dense colony or tussock.

Composite: a plant with a many-seeded flower head belonging to the *Asteraceae* family.

Cordate: means heart-shaped and generally refers to heart-shaped leaves.

Corm: a subterranean storage organ in the shape of a donut used to asexually reproduce certain plants in the family of *Liliaceae* (e.g., gladiolus).

Corolla: the showy part of a flower, usually composed of petals, but can be a tube, bell or funnel.

Crown: the base of a perennial plant that initiates growth each year.

Culm: a stalk of grass or a sedge consisting of over-lapping leaf sheaths, such as a corn stalk. Technically, such an organ cannot be called a stem.

Decumbent: prostrate except for the ascending tips of the branches.

Decurrent: pointing downward from the point of attachment.

Dehiscence: the act of dispersing pollen or seed.

Deltoid: triangular.

Dentate: refers to teeth.

Determinate: a plant that has its growth terminated by producing a terminal flower; e.g., tulip.

Dichotomous: branching by forking. Commonly used when referring to a taxonomic key where each statement has two choices.

Digitate: finger-like, or arranged like fingers, as is the case of a palmately compound leaf.

Dioecious: refers to a species that produces male and female plants.

Disc: refers to the center of a composite flower. The Black-Eyed Susan is named for its dark flower disc.

Dissected: refer to leaves that have lobes that appear to result from being cut.

Drupe: a succulent fruit with a single seed called a pit or stone, such as a cherry.

Druplet: a small drupe such a single aggregate of a raspberry fruit.

Elliptic: refers to a leaf shape that is symmetrically pointed at both ends.

Entire: a leaf that has a smooth, curved outline is said to entire.

Exserted: usually refers to extended flower parts, such as an exserted style that extends beyond the corolla tube.

Fascicle: a small bundle such as the cluster of needles produced by pines.

Fibril: a term associated with mushrooms referring to an aggregation of hyphae to form a filament.

Filament: the stalk that holds the anther; also, any thread-like structure.

Filamentous: thread-like.

Foothills: as used in this book, this is a zone of 6000 to 8000 ft.

Frond: a fern leaf.

Glabrous: smooth, without hairs.

Glaucous: a bloom or white, waxy substance covering a leaf or organ.

Globoid, globose, globus, globular: globe-shaped.

Head: a flower head or seed head that holds many flowers or seed. Most often used in reference to composite flowers such a Sunflower head, or grass such as a head of barley.

Imbricated: shingled; an arrangement of overlapping phyllaries on the involucre. An identification aid – "if they're imbricated, it can't be a *Senecio*."

Incised: refers to a leaf that has been cut sharply and deeply into lobes. It implies sharp points and straight sides.

Inflorescence: the part of the plant that produces flowers.

Involucre: a whorl of bracts, sometimes fused, about the base of a flower cluster; always prevalent in composites such as dandelions.

Keel: the lower petal of a leguminous flower.

Lanceolate: refers to a leaf that is pointed at the tip and rounded at the petiole. This coincides with the shape of a medieval lance.

Lateral: side, as in lateral branches.

Leaflet: a sub leaf such as a leaflet on the rachis of pinnately compound leaf.

Leguminous: a leguminous plant, such as peas, belong to the *Fabaceae* family. They have a distinctive flower and seed pod type that is referred to as leguminous.

Lenticles: these are sites of gas exchange that appear as white or tan spots on fruit and twigs. They sometimes serve as a means of identification.

Linear: refers to a leaf that is long and narrow.

Lobe: any rounded appendage; most often used to describe the segments of a pinnatifid leaf.

Midrib: refers to the central vein in the leaf.

Monoecious: refers to a plant that has male and female flowers on the same plant.

Montane: refers to elevations between 8000 and 10,000 ft. in this book.

N.F.: National Forest.

Nodding: generally refers to a flower with a willowy stalk permitting the flower to droop and sway in the wind.

Node: the point at which a leaf arises.

Noxious: a plant declared an undesirable weed by an official agency.

Oblanceolate: the reverse of lanceolate, where the rounded end of the leaf is near the apex and the pointed end is at the petiole.

Obovate: the reverse of ovate, where the wide part of the leaf is near the apex and the pointed end is attached to the petiole.

Oddly-pinnate: means that a pinnate leaf has an odd number of leaflets. Usually the odd leaflet is at the tip of the rachis.

Ovate: this leaf type is similar to lanceolate, but much wider. The pointed end is at the apex and the wide, rounded end is at the petiole.

Panicle: an inflorescence where the rachis has branches that re-branch.

Palmate: refers to a compound leaf where the leaflets arise from a common point, somewhat like the fingers arise from the palm.

Patch: an area colonized by a species of plant that is usually not very tall, such as a patch of clover.

Pedicle: a flower stem.

Perfect: refers to a flower that has both male and female organs.

Perennial: a plant that produces an aerial structure every year which dies back to the ground every year.

Perianth: sepals and petals of a flower, collectively.

Petal: a single 'leaf' of the corolla.

Petiole: the stalk of a leaf.

Phyllaries: the bracts that compose the involucre found on composite flower heads.

Pinnate: a compound leaf form that has a rachis with leaflets attached to both sides in ladder fashion.

Pinnafid: a leaf form that has lobes on both sides of a midrib in pinnate fashion, the difference being that pinnatifid has to do with lobes and pinnate has to do with leaflets.

Pistil: the female part of a flower consisting of the ovary, style and stigma.

Pleated: usually describes a corolla that is corrugated.

Pod: generally in reference to the fruit of *Fabaceae*, as in pea pod.

Prostrate: a horizontal growth habit of vining plants, especially those not equipped to climb.

Pubescent: hairy or fuzzy surface in the manner of peach fuzz.

Raceme: an inflorescence in which the flowers are attached to the central flower stalk by pedicles (stems), as occurs with Delphiniums.

Rachis: the axis of a pinnate leaf or inflorescence.

Ray: the single petal of composite flower as found on daises

Rec.: Recreation

Receptacle: the point of attachment of the flower parts. In composites it is the disc, in other flower types it is less conspicuous.

Recurved: generally used to describe a petal that curves backward as do the petals of the Avalanche Lily

Reduced upward: this refers to the tendency of leaves to become progressively smaller as they near the top of the stem.

Reflexed: generally used to describe a petal that is bent backward at a sharp angle. Shooting Star (*Dodecatheon*) would be good example.

Reniform: kidney-shaped as a kidney bean.

Reticulate: a netted pattern that may appear on seed, leaves, or most obviously, on cantaloupe melons.

Rhizome: a horizontal, underground stem, used as a means of extending the domain of the species, as with Quack Grass.

RMNP: Rocky Mountain National Park.

Rosette: a clump of leaves that give rise to flowering stalks. Dandelion is an example.

Rugose: wrinkled.

Runner: a horizontal, above-ground stem used to extend the domain of the plant, as found in strawberries.

Rush: a grass-like herb with a 3-locular ovary producing a single seed per locule or a single locular ovary producing 3 seeds.

S.P.: state park

Sagittate: shaped like an arrowhead.

Samara: a winged seed (fruit) such as produced by maple trees.

Sap: the 'blood' of a plant.

Saprophyte: an organism that lives on dead organisms or refuse.

Scale: a leaf or other structure that resembles a fish scale in size or arrangement.

Scape: a leafless stalk supporting an inflorescence.

Scree: gravel-like soil that is very common on tundra where there is a lot of erosion and little organic matter.

Sedge: a grass-like herb with fibrous roots and a locular ovary contaning a single seed.

Senescence: aging.

Sepal: a single 'leaf' of the calyx.

Serrated: saw-toothed.

Sessile: a flower or leaf attached directly to the stem with neither a pedicle or a petiole.

Sheath: the 'scabbard' from which a blade of grass arises. In order to chew a stalk of grass, it is first pulled from its sheath.

Shrub: a woody bush.

Spatulate: a leaf with a winged petiole and an outline of a wooden spoon. They are quite common in rosettes.

Species: a group of plants that are genetically the same. Also, the Latin name following the genus, the two of which give the plant its Latin name, as in the common sunflower: *Helianthus annuus*.

Spike: an inflorescence bearing sessile flowers, or any upright stalk that comes to a point.

Spikelet: refers to the short stem that bears the flowers in a grass inflorescence.

Spine: a sharp, stiff bristle intended for defensive purposes, such as found on cacti and thistles.

Spur: a short, woody stem, found on apple trees, which produces leaves, blossoms and apples, and the backward extension of a flower such as a Delphinium.

Stalk: a non-botanical term that refers to an upright structure. It may be a petiole (celery), a culm (grass), a scape (onion), a stem, or even a spike.

Stamen: the male part of a flower, consisting of the filament and the anther.

Stem: an organ that is capable of producing both leaves and roots. It also produced scapes, culms and flowers. Names for stems include: stem (cosmos), plate (onion), tuber (potato), runner (strawberry), rhizome (quack grass) and caudex (dandelion).

Stigma: the female part of a flower that receives the pollen.

Stipule: the bract that subtends a petiole at the point of attachment to the stem. They usually are in pairs, but can encircle the stem like a collar (*Salix eriocephala*).

Style: the part of the female flower organ that connects the stigma to the ovary.

Subalpine: in this book, this term refers to elevations between 10,000 and 11,500 ft.

Subtend: associated with; as stipules subtending a leaf.

Succulent: juicy.

Sucker: a stem or shoot arising from a root.

Tendril: a string-like modified leaf, usually as a extension of the leaf rachis, and used to elevate the plant by coiling around whatever it touches.

Tepal: the name given to petals when there is no obvious difference between the sepals and petals; a common occurrence in *Liliaceae* and *Ranunculaceae*.

Terminal: the tip or end.

Thicket: a dense stand of shrubs. Something walked around, not through.

Tiered: in rows, one above the other.

Tomentose: dense pubescence giving a woolly appearance.

Trifoliate: three-leaved, as a 3-leaf clover.

Trisected: cut into three parts.

Tuft: a dense group of needles or blades of grass; generally smaller than a clump or a tussock.

Tundra: an area permanently underlain with frozen ground.

Tussock: a large clump, usually of grass, often in marshy ground, sometimes used as stepping stones to keep feet dry.

Umbel: a group of flowers in a round, compact cluster that may either be flat, domed or globular.

Urn: an ancient, water-carrying vessel with a narrow neck and a bulbous base. A term used to describe flowers that resemble an urn, especially the classic Grecian urn.

Veins: water and nutrients are carried to all parts of a leaf through a network of veins.

Venation: refers to the type of vein pattern exhibited by a leaf, as in parallel venation.

Whorl: a cluster of leaves, flowers or needles that encircle a stem. They generally occur at nodes.

Wing: one of the lateral petals of a leguminous flower.

Winter annual: a plant that begins growth in the fall, goes dormant in winter, and resumes growth in the spring, producing seed before it succumbs. Winter wheat is a good example.

ROCKY MOUNTAIN FLORA

Life List

NUMBER:_____ **FLORA NAME** _____

LOCATION: _____

DATE: _____ ELEVATION: _____

NUMBER:_____ **FLORA NAME** _____

LOCATION: _____

DATE: _____ ELEVATION: _____

NUMBER:_____ **FLORA NAME** _____

LOCATION: _____

DATE: _____ ELEVATION: _____

NUMBER:_____ **FLORA NAME** _____

LOCATION: _____

DATE: _____ ELEVATION: _____

NUMBER:_____ **FLORA NAME** _____

LOCATION: _____

DATE: _____ ELEVATION: _____

NUMBER:_____ **FLORA NAME** _____

LOCATION: _____

DATE: _____ ELEVATION: _____

NUMBER:_____ **FLORA NAME** _____

LOCATION: _____

DATE: _____ ELEVATION: _____

NUMBER:_____ **FLORA NAME** _____

LOCATION: _____

DATE: _____ ELEVATION: _____

NUMBER:_____ **FLORA NAME** _____

LOCATION: _____

DATE: _____ ELEVATION: _____

NUMBER:_____ **FLORA NAME** _____

LOCATION: _____

DATE: _____ ELEVATION: _____

NUMBER:_____ **FLORA NAME** _____

LOCATION: _____

DATE: _____ ELEVATION: _____

NUMBER:_____ **FLORA NAME** _____
LOCATION: _____
DATE: _____ ELEVATION: _____

NUMBER:_____ **FLORA NAME** _____
LOCATION: _____
DATE: _____ ELEVATION: _____

NUMBER:_____ **FLORA NAME** _____
LOCATION: _____
DATE: _____ ELEVATION: _____

NUMBER:_____ **FLORA NAME** _____
LOCATION: _____
DATE: _____ ELEVATION: _____

NUMBER:_____ **FLORA NAME** _____
LOCATION: _____
DATE: _____ ELEVATION: _____

NUMBER:_____ **FLORA NAME** _____
LOCATION: _____
DATE: _____ ELEVATION: _____

NUMBER:_____ **FLORA NAME** _____
LOCATION: _____
DATE: _____ ELEVATION: _____

NUMBER:_____ **FLORA NAME** _____
LOCATION: _____
DATE: _____ ELEVATION: _____

NUMBER:_____ **FLORA NAME** _____
LOCATION: _____
DATE: _____ ELEVATION: _____

NUMBER:_____ **FLORA NAME** _____
LOCATION: _____
DATE: _____ ELEVATION: _____

NUMBER:_____ **FLORA NAME** _____
LOCATION: _____
DATE: _____ ELEVATION: _____

NUMBER:_____ **FLORA NAME** _____
LOCATION: _____
DATE: _____ ELEVATION: _____

NUMBER:_____ **FLORA NAME** _____
LOCATION: _____
DATE: _____ ELEVATION: _____

NUMBER:_____ **FLORA NAME** _____
LOCATION: _____
DATE: _____ ELEVATION: _____

NUMBER:_____ **FLORA NAME** _____
LOCATION: _____
DATE: _____ ELEVATION: _____

NUMBER:_____ **FLORA NAME** _____
LOCATION: _____
DATE: _____ ELEVATION: _____

NUMBER:_____ **FLORA NAME** _____
LOCATION: _____
DATE: _____ ELEVATION: _____

NUMBER:_____ **FLORA NAME** _____
LOCATION: _____
DATE: _____ ELEVATION: _____

NUMBER:_____ **FLORA NAME** _____
LOCATION: _____
DATE: _____ ELEVATION: _____

NUMBER:_____ **FLORA NAME** _____
LOCATION: _____
DATE: _____ ELEVATION: _____

NUMBER:_____ **FLORA NAME** _____
LOCATION: _____
DATE: _____ ELEVATION: _____

NUMBER:_____ **FLORA NAME** _____
LOCATION: _____
DATE: _____ ELEVATION: _____

NUMBER:_____ **FLORA NAME** _____
LOCATION: _____
DATE: _____ ELEVATION: _____

NUMBER:_____ **FLORA NAME** _____
LOCATION: _____
DATE: _____ ELEVATION: _____

NUMBER:_____ **FLORA NAME** _____
LOCATION: _____
DATE: _____ ELEVATION: _____

NUMBER:_____ **FLORA NAME** _____
LOCATION: _____
DATE: _____ ELEVATION: _____

NUMBER:_____ **FLORA NAME** _____
LOCATION: _____
DATE: _____ ELEVATION: _____

NUMBER:_____ **FLORA NAME** _____
LOCATION: _____
DATE: _____ ELEVATION: _____

NUMBER:_____ **FLORA NAME** _____
LOCATION: _____
DATE: _____ ELEVATION: _____

NUMBER:_____ **FLORA NAME** _____
LOCATION: _____
DATE: _____ ELEVATION: _____

NUMBER:_____ **FLORA NAME** _____
LOCATION: _____
DATE: _____ ELEVATION: _____

NUMBER:_____ **FLORA NAME** _____
LOCATION: _____
DATE: _____ ELEVATION: _____

NUMBER:_____ **FLORA NAME** _____
LOCATION: _____
DATE: _____ ELEVATION: _____

NUMBER:_____ **FLORA NAME** _____
LOCATION: _____
DATE: _____ ELEVATION: _____

NUMBER:_____ **FLORA NAME** _____
LOCATION: _____
DATE: _____ ELEVATION: _____

NUMBER:_____ **FLORA NAME** _____
LOCATION: _____
DATE: _____ ELEVATION: _____

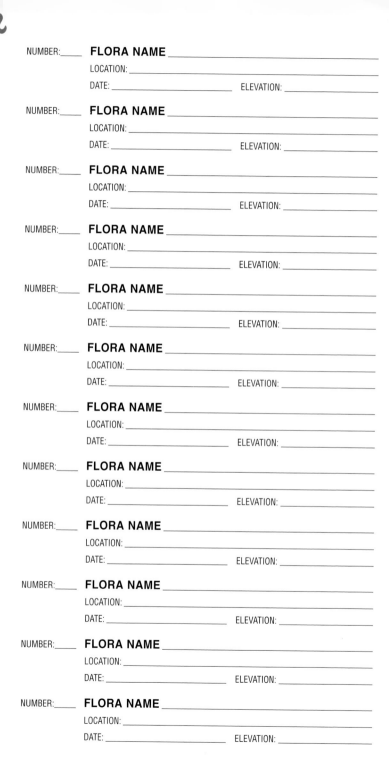

NUMBER:_____ **FLORA NAME** _____
LOCATION: _____
DATE: _____ ELEVATION: _____

NUMBER:_____ **FLORA NAME** _____
LOCATION: _____
DATE: _____ ELEVATION: _____

NUMBER:_____ **FLORA NAME** _____
LOCATION: _____
DATE: _____ ELEVATION: _____

NUMBER:_____ **FLORA NAME** _____
LOCATION: _____
DATE: _____ ELEVATION: _____

NUMBER:_____ **FLORA NAME** _____
LOCATION: _____
DATE: _____ ELEVATION: _____

NUMBER:_____ **FLORA NAME** _____
LOCATION: _____
DATE: _____ ELEVATION: _____

NUMBER:_____ **FLORA NAME** _____
LOCATION: _____
DATE: _____ ELEVATION: _____

NUMBER:_____ **FLORA NAME** _____
LOCATION: _____
DATE: _____ ELEVATION: _____

NUMBER:_____ **FLORA NAME** _____
LOCATION: _____
DATE: _____ ELEVATION: _____

NUMBER:_____ **FLORA NAME** _____
LOCATION: _____
DATE: _____ ELEVATION: _____

NUMBER:_____ **FLORA NAME** _____
LOCATION: _____
DATE: _____ ELEVATION: _____

NUMBER:_____ **FLORA NAME** _____
LOCATION: _____
DATE: _____ ELEVATION: _____

NUMBER:_____ **FLORA NAME** _____
LOCATION: _____
DATE: _____ ELEVATION: _____

NUMBER:_____ **FLORA NAME** _____
LOCATION: _____
DATE: _____ ELEVATION: _____

NUMBER:_____ **FLORA NAME** _____
LOCATION: _____
DATE: _____ ELEVATION: _____

NUMBER:_____ **FLORA NAME** _____
LOCATION: _____
DATE: _____ ELEVATION: _____

NUMBER:_____ **FLORA NAME** _____
LOCATION: _____
DATE: _____ ELEVATION: _____

NUMBER:_____ **FLORA NAME** _____
LOCATION: _____
DATE: _____ ELEVATION: _____

NUMBER:_____ **FLORA NAME** _____
LOCATION: _____
DATE: _____ ELEVATION: _____

NUMBER:_____ **FLORA NAME** _____
LOCATION: _____
DATE: _____ ELEVATION: _____

NUMBER:_____ **FLORA NAME** _____
LOCATION: _____
DATE: _____ ELEVATION: _____

NUMBER:_____ **FLORA NAME** _____
LOCATION: _____
DATE: _____ ELEVATION: _____

NUMBER:_____ **FLORA NAME** _____
LOCATION: _____
DATE: _____ ELEVATION: _____

NUMBER:_____ **FLORA NAME** _____
LOCATION: _____
DATE: _____ ELEVATION: _____

NUMBER:_____ **FLORA NAME** _____
LOCATION: _____
DATE: _____ ELEVATION: _____

NUMBER:_____ **FLORA NAME** _____
LOCATION: _____
DATE: _____ ELEVATION: _____

NUMBER:_____ **FLORA NAME** _____
LOCATION: _____
DATE: _____ ELEVATION: _____

NUMBER:_____ **FLORA NAME** _____
LOCATION: _____
DATE: _____ ELEVATION: _____

NUMBER:_____ **FLORA NAME** _____
LOCATION: _____
DATE: _____ ELEVATION: _____

NUMBER:_____ **FLORA NAME** _____
LOCATION: _____
DATE: _____ ELEVATION: _____

NUMBER:_____ **FLORA NAME** _____
LOCATION: _____
DATE: _____ ELEVATION: _____

NUMBER:_____ **FLORA NAME** _____
LOCATION: _____
DATE: _____ ELEVATION: _____

NUMBER:_____ **FLORA NAME** _____
LOCATION: _____
DATE: _____ ELEVATION: _____

NUMBER:_____ **FLORA NAME** _____
LOCATION: _____
DATE: _____ ELEVATION: _____

NUMBER:_____ **FLORA NAME** _____
LOCATION: _____
DATE: _____ ELEVATION: _____

NUMBER:_____ **FLORA NAME** _____
LOCATION: _____
DATE: _____ ELEVATION: _____

NUMBER:_____ **FLORA NAME** _____
LOCATION: _____
DATE: _____ ELEVATION: _____

NUMBER:_____ **FLORA NAME** _____
LOCATION: _____
DATE: _____ ELEVATION: _____

NUMBER:_____ **FLORA NAME** _____
LOCATION: _____
DATE: _____ ELEVATION: _____

NUMBER:_____ **FLORA NAME** _____
LOCATION: _____
DATE: _____ ELEVATION: _____

NUMBER:_____ **FLORA NAME** _____
LOCATION: _____
DATE: _____ ELEVATION: _____

NUMBER:_____ **FLORA NAME** _____
LOCATION: _____
DATE: _____ ELEVATION: _____

NUMBER:_____ **FLORA NAME** _____
LOCATION: _____
DATE: _____ ELEVATION: _____

NUMBER:_____ **FLORA NAME** _____
LOCATION: _____
DATE: _____ ELEVATION: _____

NUMBER:_____ **FLORA NAME** _____
LOCATION: _____
DATE: _____ ELEVATION: _____

NUMBER:_____ **FLORA NAME** _____
LOCATION: _____
DATE: _____ ELEVATION: _____

NUMBER:_____ **FLORA NAME** _____
LOCATION: _____
DATE: _____ ELEVATION: _____

NUMBER:_____ **FLORA NAME** _____
LOCATION: _____
DATE: _____ ELEVATION: _____

NUMBER:_____ **FLORA NAME** _____

LOCATION: _____

DATE: _____ ELEVATION: _____

NUMBER:_____ **FLORA NAME** _____

LOCATION: _____

DATE: _____ ELEVATION: _____

NUMBER:_____ **FLORA NAME** _____

LOCATION: _____

DATE: _____ ELEVATION: _____

NUMBER:_____ **FLORA NAME** _____

LOCATION: _____

DATE: _____ ELEVATION: _____

NUMBER:_____ **FLORA NAME** _____

LOCATION: _____

DATE: _____ ELEVATION: _____

NUMBER:_____ **FLORA NAME** _____

LOCATION: _____

DATE: _____ ELEVATION: _____

NUMBER:_____ **FLORA NAME** _____

LOCATION: _____

DATE: _____ ELEVATION: _____

NUMBER:_____ **FLORA NAME** _____

LOCATION: _____

DATE: _____ ELEVATION: _____

NUMBER:_____ **FLORA NAME** _____

LOCATION: _____

DATE: _____ ELEVATION: _____

NUMBER:_____ **FLORA NAME** _____

LOCATION: _____

DATE: _____ ELEVATION: _____

NUMBER:_____ **FLORA NAME** _____

LOCATION: _____

DATE: _____ ELEVATION: _____

NUMBER:_____ **FLORA NAME** _____

LOCATION: _____

DATE: _____ ELEVATION: _____

Flora Index